Social Work Case Management

Case Studies From the Frontlines

Michael J. Holosko
University of Georgia

SAGE

Los Angeles | London | New Delhi
Singapore | Washington DC | Melbourne

FOR INFORMATION:

SAGE Publications, Inc.
2455 Teller Road
Thousand Oaks, California 91320
E-mail: order@sagepub.com

SAGE Publications Ltd.
1 Oliver's Yard
55 City Road
London, EC1Y 1SP
United Kingdom

SAGE Publications India Pvt. Ltd.
B 1/I 1 Mohan Cooperative Industrial Area
Mathura Road, New Delhi 110 044
India

SAGE Publications Asia-Pacific Pte. Ltd.
3 Church Street
#10–04 Samsung Hub
Singapore 049483

Printed in the United States of America

ISBN: 978-1-4833-7447-5

This book is printed on acid-free paper.

Acquisitions Editor: Nathan Davidson
Editorial Assistant: Alissa Nance
Production Editor: Bennie Clark Allen
Copy Editor: Lana Todorovic-Arndt
Typesetter: Hurix Systems Pvt. Ltd.
Proofreader: Susan Schon
Indexer: Jeanne Busemeyer
Cover Designer: Gail Buschman
Marketing Manager: Jenna Retana

Certified Chain of Custody
Promoting Sustainable Forestry
www.sfiprogram.org
SFI-01268

SFI label applies to text stock

17 18 19 20 21 10 9 8 7 6 5 4 3 2 1

Contents

Foreword

It is indeed a privilege to have been asked by SAGE Publishing to write the foreword to Michael Holosko's must-read text, *Social Work Case Management: Case Studies From the Frontlines.* Professor Holosko has come up with yet another innovative and practice-relevant book that I believe will shape the future of case management in our profession. Both BSW and MSW practitioners and case managers practicing today are advised to read this thoughtful, creative, and well-written addition to our professional literature. Written purposely in a much appreciated conversationally informed tone—instead of a stodgy academic one—there are six aspects of this text that should be emphasized to readers at the outset.

The first is our profession's longstanding history and relationship with case management. As thoughtfully elaborated early on in the book, case management functions were occurring in societies prior to the advent of social work. And from our early history as a profession, social work theory and methods were strongly aligned to what eventually became known as case management. Today, many social workers are occupationally identified as "case managers," as illustrated in the riveting 22 case studies included in the text (Chapters 5–26). As echoed repeatedly by Professor Holosko, our future is burgeoning in this field in North America and China.

Second is the inherent participatory nature of the book's core content—a joining together of clients with seasoned practitioners. Whether it is providing empathy and rapport, timely knowledge, referrals, resources, and whether the mutual processes are brokering, advocating, meshing family/organizational/other systems with the individual client, case managers have a vast repertoire of unique knowledge and skills, which are explicated in the text. Since social work practitioners know community systems well, have a broad, eclectic sense of theory and methods that they apply, and practice the very best of advanced generalist principles that the profession possesses, this is the essence of our important case management work.

Third, the book has important relevance to today's current definition of direct practice. As noted throughout the text, case managers need to extensively document what they do. Bureaucratic systems can be insensitive, if not outright hostile to the individualized needs of people they serve. We come to appreciate that social work case managers play essential roles in mediating and navigating these daily challenged conflicts, simultaneously maximizing their clients' capacities to grow and thrive with often-limited available community resources. Our clients are frequently vulnerable, and, as these various chapters remind us, their needs are also differential. In short, social work case management is a viable professional platform through which client needs are addressed today. In Chapter 4, Professor Holosko presents a simple yet creative Task Centered Case Management Model to frame our current practice in this field.

And so, case management is above all else an application of professional knowledge practiced with unique personal and professional skills. Although such knowledge may be objectively claimed, it may be subjectively interpreted. Professor Holosko constantly reminds us that it can be generated via the interactions and communication between people. Or as noted in the book, it can be all of these things concurrently (Graham, 2006; Park, 2001)! Indeed, the best types of knowledge are those that illuminate the broadest forms of relevance coupled with insights, and apply these judiciously and wisely. Holosko's well-crafted text, to his credit, achieves the important goal of explaining *how* and *why* we think—about *how* and *why* we practice case management in today's health and human service systems. For much of our discipline's history, there has been a decided schism between academic social work and what is actually practiced in the field. By consciously pairing practitioners with scholars, Professor Holosko seeks to join together our most viable sources of shared knowledge. This then, is the fourth point needing to be emphasized to readers: the book's joint authorship, across 22 chapters, of practitioner and scholar, leading to still deeper insights into the nuanced essence of social work case management practice. What is more, readers learn about case management practiced with a breadth of clients, including at-risk youth, child welfare, HIV/AIDS, mental health, work with the homeless, and also how to use more advanced generalist principles that transcend any of these unique practice areas. The topics presented cover a broad range of practice domains in two countries with similar but also manifestly distinct social, political, and economic histories.

This leads to a fifth point I noted when reading this text—the book's innovative practice insights. To know a domain is to have exerted intellectual and practical energy to that pursuit. There is such diversity in the fields of analysis presented, and a great deal of detailed yet necessary nuances explained regarding different facets of case management practice, from one domain to the next. His book comes with thoughtful introductions, contextual frameworks for knowledge, and conclusions; a most useful glossary of frequently used case management terms; and thoroughly insightful chapters that equip a reader with topical and pragmatic practice-relevant concerns. Undeniably, we see that there are diverse fields of case management practice presented across the text. Yet, there are also commonalities among these chapters, including helpful job descriptions, and the 22 practice chapters are carefully edited to provide coherence across author domains.

The sixth and final point is the need to do things differently, and better, in our field—to always strive to improve. Early chapters outline the contemporary contexts of globalization and neoliberalism and the need for value-based social justice. Through this lens, and because it always involves mobilizing resources and therefore, assertively shifting power to clients—case management in its best sense is presented as a tool for challenging those forces that are contrary to our profession's commitment to social justice. This is not to suggest that case management is a "magic bullet," or panacea; but rather, in addition to other strategies for social justice practice, it may be one of several approaches that the profession deploys to achieve greater ends. His text equips today's social workers to be skilled, knowledgeable, and effective case management practitioners, which resonates with the core values of our profession. This book is written by a social worker for social workers interested in understanding the realities of conducting case management in today's changing landscape. It is not only important and essential to our profession, but it is empowering to the vulnerable clients we work with daily and to those social work professionals who choose to practice in this growing, exciting, and challenging field.

John R. Graham, PhD RSW (AB)
Professor and Director
School of Social Work
University of British Columbia
Okanagan Campus

❖

REFERENCES

Graham, J. R. (2006). Spirituality and social work: A call for an international focus of research. *Arete: A Professional Journal Devoted to Excellence in Social Work, 30*(1), 63–77.

Park, P. (2001). Knowledge and participatory research. In P. Reason & H. Bradbury (Eds.), *Handbook of action research: Participative inquiry and practice* (pp. 81–90). Thousand Oaks, CA: Sage.

Social Work Case Management

SAGE was founded in 1965 by Sara Miller McCune to support the dissemination of usable knowledge by publishing innovative and high-quality research and teaching content. Today, we publish over 900 journals, including those of more than 400 learned societies, more than 800 new books per year, and a growing range of library products including archives, data, case studies, reports, and video. SAGE remains majority-owned by our founder, and after Sara's lifetime will become owned by a charitable trust that secures our continued independence.

Los Angeles | London | New Delhi | Singapore | Washington DC | Melbourne

Preface

No matter how one looks at the future North American labor force projection data, social work is deemed to be a high-demand profession up until approximately 2030. The target areas for our growth include health care, followed by mental health, addictions, and gerontology. Historically, our profession's main practice domain has been child welfare, but in the past 50 years or so in North America, social work has gained considerable traction and prominence in many areas of practice, including the burgeoning growth area of case management.

This book fills a distinct literature void in this area as there is no text written about social work case management that is anchored by an empirically tested social work model. It was written by social workers, for social workers, and it presents a framework to practice social work case management in a variety of health and human service organizations.

The text is organized into three subsections. Part I presents the contextual chapters that are the framing or scaffolding for all of the material presented in the rest of the text. Chapter 1, "Current Trends Shaping Social Work Case Management," identifies international trends, for example, neoliberalism and globalization, as well as more local national trends, for example, "do more with less daily," "use more integrative approaches to service delivery," etc. It reminds us that we do not practice our noble craft in a vacuum and also that social work's knowledge, values, and skills have an excellent "goodness-of-fit" with case management.

Chapter 2, "The History of Social Work Case Management," describes in detail, how our profession since the 1990s up until today in North America has evolved and endured through various social, political, and economic changes, as well as legislation changes, to become what it has become today. It echoes the simple adage that "history does matter," and harkens the message clearly that social work case management's "time has come." Chapter 3 is titled "Task-Centered Case Management." This presents the backbone of the text and is the social work practice model developed from William Reid's timeless, visionary Task Centered Practice Model. With permission from Dr. Reid's partner, Anne "Ricky" Fortune at SUNY Albany, I contemporized it for today's practice reality, and labeled it the Task-Centered Case Management Model. The chapter concludes with a practice approach that promotes conversations for change called Motivational Interviewing. This approach fits well with what we do daily in social work and applies fittingly to Task-Centered Case Management.

Part II of the text presents 22 chapters all written by social workers currently practicing case management in a wide variety of settings in Canada, China, and the United States. Each chapter was formatted using the following main subheadings: the clientele, practice roles and responsibilities, role development potential, and case example. Under these subheadings, these case managers also addressed related issues such as the day-to-day challenges in doing their work, their personal and professional stress in doing this work, and the adequacy of their BSW and MSW education and training. The case examples offered herein are vivid and riveting accounts, and they really exemplify their work realities from the perspective of their own voice and practice lens.

The final subsection and the concluding Chapter 27 is titled "Social Work Case Management: Onward and Upward!" It first gleans across the previous 22 case example chapters and summarizes their main qualitative findings. Second, it uses the portal of learning competencies to dig down further into the educational requirements needed for BSW and MSW curricula, as to date such content has not been meaningfully infused in our curricula.

The text was intentionally written in a candid and informed conversational tone, to engage readers more meaningfully in the content. It also includes a glossary of 101 commonly used case management terms for students and practitioners to have at their fingertips, to better understand this content that grows in its nuances and complexities each day, as our external practice worlds continue to change.

Finally, this text was written for community college social service students, BSW and MSW students, practitioners, educators, field instructors, and supervisors. Case management looms large on our professional horizon, and we need to move forward with more resolve and urgency to be part of this movement afoot in North America. As you will read, we do have the necessary knowledge, values, and skills to do this job, and we now need the educational knowledge to go about our work in this important task. After reading this text, it is hoped that each and every social worker will be proud of not only who we are as a profession, but what we can do as a profession, particularly in the area of social work case management. I certainly was!

I leave you with a quote from Malcom Forbes that to me is the story behind this text.

"The best vision is insight."

—*M. J. H.*

Acknowledgments

There are so many individuals who should be acknowledged for helping me with this manuscript and who worked in various ways to help me complete this project. Some were business people, some were spiritual people, some were motivational people, some were idea-sharing people, some were technical people, some were formatting and typing experts, some were social work case managers, and some were the very clients of social work case managers.

The first person who encouraged and reached out to me to write this text was Kassie Graves at SAGE Publications. We spent many hours talking about the importance of this text, and through her guidance and coaching and insisting that the text be anchored by a clearly defined social work case management model, the idea came to fruition. Nathan Davidson picked up the baton when Kassie left and continued to marshal and shepherd this work diligently to completion. I'm very thankful for SAGE to have been so supportive of this initiative from its inception. I would like to gratefully acknowledge Bennie Clark Allen, Kylie Bethel, and Pat Bobrowski at SAGE for their overt professionalism, author empathy, and timely assistance in completing this book.

My partner Deborah Ann Holosko has been a social work case manager in Canada and the United States for 15 years, and always believed strongly in the importance of having our profession be more recognized for doing such noble and important work. She herself was very insightful throughout this process, and offered numerous practical suggestions about the current climate that case managers work in, and the many struggles and rewards that they have daily. I also would like to thank the University of Georgia, in particular the resources from the endowed Pauline M. Berger Chair, for allowing me to hire and support a cohort of wonderful graduate students who worked as research assistants, typists, graphic artists, and provided much needed "student voice" to the material in every phase of the process. These included Joelle Pettus, Anna Rumminger, J. Lloyd Allen, and Jessica Parker. I couldn't have proceeded too far in this endeavor without their dedication and help.

I would also like to thank at this time my oh-so-visionary MSW and PhD professors at the Universities of Toronto and Pittsburgh. Some 38 years ago, you taught me that macro practice and micro practice was a false dichotomy, and that these were actually two domains of practice that were overlapping circles. This eclipsed shaded area of these circles is where I have spent my entire academic career—and this text is a testimony to their wisdom. I would also like to thank my colleague and friend Judith Dunlop for her continued support and intellectual ideas about real-world macro and micro practice that I processed with her for many hours until this text's completion.

I would also like to personally thank Anne "Ricky" Fortune, who is William Reid's partner. She gave me her blessing and support to contemporize his visionary Task Centered Practice Model for this text. Finally, I would like to thank the case managers and coauthors who wrote the poignant, honest, client-centered, and unique case examples in each chapter of Part II. Your insights and accounts were so passionate and important to the field of social work in general, and to the noble work of case managers in particular.

This text was written by a social worker for social workers, and it is targeted for BSWs and MSWs who wish to pursue careers as social work case managers upon graduation. It is replete with information about the history, context, realities, nuances, and case examples of social work case management. Hopefully, such information will be embraced in the professional toolkits that you carry forward for your important work with vulnerable clients in this area.

I leave you with a quote from Mahatma Gandhi that describes the real story behind this text:

> "*An ounce of practice is worth more than tons of preaching.*"

SAGE Publishing gratefully acknowledges the following reviewers for their kind assistance:

Sherrie L. Foster, *Tennessee Technological University*

Christopher C. Garland, *Northeastern State University*

Annalease M. Gibson, *Albany State University*

Bonnie F. Hatchett, *University of Arkansas/Pine Bluff*

LaKeisha L. Harris, *University of Maryland Eastern Shore*

Steven Hoffman, *University of Texas at San Antonio*

Diane M. Knust, *University of Minnesota*

Jeffrey Longhofer, *Rutgers University*

Amy Meyers, *The College of New Rochelle*

Tierra M. Parsons, *Johnson C. Smith University*

Nicola Ranson, *National University*

Melanee W. Sinclair, *Bethany College*

preferably, a client and members of his or her support network. They may also be required at routine intervals, are often recommended during times of significant change, crisis, or lack of progress, and are documented in progress notes or on a case conference form.

17. **Case Management:** A collaborative process that assesses, plans, implements, coordinates, monitors, and evaluates the options and services required to meet an individual's health needs, using the communication and available resources to promote quality, cost-effective outcomes. Case management occurs within a single, larger organization, or within a community-based program that coordinates services among service providers, also known as administrators, managers, care coordinators, care managers, rehabilitation counselors, patient advocates, systems navigators, client navigators, patient navigators, health care navigators, utilization reviewers, patient monitors, insurance benefit managers, vocational evaluators, admissions liaisons, bill auditors, and work-adjustment specialists.

18. **Case Manager:** A trained health care professional responsible for coordinating the care delivered to an assigned group of clients/patients based on diagnosis or need. Other responsibilities include the following: patient/family education, re-assessment, case conferences, advocacy, delays management, care and outcomes monitoring and management.

19. **Certified Case Management/Manager:** A certified health care professional designated due to his or her experience and knowledge of case management. Certification is the act of confirming that someone has met a certain set of predetermined criteria by the certifying body and is recognized as an acceptable standard of practice by general consent of the population it certifies.

20. **Chronic Disease:** Diseases characterized by complex causality, multiple risk factors, a longer latency period, a prolonged course of illness, functional impairment or disability, and in most cases, the unlikelihood of eventual cure.

21. **Client:** The individual or family who receives case management services, also known as patient, consumer, service user, peer, resident, beneficiary, (service) recipient, customer, advocate, participant, or member. Social workers retain the use of the word client, but given that the majority of case management occurs in health care settings, patient is more frequently used.

22. **Client Consent (for Case Management):** A designed and approved form presented and discussed with a client that describes the case management services, the voluntary nature of the program, and the right to decline all, or part of those services. The client's signed agreement is required to participate in the case management program and its processes.

23. **Clinical Case Management:** Case management that generally provides one-on-one service in a medical clinical setting delivered to individuals in clinical

settings, for the purpose of preventing the onset of progression of a health condition or illness.

24. **Co-insurance:** The percentage of costs a patient pays out-of-pocket for their medical care.

25. **Comprehensive Individualized Service Plan (CISP):** A plan developed by a case manager on behalf of the client that is reviewed and approved in writing by the client and case manager's supervisor. The plan normally documents: the actions/ activities required to meet identified service needs; the community programs, persons/and/or agencies to which the beneficiary will be referred; a description of the nature, frequency, and duration of the activities; service eligibility; and assistance necessary to achieve targeted short- and long-term outcomes.

26. **Continuing Care:** This refers to directly furnishing or indirectly making available, upon payment of an entrance fee and under a residency agreement, housing and health related services, including nursing or assistance with activities of daily living (ADL) to the continuing care retirement community provider that is furnishing care, whether provided in the community or in another setting designated by the residency agreement.

27. **Continuum of Care:** This matches ongoing needs of individuals being served by the case management process with the appropriate levels and types of health, medical, financial, legal, and psychosocial care for services across multiple settings.

28. **Co-occurring Disorder:** Any two (or more) behavioral health disorders experienced by the same person at the same time. This is most commonly used to refer to co-occurring mental illnesses and chemical dependency.

29. **Cost Containment:** Control or reduction of inefficiencies in the consumption, allocation, or production of health care services that contribute to higher than necessary costs. Inefficiencies can occur when health services could be delivered in less costly settings without loss of quality, and inefficiencies in production exist when the costs of producing health services could be reduced by using a different combination of resources.

30. **Crisis Intervention:** An immediate response by a health care service provider to address a client's emergency needs, that is, emergency medical situation, domestic violence, mental health crisis, etc.

31. **Cultural Competency:** The ability to make services respectful of a client's cultural beliefs and behaviors, whether influenced by gender, ethnicity, poverty, language, disability, sexuality, age, or other cultural influences, so that services are sensitive, comfortable, and acceptable to clients. Service delivery is both designed and implemented with the understanding that culture and language have considerable impact on how clients access and respond to health and human services.

32. **Custodial Care:** Care provided primarily to assist a client/patient in meeting the activities of daily living (ADL), but not requiring skilled nursing care.

33. **Developmental Disabilities**: A broad range of conditions evident at birth or early in childhood that can result in lifelong deficits in mental, psychosocial, and physical functioning. Individuals with mental retardation, cerebral palsy, autism, epilepsy (and other seizure disorders), sensory impairments, congenital disabilities, traumatic brain injury, or conditions caused by disease (e.g., polio and muscular dystrophy) may be considered developmentally disabled.

34. **Disability:** A limitation or inability to perform socially defined activities and roles expected of individuals in the manner considered "normal," resulting from impairment or chronic illness. It can also refer to any restriction or lack (resulting from an impairment) of ability to perform an activity in the manner or within the range considered normal for a human being. A disability may or may not be a handicap to an individual, depending on one's adjustment to it.

35. **Disability Income Insurance:** A form of health insurance that provides periodic payment to replace income, when an insured person is unable to work as a result of illness, injury, or disease.

36. **Discharge Planning:** A formal process of assessing the client/patient's needs of care after discharge from a health care facility, ensuring that the necessary services are in place before discharge. This process ensures a timely, appropriate, and safe discharge to the next level of care, or setting including appropriate use of resources necessary for ongoing care.

37. **Disengagement:** The closing of a case is a process of gradual or sudden withdrawal of services, as the situation indicated, on a planned basis.

38. *DSM-5*: This refers to the authoritative document called the *Diagnostic and Statistical Manual of Mental Disorders* published by the American Psychiatric Association, which is the formal legal document that describes all diagnostic, symptoms, and mental health classification terminology for these disorders.

39. **Evidence-Based Practice (EBP):** Treatments for which systematic empirical research has provided evidence of statistically significant effectiveness as treatment for specific problems. Also called evidence-informed practices.

40. **Extended Care Facility:** It is a skilled nursing facility that provides post-hospital services reimbursable by Medicare.

41. **First-Level Reviews:** These are conducted while a patient is in the hospital and care is reviewed for its appropriateness.

42. **Fiscal Authority:** This gives a case manager control over the funding used to purchase services, either for the client, for a caseload, or for all the clients of an agency.

43. **Follow-up:** The process of evaluating a client's status including their physical health and the stability of the client's functioning after termination of case management. Follow-up may be performed to collect program evaluation measures pertaining to client outcomes, and must be recorded in the client's file.

44. **Functional Limitations:** This results from impairment or chronic illness and is a restriction or lack of ability to perform an action or activity in the manner or within the range considered normal.

45. **Goals:** A statement of broad outcomes that a client and case manager have agreed upon in the CISP (see CISP above). These should be simple, measurable, and achievable and are the basis for the tasks and activities that client and case manager will undertake.

46. **Harm Reduction:** An individualized, client-centered approach requiring a non-judgmental assessment of the client's current behavioral practices, and working toward small gradations in risk reduction in order to achieve behavioral changes in a manner consistent with the client's abilities and desires.

47. **Health Outcomes:** A change in the health status of an individual, group, or population attributable to a planned intervention or series of interventions, regardless of whether such an intervention was intended to change health status.

48. **Health Promotion:** The process of enabling people to increase control over, and improve their health. It involves the population as a whole in the context of their everyday lives, rather than focusing on people at-risk for specific diseases, and is directed toward action upon the determinants or cause of health.

49. **HIPAA:** The federal government's *Health Insurance Portability and Accountability Act* (1996) that requires all health care professionals to protect the full privacy of patients and clients. In relation to case management, *HIPAA* addresses worker compensation populations, the treatment of protected health information, and the manner in which case managers can ensure that they provide appropriate services while navigating *HIPAA's* requirements.

50. **Immediate Needs:** These are client-identified issues that must be addressed at once, to stabilize the client's situation and facilitate further engagement.

51. **Implementation:** The process of executing specific case management activities, and/or interventions that will lead to accomplishing the goals set forth in the Comprehensive Individualized Service Plan (CISP).

52. **Independent Living:** A service delivery concept encouraging the maintenance of control over one's life, based on choice of acceptable options that minimize reliance on others performing everyday activities (ADLs).

53. **Individualized Plan of Care:** Similar to a Comprehensive Individualized Service Plan (CISP). This is agreed-upon set plan for a specific individual that pertains to the sole care of that individual.

54. **Individuation:** The idea of an individual separating themselves from others and viewing their life and incidences as unique. In case management, individuation can lead to individualized plans of care.

55. **Intake:** An initial appointment where new clients meet with the health care professional case manager to provide basic information about themselves and their concerns.

56. **Intensive Case Management (ICM):** This is a community based program of care which aims to provide long-term care for severely mentally ill people who do not require immediate admission. ICM evolved from two original community models of care, Assertive Community Treatment (ACT) and Case Management (CM), where ICM emphasized the importance of small caseloads and higher intensity inputs.

57. **Learned Helplessness (among people):** This concept applies to many situations with human beings. It refers to the internalized beliefs that some clients may feel when they have no control over their situations. They then begin to behave in powerless or incompetent ways, and overlook opportunities for growth, relief, or positive change.

58. **Legal Authority:** A legislative mandate that designates an organization responsible for a particular service or a particular population.

59. **Level of Care:** The intensity of effort required to diagnose, treat, preserve, or maintain an individual's physical or emotional status.

60. **Level of Service:** Based on the patient's condition and the needed level of care, these are used to identify and verify that the patient is receiving care at the appropriate level.

61. **Long Term Care:** Ongoing health and social services provided for individuals who need assistance on a continuing basis because of physical or mental disability. Services can be provided in institutions, the home, or the community, and include informal services provided by family or friends, as well as formal services provided by professionals or agencies.

62. **LPN:** A certified and degree granted Licensed Practical Nurse. They have specialized nursing training and are able to dispense most medications.

63. **Managed Care:** Systems and techniques used to help direct the utilization, cost, and quality of health care services. These include a review of medical necessity, incentives to use certain providers and case management. Managed care encompasses many types of organizations, but it is generally used to describe the activity of organizing doctors, hospitals, and other providers into groups to enhance the quality and cost-effectiveness of health care.

64. **Medical Necessity on Admission:** A formal review used to determine that the hospital admission is appropriate, clinically necessary, justified, and reimbursable.

65. **Medical Power of Attorney (MPOA):** A legal instrument that allows one to select a representative to make healthcare decisions for you if (and only if) you become unable to make those decisions yourself.

66. **Mental Health Assessment:** By using numerous tools and recommended protocols, trained case managers can assess the mental health capacities of their clients. These are normally conducted in the following main areas of functioning: personality, disability, neuropsychological, cognitive, and situational problems. Case managers must refer to the DSM-5 for the clarification of any and all mental health disorder symptoms.

67. **Monitoring:** A process in which the case manager maintains regular contact with the client, the family, and the providers of service in order to ensure that the services are appropriate and meeting the individual client's current needs.

68. **Narrative Summary:** Documentation collected by the case manager that provides an overview of issues presented by the client during an assessment. It may prioritize needs and include a plan for following up on them.

69. **NASW Standards for Case Management:** These document and explain 12 key social work standards including: 1) Ethics and Values, 2) Qualifications, 3) Knowledge, 4) Cultural and Linguistic Competence, 5) Assessment, 6) Service Planning, Implementation, and Monitoring, 7) Advocacy and Leadership, 8) Interdisciplinary and Inter-organizational Collaboration, 9) Practice Evaluation and Improvement, 10) Record Keeping, 11) Workload Sustainability, and 12) Professional Development and Competence.

70. **Nurses:** Individuals holding various types of certified nursing degrees in which case management may be practiced include: Registered Nurse (RN), Licensed Practical Nurse (LPN), Certified Nurse Assistant (CNA), Licensed Vocational Nurse (LVN), Nurse Practitioner (NP), Advance Practice Nurses (APN), Clinical Nurse Leaders (CNL), Clinical Nurse Specialists (CNS), Certified Nurse Midwives (CNM), Certified Registered Nurse Anesthetists (CRNA).

71. **Objectives (in CISP):** A short-term (about 6 months or less) desired outcome, agreed upon between a case manager and a client that contributes to the achievement of a broader goal in a CISP. Objectives are concrete and may require one or more activities to reach the desired result.

72. **Outcome:** The result and consequence of a health care intervention process. A good outcome is a result that achieves the expected goal. An outcome may be the result of care received or not received. It represents the cumulative effects of one or more processes on a client at a defined point in time. CISPs and interventions specify whether they are short or long term.

73. **Outcome Measurement:** The systematic, quantitative observation at a point in time, of positive and negative short and long term outcome indicators in a CISP.

74. **Outreach:** A process of creating proactive awareness in the professional community and in the general public, about the availability of services in order to identify and establish contact with those who are deemed appropriate for case management services.

75. **Payers:** Those agencies or companies that incur financial outlays so that clients will receive services.

76. **Planning:** The process of determining goals, specific objectives, and actions designed to meet the client's needs as identified through the case management assessment process. The plan should be action oriented, measurable, and time specific in the CISP.

77. **Power of Attorney:** A written authorization to represent or act on another's behalf in private affairs, business, or some other legal matter such as health care capacity. The person authorizing the other to act is the principal, grantor, or donor (of the power). The one authorized to act is the agent or attorney—or, in some common-law jurisdictions, the attorney-in-fact.

78. **Practice Guidelines:** Systematically developed statements, best practices, laws, and/or policy recommendations, on medical practices to assist a practitioner to make evidence-informed decisions about appropriate diagnostic and therapeutic health care services for specific medical conditions.

79. **Pre-authorization:** A process in which a member, doctor, or hospital calls the client's benefit plan administrator for permission to carry out a treatment or procedure that will be covered under the benefit plan.

80. **Pre-screening:** A process through which a person's need for case management is initially evaluated.

81. **Primary Prevention:** The onset and development of a health problem or disease that is eliminated or inhibited by altering susceptibility, or reducing exposure for susceptible persons.

82. **Provider:** A doctor, hospital, laboratory, or other person or company that takes care of health care needs.

83. **Quality of Life:** An individual's perception of their position in life in the context of the culture and value system where they live, and in relation to their own goals, expectations, standards, and concerns. It normally appraises the following: health status, psychological state, level of independence, social relationships, personal beliefs, and relationship to salient features of the environment.

84. **Re-assessment:** A process whereby client status, function, and outcomes are reviewed according to an established time frame, or due to an unexpected crisis.

85. **Referral:** A process through which various persons in the community in need of case management services are referred to a program.

86. **Representative Payee:** An individual or organization that received social security and/or SSI payments for someone who cannot manage or direct someone else to manage his or her money.

87. **Secondary Prevention:** A set of measures available to individuals and communities for the early detection and prompt intervention to control disease and minimize disabilities.

88. **Self-Determinism:** An ethical approach to service delivery and care management that supports the client in determining their own future, by designing their own plans and choosing the assistance that they desire.

89. **Service Coordination:** A process through which the case manager arranges and/or authorizes services and implements the service plan (CISP) using various providers necessary to meet the client's needs.

90. **Service Plan (SP):** An agreed-upon written strategy developed jointly with the client and case manager outlining the goals and objectives for treatment. It can also be used to assess progress and any problems that may arise during the treatment.

91. **Skilled Care:** Patient care services that require delivery by a licensed physician regarding the necessity for a treatment that has been recommended by another physician. These may be required by some health plans for certain high-costs cases, such as cardiac surgery.

92. **Skilled Nursing Facility:** An institution that has a transfer agreement with one or more hospitals, and provides primarily in-patient skilled nursing care and rehabilitative services, and meets other specific certification requirements.

93. **Social Work Case Management:** Case management performed by a trained BSW or MSW health care professional.

94. **Specialist Case Manager:** A care management system in which a client is assigned several different case managers, depending on the unique needs and services reflected by the assessment and CISP.

95. **Stages of Case Management:** At a simple level, case management has minimally five sequential stages that include the following: 1) assessment and engagement, 2) developing goals and objectives, 3) intervention and implementation, 4) re-assessment, and 5) case closure.

96. **Subacute Care Facility:** A health care facility that is a step down from an acute care hospital and a step up from a conventional skilled nursing facility intensity of services.

97. **Task Environment:** This refers to the external organizational domain, or those organizations/agencies in the community that a health and human service organization (HSO) interacts and transacts with to fulfill its mission. The main areas in which these organizations are categorized include competing, complementary, referring, receiving, fiscal, or authoritative and legitimization.

98. **Termination:** The formal process of ending case management or health care services with a client. Termination may occur for reasons such as client or family non-compliance, client or case manager withdrawal, lack of eligibility for services, client attainment of goals, rehabilitation, or death of the client.

99. **Tertiary Prevention:** The reduction of health care problems in persons with some form of disability by attempting to restore stable and/or effective functioning.

100. **Utilization Review:** A process in which an insurance company reviews health care services provided by a doctor or hospital. The company conducts these to ensure that it is paying for appropriate health care services that produce desired cost-effective outcomes.

101. **Vocational Rehabilitation:** Cost-effective case management by a skilled professional who understands the implications of the medical and vocational services necessary to facilitate an injured worker's expedient return to suitable gainful employment, with a minimal degree of disability.

Part I

Trends, History, Social Work Case Management Model, and Practice Competencies

Current Trends Shaping Social Work Case Management

"Everything should be made as simple as possible, but no simpler."

—Albert Einstein

Trends Influencing Social Work Case Management (SWCMG)

The North American health and human services organizations (HSOs) in which professionals are employed are usually stressful settings in which to work (Holosko, 2006). They are generally characterized by ongoing annual funding and budget cuts, more stringent eligibility criteria for service provision, shortened time frames for interventions, increased caseload numbers, numerous regulatory policies and procedures that are constantly being amended, less time for supervisors to consult with their front-line workers, and increased organizational settings in which to work and collaborate (Preston, 2010; Savaya, Gardner, & Stange, 2011). When changes in policies, budgets, or service provision happen, front-line workers, supervisors, and managers are forced to respond rapidly and adapt to them. Many human service workers feel that such changes seem to occur almost on a daily basis.

HSOs are profoundly influenced and shaped by a variety of trends that impact the *where, when,* and *how* SWCMG is practiced in this era of changing health care reform (Cesta, 2012). Almost a decade ago, Hoge, Huey, and O'Connell (2004) advocated that behavioral health workforce personnel require an understanding of the diverse paradigms of various economic forces and trends that influence health care delivery, in order to be competent working in this area. Understanding such trends seem even more important today, given their frequency and occurrence. Sometimes such trends are clearly presented to HSO employees, and/or are time framed; for example, the agency will go paperless by July 15th. Other times, they and their implications are unclear to both the HSOs themselves and their employees; for example, next year's state budget will have severe cuts to all state-funded mental health agencies. In such cases, these decisions are often made well beyond the agency walls—from "places above." Thus, like many other employees, social work case managers (SWCMs) work in settings rife with overt organizational change and uncertainty, for example, fiscally, politically, administratively, and policy-wise.

This chapter first identifies these various external trends and shows how they flow downward and eventually influence SWCMG practice. Second, it identifies selected practice transitions that SWCMs have to embrace to accommodate these trends. Finally, it concludes with a rationale for better SWCMG education and training across all social work curricula to meet the demands for employment in this burgeoning growth area. The trends described herein influence different health and human service professionals in various ways; however, this chapter emphasizes how they impact social worker practitioners in general, and SWCMs in particular. We preface this discussion by stating that the trends presented are certainly not the only ones impacting social workers and SWCMs, but ones that have been well cited in the extant literature in this field.

International Trends: Neoliberalism and Globalization

Neoliberalism

Somewhere, in the conceptual stratosphere above, social workers have often heard how the two topical buzz words *neoliberalism* and *globalization* have impacted social welfare policies and practices. Just how they have done this is less clear. Schriver (2013) noted that the worldwide trends of these rather nebulous concepts appear much better known outside of the United States than they are in America. However, given their prominence in shaping national social welfare policy in many developing and underdeveloped countries of the world, they merit attention in any discussion of macro trends influencing social work and SWCMG practice. It is important to first note (and distinguish) that the term liberalism is a *political* doctrine, and neoliberalism is an *economic* doctrine. Further, these very different concepts are often blurred because they both have the word liberal within them. Another point of conceptual fuzziness here is when liberalism gets applied to the field of economics, it refers to policies meant to encourage entrepreneurship by removing government controls and interference, which positions the term to more of a right-wing conservative notion than its truer liberal left-of-center political meaning. The concept of liberalism clearly embodies a political philosophy favoring individual freedom and liberty, equality, and capitalism (Hartz, 1955, as cited in Nilep, 2012), which has a long and deep effect in American history.

Turning to the concept of neoliberalism, neo means "new," so this "new liberalism" was an economic shift from the previously described political concept above. Neoliberalism is about the freer movement of goods, resources, and enterprises in an effort to find cheaper labor and resources and, therefore, ultimately maximize profits and efficiencies (Holosko, 2015). The key assumptions or elements of neoliberalism described by Martinez and Garcia (1997) from the *Corporate Watch* include the following:

1. *The rule of the market:* The freedom for capital, goods, and services, where the market is "self-regulating." It also includes the de-unionizing of labor forces, removal of financial regulations, and more freedom from state or government.

2. *Cutting public expenditures for social services:* This means reducing the so-called social safety net for the poor including health, human services, and education.

3. *Deregulation:* It involves the reduction of government regulation of anything that could diminish profits, including the protection of the environment and safety on the job.

4. *Privatization:* It includes selling state-owned enterprises, goods, and services to private investors including banks, key industries, railroads, toll highways, electricity, schools, and hospitals.

5. *Eliminating the concept of "public good" or "community":* In short, these should be replaced with "individual responsibility," at any cost.

As the concept relates to our post welfare states of its current citizen regimes, neoliberalism is also used to describe social welfare, welfare policy, ideology, or governmentality (Holosko & Barner, 2014; Larner, 2005; SUNY Levin Institute, 2013).

Globalization

A consensual definition of globalization is, "a process of interaction and integration among the people, companies, and governments of different nations, a process driven by international trade and investment, and aided by information technology" (Holosko & Barner, 2014). This process has had profound effects on the environment, culture, economic development, prosperity, and human physical well-being in societies around the world (SUNY Levin Institute, 2013). Although neoliberalism and globalization were presented separately above, given their similar economic growth and trade imperative, in the past 15–20 years, these concepts have been inextricably braided (Holosko & Barner, 2014). In short, globalization is the reigning socio-historical re-configuration of social space, and neoliberalism is the policy approach to it. The term now used to promote their interrelationship is *neoliberal globalization* (Scholte, 2005).

When examining the literature about the so-called pluses or minuses of neoliberal globalization over time, the minuses far outweigh the pluses. This is particularly true in the area of social welfare, as in the past 25 years we have seen: more poverty worldwide than ever before, greater discrepancies between economic and social groups, more income inequality between the rich and poor, less human security and human rights, less social justice, poorer environmental health, and poorer safety and employment policies (SUNY Levin Institute, 2013). However, during this same time, there have been some noteworthy gains made in commerce, trade, finance, investment, technology, international law, military alliances, transportation, banking, and energy (Holosko & Barner, 2014). But, a closer look at *who* has made these latter gains clearly reveals that it is almost always the wealthier and dominant countries and corporations of the world, from which observers have now coined the phrase *economic colonialism* (Schriver, 2013). Unfortunately, although such economic concerns are important, they are not the life blood of social work practice, and/or social welfare policies. In sum, it is not a stretch to say that overall, social welfare and its clients have not fared well at all under the umbrella of neoliberal globalization.

National and Local Trends

The demand for social workers in general, and SWCMs specifically, will increase considerably in the next 10 years in America. In the recent U.S. Department of Labor, *BLS Occupational Outlook Handbook, 2012–13 Edition, Social Workers* (www .bls.gov/ooh/Community-and-Social-Service/Social-workers.htm#tab-6), it is projected that the employment of social workers is expected to grow by 25% from 2012 to 2020, faster than the national average for all occupations. It is also noted that this will be apparent in the areas of a) health care, expected to grow by 34%, b) mental health and substance abuse services by 31%, and c) social and family services by 20%.

In an effort to be proactive to these trends looming on the horizon, as they merged with the onset of *The Affordable Care Act* in September 2013, the Council on Social Work Education (CSWE) hosted a White House de-briefing in Washington, DC, titled "Addressing the Social Determinants of Health in a New Era: The Role of Social Work Education."

> This discussion focused on preparing the next generation of social work practitioners for the new paradigm in health professional education and collaborative practice to meet the needs of all Americans. The goal of the event was to come away with a shared understanding of the future of health care in the United States, broadly defined, and identification of a path forward for social work education in this new era. (CSWE, 2013, p. 1)

In addition to other featured panels on shifting demographics, mental health needs and building capacity, one titled "New Expectations for Health Care" addressed what the new era of health care looks like with respect to integrated care, interprofessional health care teams, and consideration of social determinants of health (CSWE, 2013, p. 4). In the past decade or so, two emergent trends in SWCMG have evolved, and they seemed well positioned to respond to this national imperative. These include a) re-engineering the goodness-of-fit between social work and case management, and b) promoting self-advocacy in case management planning and intervention.

The Goodness-of-Fit Between
Social Work and Case Management

Since the inception of social work practice in North America, whether our front-line workers were called "friendly visitors," "settlement house workers," "caregivers," "caseworkers," "social caseworkers," "social workers," or "case managers," one of the key and long standing attributes of our profession has been its ability to adapt, modify, and re-engineer itself across a broad range of fields of practice, vulnerable populations, and settings. Indeed, it has been argued that our profession's malleability legacy has been a unique part of its historical growth since its inception (Lubove, 1969). Since the 1900s onward in North America, the field of case management has had a parallel professional trajectory in adapting, altering, modifying, educating, and training workers, as it evolved from community settings, to hospital settings, to mental health settings, and finally to social welfare institutions of care—all of which are still the domains where SWCMG is currently primarily practiced. The profession of social work has evolved by literally living its hallmark adage of "always take the client s/he is at," and in turn, help them move to a better place in their lives. This pervasive person-centered mission transcends all of both social work and SWCMG practice as we know it today.

Beneath this overarching mission, the profession has anchored itself in various practice approaches, core values, and a tried and true intervention model called the problem-solving approach for practice. Taken together, these collectively serve as the rationale why social work and case management are indeed such an appropriate goodness-of-fit. Some of the other noted practice perspectives the profession has used (and still uses today) include social casework, person-in-environment, ecological, ecosystems, biopsychosocial, task-centered practice, feminist, solution-focused brief therapy, systematic family therapy, and more recently (in the last 20 years or so) strengths-based, social justice, resource procurement, barrier identification and removal, environmental, and neuroscience. Underlying these varying perspectives are a set of humane core values from which we have never wavered. These include self-determinism, autonomy, respect, genuineness, individuation, service, dignity and worth of individuals, social change, importance of human relationships, social and economic justice, integrity and competence. Our professional code of ethics firmly holds all of these values dearly, and for those of us in the profession, they help explain how we do, and what we do to others.

As indicated, although it has been often deemed a solution-focused approach, the overarching model currently used to describe our day-to-day person-centered work with clients is more frequently known as the problem-solving approach. This minimally includes the sequential steps of engagement; assessment; planning and contracting; action/doing, or intervention; monitoring and evaluation; and termination. In sum, the above noted practice perspectives, core analyzing values and scaffolding person-centered problem-solving model of social work practice, coupled with the profession's unique ability to re-engineer itself, has had applications in all fields of health and human service practice. These have also stead the growth of the profession very well and, by default, have stead those social workers who practice case management very well also.

Promoting Self-Advocacy in SWCMG
Case Planning and Intervention

One of the more pervasive trends clearly emergent in the past decade in North American SWCMG is the shifting of care responsibilities to the actual "person-in-care." In most health and mental health settings, these "persons" are typically called "patients," in elderly care settings they are often called "residents," in criminal justice systems they are "inmates," and in social welfare service organizations, they are normally called "clients." Thus, it is the organizational domain who labels the "persons-in-care" who receive case management services.

Health care organizations generally, and nurses specifically who work within them, promote, provide, and drive the entire case management field more so than any other profession. As one cognate professional in the health care arena, SWCMs are far fewer in number than their nurse case management counterparts and work typically in collaboration with them to provide various case management services. In some settings, like hospitals, SWCMs provide a range of complementary case management services with nurses normally attached to a particular unit such as an emergency room (Fusenig, 2012). They also provide more traditional case management tasks and functions in various other units of the hospital—for example, acute care, aging services, children services, etc.—such as assessment, discharge planning, in their roles as members of the overall social work department.

Given the prominence of case management in health care in North America, as well as the large disproportionate body of literature published on it in this area, social work looks to SWCMG in health care for leadership in the area of trends in other areas of case management. Typically, the international and national external trends previously noted in this chapter trickle down through health care first, followed by mental health, and then eventually family and social service agencies. These three occupational areas currently employ the largest number of social workers who are typically called "case managers" in their respective job titles.

As indicated (in the title of this subsection on national trends), the issue of self-advocacy in health care planning is a major concern that SWCMs deal with on a daily basis. In North America, Canada refers to this normally as *care coordination*, and in the United States, it is usually referred to as *patient advocacy*. This approach is one where the patient is a full and active participant in his or her care planning and intervention decisions. Thus, the ownership of caring for the person-in-care, shifts from care providers, to *care providers and their patients* (Bodenheimer & Abramowitz, 2010; British Columbia Ministry of Health, 2011). As such, patients are proactively educated and trained about how to care for themselves when they receive case management services. Consequently, SWCMs encourage and facilitate their patients to move from a passive, to a much more assertive and active role in their own care. In this model, SWCMs, *in full partnerships with their patients* assess their needs, determine their service eligibility, procure and negotiate resources, develop plans for care, develop treatment goals, initiate interventions needed, and in doing so, they educate and train patients about a) what their formal and informal support systems are; b) what barriers exist for care; c) what care arrangements the patient is responsible for; d) ways to empower patients to affect their self-care; and then, e) follow-up and evaluate the agreed-upon care-planning arrangements and intervention activities. In addition, the entire process is time-framed, both output and outcome driven, and transparent.

Further, this model promotes self-direction and personal management, self-efficacy, a personal investment in overall care planning, self-actualization, and more personal accountability. Empirical studies conducted on this proactive patient-empowered approach to case management practice have shown better illness prognosis, more positive health outcomes, greater patient satisfaction, and shorter time frames for achieving stability, and recovery benchmarks (Anderson & Funnell, 2010; Fleming-Castaldy, 2010; Holman & Lorig, 2000; Kendrick, Petty, Bezanson, & Jones, 2006; Leske, Strodl, & Hou, 2012). This groundswell national case management trend is not only prominent in health care where fee-for-service and eligibility criteria direct patients through various systems of care, but also in other settings where SWCMG is practiced.

The two main models where SWCMG is practiced today were astutely first described by Rose and Moore (1995) as "client driven" and "provider driven." The former is the model that most SWCMs are more comfortable with; as normally, in this model, client needs are identified and accessed mutually, treatment goals are developed, links to formal and informal services are identified, and the monitoring of outcomes are done in full partnership with client input into this process. The essence of this SWCMG-client work focuses on identifying client strengths and obstacles to the obtainment of goals, developing social networks, freeing the client from clinical judgments and contempt, and assessing the role of each service system intervention as either a support or obstacle (pp. 228–229).

Conversely, the so-called provider-driven models are cost and eligibility driven, as restrictive and narrow parameters are set on the decisions made in the entire case management process, where a limited (by resources and options) menu of fee-for-service choices are offered to clients. The SWCM-client work in this model focuses on identifying problems, making resources and referrals for services, ensuring client adherence and compliance to treatment plans, and monitoring time-framed outputs and outcomes (Rose & Moore, 1995, p. 229). As previously noted, this model is more closely aligned to health care, but in actual practice many SWCMs are employed in North American settings that have features of both models.

The above-mentioned international trends, in turn, trickle down to influence national and state trends, then eventually impact local trends, where SWCMs practice. Thus, how they actually shape day-to-day practice where social workers and SWCMs are employed will be presented.

How Trends Shape Social Work and SWCM Practice

Table 1.1 distils four selected trends at the local levels of social work and SWCMG practice and not only describes them in terms of their impact, but candidly offers the "stories behind the trends."

❖ **Table 1.1**   Four Selected Neoliberal Globalization Trends Influencing Social Work Practice

Selected Trends	The "Stories Behind the Trends"
1. Increase in Service Demands ↑ Decrease Funding ↓	1. Do More with Less 2. Think Smarter
2. Community "Problem Reconfiguration"	1. Communities Lag Behind the Concepts 2. Matching Mandates to Problems
3. Integrative Approaches to Service Delivery	1. Define Partners and Stakeholders 2. Develop Joint Agreements
4. "Era of Legitimacy"	1. Evaluation of Program and Services 2. Interventions → Outputs → Outcomes

Source: Feit, M. D., & Holosko, M. (2013). *Distinguishing Clinical from Upper Level Management in Social Work.* London, U.K.: Taylor & Francis. Pages 18–34.

Trend 1: Increase in Service Demands ↑ Decrease Funding ↓

Each day, more and more vulnerable individuals require more and more social welfare services all over the world (Feit & Holosko, 2013). Social welfare, defined broadly here, is taken to include education, health, housing, and social services. Although "real spending" as a percentage of GDP reflected in constant dollars (and adjusted for inflation) has grown in North America, per capita spending for social welfare (actual dollars per person) has not significantly changed in the past 25 years or so (Holosko & Barner, 2014). This is particularly true for the two most vulnerable groups in our society, the very young and very old (Pati, Keren, Alessandrini, & Schwarz, 2004).

At the organizational level, HSOs a) often compete fiercely for limited funds; b) are forced to find creative ways to offset their annual escalating costs through revenue sharing, limiting eligibility criteria, re-prioritization and re-structuring their organization's mandate; c) use more and more non-professional, and/or volunteer staff; d) borrow money against their limited budgets; and e) actively seek out more funding avenues, for example, external grants, private donations, cost-shared arrangements, and contractual services (Holosko & Barner, 2014). Heller (2006) referred to these responses as seeking more "fiscal space," or finding additional resources to service clients in these troubled neoliberal financial times.

The stories behind this trend are rather bleak as with such limited resources, and in our altruistic efforts to do our allegedly important mission-driven and client-centered work, HSOs are fiscally and politically scrambling just trying to survive—let alone thrive, in today's climate. Indeed, SWCMs (like other human service employees) are constantly under pressure to do more with less, as their caseloads and waiting lists for services increase daily. As previously indicated, financial uncertainty is both ubiquitous and pervasive in most HSOs, and there isn't a supervisor or administrator in any HSO who would not be elated if their annual funding was re-approved next year with a "zero percent increase"—as they have come to realize that there could be far worse scenarios.

This trend, impacting the domain in which SWCMs' work is conducted, creates challenges for all human service workers, as if they continue to do too much more—with no complementary supports or resources, they may find themselves compromising the very services they are mandated and ethically bound to deliver to clients (Allen & Smith, 2008; Holosko & Barner, 2014). Finally, SWCMs can only be asked to "think smarter" and "be more efficient" a finite number of times, or the proverbial double-edged sword of quantity vs. quality is sure to cut someone in an injurious way—and it's most likely to be our clients. We contend that this first trend, although intimately related to the others noted in Table 1.1, holds significantly more gravity than do the other three. It is also one that SWCMs are very aware of, given that it affects all areas of their direct and indirect practice with vulnerable clients on a daily basis.

Trend 2: Community "Problem Re-configuration"

There has been a decided shift in the current devolution-revolution of health and human services to developing social welfare programs, interventions and services in communities, not from a population or demographic imperative, but from a problem re-configuration one. Here, a community's problems are prioritized, based on the so-called problems of individuals in the community. So, depending on "the problems that the community has," and its existing infrastructures—if one is fortunate enough to end up with a problem that the particular community "has identified"—care can be accessed. Conversely, if one's problems do not match up with "the community problems"—clients must travel (if they can) to usually adjacent communities to receive care (Feit & Holosko, 2013). For example, in Canada's and Sweden's universal health care systems, smaller towns and cities cannot afford highly specialized health care for all citizens. As a result, many citizens needing such care are accustomed to driving, or being airlifted to proximal communities that have the specialized care that they require and have come to expect (Holosko, 1997).

The stories behind this reality are noted in Table 1.1. First, communities clearly lag behind this concept, and they have difficulties matching their infrastructures and mandates to the ever-changing "problems of the community." To exemplify the stories behind this trend, Brown and Stevens (2006) studied seven U.S. communities who aimed to expand health coverage to the uninsured and improve their care (the main current political agenda of President Obama). Funded by the Robert Wood Johnson Foundation's *Communities in Charge* (CIC) program, when these communities (with identified community problems) were evaluated, they concluded that:

> Despite solid leadership and carefully crafted plans, political, economic, and organizational obstacles precluded much expansion of coverage and constrained reforms . . . CIC's record offers little evidence that communities are better equipped than are other sectors of U.S. society to solve the problems of un-insurance. (p. W150)

SWCMs, by virtue of how they practice, become acutely aware of the limited resources available to clients in their own communities. This forces them by default, to expand on their definition of just what "local community care" is—to a more expansive one, involving a greater geographic area beyond the local community.

This in turn, presents a new set of resource challenges such as networking with these new service providers, new waitlist protocols, service availability, access to services, cost, formal and informal supports for clients in these new geographic areas, referrals, and transportation for services.

Trend 3: Integrative Approaches to Service Delivery

Due to the current trends of devolution and fiscal cutbacks for North American HSOs, services and providers have become collaboratively bundled together with multiple agencies offering defined systems of care in their respective communities (Cook, Michener, Lyn, Lobach, & Johnson, 2010). These are often referred to as cross-sectional collaborations—networks, alliances, or partnerships among public, secular and faith-based non-profits, and for-profit organizations. They either consist of distinct organizations that develop relationships with each other to meet client needs called "self-organizing networks." Or, they are community organizations sub-contracted with a lead organization, which is expected to create a mandated community-based network of service providers (Provan & Milward, 1995; Whelan, 2011). The latter (lead organization model) is the more preferred approach as frankly, it is cheaper. But ideally, both arrangements are expected to yield the benefits of increased efficiency, innovation, local adaptation, increased flexibility, and enhanced community ties (Graddy & Chen, 2006, p. 534).

This idea is certainly tenable and required in today's reality, but the concept appears to be ahead of the community's ability to implement it. The previously noted proverbial "clouds of uncertainty" about integrative service approaches hover large over issues of costs, organizational, programmatic, and community influences, democratic and consensual accountability, efficiency and effectiveness, integrative models that are viable and ones that are not, organizational and community care constraints and contingencies, community capacities, access, outcomes, policy considerations, and network size and scope (Bryson, Crosby, & Stone, 2006; Knitzer & Cooper, 2006). Despite such uncertainties, HSOs continue to move forward with this seemingly altruistic community-spirited ideal, which has profound implications for how SWCMs provide services to their clients.

In addition, the neoliberal deficit reduction strategies of federal, state, and local governments has led to a resurgence of interest in community collaboration (Foreman Kready, 2011). Increasingly, mandates for collaboration are linked to conditions of funding. As governments mandate collaborative networks as implementation mechanisms for integrating social welfare services, empirical studies about how inter-organizational collaboration is implemented among community partners is an emerging research, policy, and practice area (Babiak, 2009; Bryson, Crosby, & Stone, 2006; Sytch, Tatarynowicz, & Gulati, 2012).

Many, social workers and SWCMs are very mindful of some of the more important issues about the real "stories behind the story of collaboration" (Holosko, 2009). Here are a few:

1. *Funding issues require collaboration:* Regardless of the "will" to collaborate, such partnerships are tied to funding. Those HSOs who do so will thrive, and those who do not will

inevitably wither away. Thus, developing relationships with partners in the community however strained, is integral to local organizational survival.

2. *Voluntary vs. mandatory collaboration:* Although different joint agreements are voluntary and some are mandatory, the nature of the collaborative relationship transcends this distinction (Dunlop & Holosko, 2004). This means that agencies collaborate to ensure funding and typically will do anything they can to make the collaborative relationship work.

3. *All communities are not created equal:* Communities vary greatly in their demographics, organizational relationships, service networks, pre-existing partnerships, resources and infrastructures, and collaborations seem to magnify such inequalities. Thus, some communities are able to develop more effective collaboration networks than others.

4. *Evaluation complexities:* Evaluating collaborative initiatives has been challenging to say the least, as these initiatives are typically multi-site, multi-level, with different programs/goals/objectives/costs/outcomes/services/stakeholders, etc. The assumption put forward here is that complex community-based collaborations are more efficient than singular service delivery models. However, this has never been empirically determined or validated (Holosko & Feit, 2006).

5. *Collaborations are more likely to succeed when they have legitimacy:* Finally, Human and Provan (2000) cited three necessary conditions for collaborative network survival: 1) legitimacy of the *network as a form* that can attract internal and external supports, 2) legitimacy of the *network as an entity* responsible to both insiders and outsiders, and 3) legitimacy of the *network as an interaction* that builds trust among members to freely communicate with one another. Although somewhat dated, these conditions hold true today.

Trend 4: Era of Legitimacy

Never before in our North American social welfare history has evaluation and its focus on outcomes been "part and parcel" of the mandated delivery of our intervention's programs and services. Indeed, we are no longer on the frontier of program and practice evaluation activity, but are in the midst of a groundswell of such activities becoming mandated in federal and state social welfare initiatives, programs, and services. In turn, public scrutiny for the financing and efficiency of outcomes is more apparent than it ever was before. We have evolved from offering social welfare programs directed by the rather noble motives of altruism and case wisdom, or "a need for such services," to much more cost legitimizing ways of providing health and social services. These include the empirical testing of all interventions; developing more empirically defined protocols for our interventions; increasing treatment fidelity, developing pilot projects to justify larger initiatives; ensuring interventions are tied to defined frameworks (i.e., logic models) and outcomes; developing organizational and community capacities to ensure success of interventions; funding initiatives with the assurance of self-sustainability over a shorter time period; ensuring that funded social welfare initiatives include timely best and/or promising practices; and ensuring that funded programs/services are both effective and efficient.

Presently, SWCMG requires not just a traditional focus on inputs and outputs, but also on outcomes and their sustainable impacts (W. K. Kellogg Foundation [2006] website reference for the program logic model framework: http://www.wkkf.org/

knowledge-center/resources/2006/02/wk-kellogg-foundation-logic-model-development-guide.aspx). And these must be assessed empirically with a view to what it costs to provide such interventions. Clements, Chianca, and Sasaki (2008) said it more succinctly: "evaluations should estimate the total impacts that can be attributed to an intervention and also estimate the intervention's cost effectiveness. . . . Also, evaluations of this nature are likely to be more helpful for program managers" (p. 196). Given that the current SWCMG model is now being driven by costs, it appears that soon, the cost benefit or cost effectiveness of all social work interventions will need to be tabled as a bona fide agenda for all case management services.

In conclusion here, with *The Affordable Care Act* currently unfolding in the United States, the issue of providing local systems of care models that are cost effective are paramount to this initiative. Given our knowledge of how formal and informal systems are linked to clients with resources and services, social workers and SWCMs are in ideal positions to take a leadership role in the delivery of the next generation of health care in America. This sub-section provided the context for how community trends shape this reality. Hopefully, having better awareness and thinking out of the agency box, which SWCMs routinely do, in order to administer timely care to their clients, will become the norm for all health care professionals, in the near (and very soon) future.

Practice Transformations

Chapter 1 briefly outlined the history of social work practice in North America, and the more elaborate history of SWCMG practice. As was noted, the so-called managed care movement that predominated the health and mental health institutions in the 1970s and spawned fee-for-service insurance providers and HMOs, cost efficiency measures, the expansion of private hospitals, and the growing specialization of tasks and functions required social workers to practice effectively in such settings. Since then, SWCMG became re-defined iteratively through both pieces of enacted federal legislation significantly including: *Community Mental Health Centers Act* (1963), *The Deficit Reduction Act* (1984), *The Americans with Disability Act* (1990), *Personal Responsibility and Work Opportunity Reconciliation Act* (1996), *Mental Health Services Act* (2004, 2009), and recently *The Affordable Care Act* of 2010, as well as numerous state-wide policy and best practice changes and their various revisions over time.

In addition to the previously mentioned flexibility of the social work profession to continually adapt in its professional survival, the profession with the advent of case management as we know it today has had to make some practice modifications that have helped to solidify its prominence in SWCMG services overall—and many of these adaptations have been made in the "trending domain" area of case management practice—that being health care.

After interviewing 12 SWCMs currently practicing in this area in the United States and Canada (for this text), it became clear that social workers have had to constantly modify, adapt, learn, re-learn, and transform their practice thinking in order to be both current and relevant in practicing effectively as SWCMs in today's reality. Thus, we present an overarching Table 1.2 delineating 10 such transformations. We realize that these are not the only SWCMG transformations necessary, but are ones that currently

❖ **Table 1.2**   Ten Selected CMG Practice Transformations Necessary for Social Work Case Management Practice (SWCMG)

Traditional SW Perspectives	→	SWCMG Transformations
Individual With a Problem	→	Problems of Individuals
Client	→	Consumer/Customer
Person-in-Environment	→	Person-in-Care-in-Environment
Care System	→	System of Care
People Changing	→	People Processing/Sustaining
Programmed Decision Making	→	Shared Decision Making
Output Oriented	→	Time-framed, Output, and Outcome Driven
Singular Role Delineation	→	Role Blurring at Multi-Levels
Generalist Practice	→	Advanced Generalist Practice
Bureaucracy	→	Technological Bureaucratization

fall directly out of the noted preceding trends, the literature on this subject, and ones conveyed to us by the 12 SWCMs we interviewed. Indeed, our profession seems to role model the very resiliency we have some to expect from many of our clients.

As indicated in Table 1.2, these transformations are localized where the actual faces of our clients meet the faces of SWCMs. Thus, we also wanted to illustrate a clinical/direct or micro practice focus to these transformations, as others have used more meso and macro lenses to examine the impact of trends in other practice areas (Holosko & Barner, 2014).

Individual → Problem of Individual

Although social work's core humanistic and altruistic values involve positioning the person above all other considerations, the first trend repositions a person with a problem to the problem(s) of a person. Historically, since the history of case management (CMG) is driven by health care more so than human service organizations, the latter approximates what we have termed the so-called medical model. This is defined as, "the traditional approach to the diagnosis and treatment of illness as practiced by physicians in the Western world; that focuses on the defect or dysfunction" (*Stedman's Medical Dictionary for the Health Professions and Nursing*, 2012).

Although the problems of individuals usually drive SWCMG, this is not to say that social workers cannot, and/or should not maintain a strong professional commitment to providing person-focused and not necessarily patient-focused care (Hsieh, 2006; Kitwood, 1997; Parker, 2001; Starfield 2011). Indeed, SWCMs learn to work "within the contradictions" of their existing agencies and settings, by keeping the person foremost in any discussion of the problem. In many health care settings, SWCMs have to constantly remind clients, families, colleagues, and other health professionals of their core person-centered values and how they are unique to social work, how they can complement and add value to the existing care system, and more importantly, how they can benefit clients in their existing care systems. This is where tact, diplomacy, deft and selective communication skills, values and knowledge are used simultaneously with each *client,* not *patient* (as agencies may force us to use this label) we see. As stated poignantly by Parker (2001):

> It is crucial in contemporary social and healthcare to retain a clean sense of the person with whom we are working at any point in time. We must also keep firmly fixed in view what we are working to achieve and what the impact of the illness is on that particular system and network of individuals. . . . A shift in culture and thinking does not deny the importance of medical advance but adds a holistic and human element that brings the person to center stage. (p. 341)

So despite this paradigm shift, SWCMs work thoughtfully and deliberately to continue to "keep the light always shining on the person," and not their problem foremost. Indeed, this is a defining professional characteristic of how social workers practice CM, different than other cognate disciplines.

Client → Consumer/Customer

Trend 2 in Table 1.2 illustrates the transition for SWCMs to shift from a client to a customer, or consumer focus. Any way you look at this, it smacks of a corporate/business model, where somehow people have exchanged money by cash or insurance, and they received a product. Although this formula seems simple, it presents some real challenges for SWCMs who interact with vulnerable individuals on their caseloads each day.

The first is that we have been trained in BSW and MSW programs that these are our *clients,* not customers. Second, our profession acknowledges that many of the activities that we routinely assist clients with are impossible to have a monetary or discrete cost asset value. These are things like timely information offered to clients to make better informed decisions; empowering individuals; assisting clients to be less angry, less violent, less anxious, less depressed, less dependent; or conversely, more thoughtful, more goal oriented, more supportive of friends and family, more spiritual, more educated, more employable—and the list goes on here. So how would one be able to evaluate our effectiveness on one, two, or three of these things, and/or how would one go about doing that (Hsieh, 2006)? Second, as consumers (the other half of the term), what did they actually "consume" during their process of therapeutic engagement with SWCMs?

So what is the resolve for SWCMs who are being nudged to move in this direction? Our contention is that this is similar to "working within the contradictions" of our organizations mentioned earlier. Thus, we must strive to continue to re-frame in our hearts and minds that these are our clients foremost—people in need, who require timely and humanistic services, and whatever the organization or agency calls or labels them, and as long as these labels do not inhibit our service or dismiss/minimize our clients in any way—as they say in street lingo—we need to learn to "live with it."

In an effort to assess and clarify how health care consumers perceived of themselves, West (2014) stated:

> The consumer metaphor fits imperfectly with the healthcare system and with the experiences of healthcare users, and carries with it a host of associations that shape U.S. healthcare policy debates in particular ways. If ideological discourse is created in an attempt to smooth over contradictions and uncomfortable truths, then we ought to examine its limits, as users either adopt a consumer discourse about health in making sense of their own experiences and perspectives on the healthcare system or identify its gaps and disjunctures. (p. 300)

Person-in-Environment (PIE) → Person-in-Care-in-Environment (PICIE)

Trend 3 shifts one of our traditional cornerstones of social work practice (Bartlett, 1970; Boehm, 1954). Recognized as the main domain and providence of social work practice, the primary focus of person-in-environment (PIE) is the interaction(s) between the person and his or her environment that encapsulates a more holistic understanding of the client and his or her problem in the context of their environment (Ramsay, n.d.).

PIE has indeed been the leading paradigm of social work practice, but with the advent of CM, our overt care-centered focus pushes the original model to envelop broader environmental and contextual considerations throughout each phase of SWCMG. Indeed, we concur that the existing PIE model even in traditional non-case management settings (not health or mental health), needs expansion to better understand: how evidence-based practice may be used more effectively within it (Simmons, 2012); how psychosocial aspects may be better addressed within it; how various levels of the environment may be more understood from the multi- and interrelated dimensions in a more integrative approach (Ashford & LeCroy, 2010); how psychosocial functioning and timely psychotherapy can be better understood from the broader environment (Saari, 2002); and, how the environment could be better expanded to include its ecological context for social workers concerned about sustainability (Jones, 2008).

The SWCMG Person-in-Care-in-Environment (PICIE) model is one that considers many levels of care and environmental supports that any client has simultaneously. For example, during the assessment step, appraisals of psychosocial variables, biological variables, mental and environmental health variables, capacity/capabilities/decision-making variables, as well as motivation to want help, are considered and carefully appraised by SWCMs. Obviously, in health care settings these are more routinely assessed by using additional standardized tests and protocols, inventories, scales, etc. However, outside of traditional health care settings, considerations of many of these various assessment criteria are also appraised by skilful SWCMs, without directed or regulatory requirements, having minimal training, or by using only tests or time-framed protocols. As such, much of this is learned "on-the-job," and involves the judicious use of accrued "case wisdom" and timely supervision.

The PICIE model also expands the client's environment appraisal to move beyond the immediate environment (i.e., household members, family, and friends) to the secondary environment (i.e., formal and informal care systems in the environment, neighbors, work, social media help, and the internet, etc.). Careful assessment of these expanded environments and how they relate to the care needs of clients requiring CMG services is the norm in SWCMG practice.

Care System → System of Care

Trend 4 shifts the traditional focus of SWCMG from a care system, to a system of care. The system of care movement has been in a process of development in both health and social welfare care of children and their families, adults, and the elderly. Table 1.3 shows how system of care reform efforts interface with SWCMs in our "communities of care."

As indicated in Table 1.3, such reform efforts shape the context for how we provide SWCMG services. We anticipate that these reforms will see more changes as *The Affordable Care Act* unfolds more completely in the United States in the next few years. But referring back to sub-section one of this chapter, "context is everything," and as

❖ **Table 1.3** Characteristics of Systems of Care as Systems Reform Initiatives

From		To
Fragmented Services	→	Coordinated Service Delivery
Categorical Programs/Funding	→	Multidisciplinary Teams/Blended Resources
Limited Service Availability	→	Comprehensive Services
Crisis-Oriented Approach	→	Focus on Available Care Responsive Services
People Out-of-Home	→	People Within Home as Long as Possible
Client Care	→	Community-Based Care
Creation of "Dependency"	→	Creation of "Self-Help" and Active Participation
Client-Only Focus	→	Client and Supports as Focus
Needs/Deficits Assessments	→	Strengths-Based Assessments
Families as "Problems"	→	Families as "Partners" and Therapeutic Services
Cultural Blindness	→	Cultural Competence
Highly Professionalized	→	Formal, Informal, and Natural Support Coordination
Client Must "Fit" Services	→	Individualized Approach for Eligible Services
Input-Focused Accountability	→	Outcome/Results-Oriented Accountability
Clients With Problems	→	Clients as Partners in Solving Problems

Source: Adopted from Pires, S. (1996). *Characteristics of systems of care as systems reform initiatives.* Washington, DC: Human Service Collaborative.

we continue to practice daily with clouds of fiscal uncertainty, such trends may change as governments change, policies change, and as political parties change. This is the work we have chosen, but now we at least have more enlightenment about what and how these trends change iteratively and shape our SWCMG practice daily.

People Changing → People Processing and People Sustaining

Trend 5 offers another interesting paradigm shift for SWCMs to consider, that being moving from a traditional "people-changing" paradigm, to a "people-processing" and "people-sustaining" one. The origin of this term comes from Hasenfeld (1983) who encouraged our profession to not only look at the client as the unit of analysis, but hover above the client to obtain another view, that being the organization and its community domain as the unit of analysis. Hasenfeld (1983) developed the notion of exchange relationships between organizations as being the interactive lifeblood of any health and human service organization. All SWCMs know that as they shepherd, coordinate, navigate, negotiate, broker, mediate, collaborate, etc., with more clients daily in their systems of care, that organizational exchanges are essential to the overall CMG process. Relationships with partners and collateral agencies, including various contacts/support people, decision-making people, authority figures, care providers, etc., are how most SWCMs spend most of their hours each day. Indeed, although client access is an important occupational concern for all CMG (Hsieh, 2006), most SWCMs spend more than 85% of their time tending to the various exchange relationships with a host of individuals in the communities of care in which they work, or they cannot do their jobs effectively (personal communication, D. Holosko, 2014).

SWCMs like other SWs are well aware that for accountability purposes "body count data" prevails—or more simply the more people you see, the more funding you receive (Holosko, Bulcke, & Feit, 1997). So a constant and increased admission stream of clients is always needed or funding will be curtailed, for the most part. However, this tends to present us as being overly concerned about just being people-processing types only, which is not true. It also, by default, infers that a) somehow people processing is not a nice term or notion, and b) the other terms people changing and people sustaining are more humane (in an odd sort of way).

SWCMs who adhere strongly to their core set of professional values see all of these three from a decided strengths-based perspective. For if we don't move clients through their systems of care, we would be negligent in actually getting them care. Second, we have lost the idealized notion that all clients will change, and will change "for the better" after we intervene with them. That simply is not true. Case wisdom reminds us that some clients resist change, placate change, deny change, fake change, fear change, and/or oppose those who want them to change. We have also realized that many clients are stuck in negative places that they choose to be stuck in, as it is "familiar territory" to them. Others are very content to be stuck in what Seligman, Maier, and Geer (1968) referred to as "learned helplessness," where they simply bumble along with no resolve to change anything about themselves at all. In short here, SWCMs do not see people processing as anything more than a positive step for many clients.

Finally, for many clients "no change" or "people sustaining" are very positive. Being stable on psychiatric medications, having a positive and enduring support system, being semi-independent, being motivated to be active partners in their care without knowing full well what is involved in that partnership, are very sustainable examples of care that help many clients. In short, SWCMs come to view people processing, changing, and/or sustaining as "part-and-parcel" of the essence of effective practice, as when these are anchored in our core values, all can be framed from a decided strengths-based perspective.

Programmed Decision Making → Shared Decision Making

In every client–worker relationship is a perception that there is a power dependency dynamic, where the worker holds the ultimate authority and the client has limited or no power (Lupton, 2011). As indicated in the first sub-section of this chapter on trends and their influence, a fundamental paradigm shift in CMG in general, and in SWCMG in particular, which is "front and center" in this field, is that clients must become *full partners in this relationship from the onset and share in the decision making for their treatment plan.* The skilled SWCMG does not shift any (of his or her) authority/work/tasks/responsibilities to the client, but shares the important responsibility with the client to first "own their problem." Then, the SWCMG and client can more readily become proactively involved in a variety of necessary ongoing shared decisions to affect their meaningful client-centered care plan of action.

The current literature on user involvement in health, social service care, and planning rests clearly on the premise that user involvement, education, and shared decision making is a good and necessary thing to promote in all helping relationships, and it is likely to result in more positive impacts (Rhodes, 2012, p. 187). In this regard, a flexible communication strategy is required by all SWCMs to meet the needs of different client populations in many different contexts, as the first step to developing a genuine collaboration in an open and honest relationship. Thus, it is an essential prerequisite for clients and SWCMs to work *together* to make *all*-important medical decisions (Minogue et al., 2009; Morgan & Jones, 2009). In the medical literature, it is well documented that shared decision making has resulted in positive outcomes such as lower health care use, lower health care costs, and fewer hospital admissions among others (Scott, 2013).

Indeed, essentially all SWCMG has moved away from programmed to a shared decision-making model, and the general steps in this process are normally as follows:

1. *Make yourself accessible to clients:* First and foremost, SWCMs must ensure that their access is always available for clients and family systems.

2. *Develop good "listening ears":* Listening carefully to clients and client systems about what their needs, issues, concerns are, and what their ways of communicating are, is essential in developing any helping relationship with any client in any setting.

3. *Establish trust in each phase of the process:* SWCMs certainly understand the importance of building trust relationships with their clients. Using skills such as empathy,

As you can surmise, the information age impacts SWCMs significantly, with increased paperwork, bureaucratization, and computerization. Ongoing training and education to stay abreast with these realities are the norm for SWCMs employed in a range of health and human service settings.

Concluding Remarks

As indicated throughout this contextual chapter, like other social workers, SWCMs do not work in a vacuum. They are influenced daily by international, national, political, organizational, policy, and resource trends. This chapter identified selected main contextual trends that shape our day-to-day practice. What we have come to realize as a profession is that in order to professionally survive, social workers must continue leading with the hallmark characteristic of our profession's DNA that is to continue to adapt and transform. We are fortunate that this is part of our profession's legacy.

We then presented 10 key transformational trends that SWCMs must fully embrace in order to adapt in this regard. Although targeted to the "trending domains" (those areas that lead other areas of CMG practice) of health and mental health, we contend that existing curriculae in North America BSW and MSW programs are sorely lacking in preparing social workers to work effectively in this area. Indeed, this was a main rationale for writing this text, and as you read on, we hope that you will gain the necessary knowledge and skills to offset this deficit in your existing education.

❖

REFERENCES

Allen, B., & Smith, A. (2008). *Special report: Reduced funding cripples Head Start from reaching its potential.* Alexandria, VA: National Head Start for America Press.

Anderson, R. M., & Funnell, M. M. (2010). Patient empowerment: Myths and misconceptions. *Patient Education and Counseling, 79*(3), 277–282.

Ashford, J., & LeCroy, C. (2010). *HBSE a multidimensional perspective* (4th ed.). Belmont, CA: Cengage Learning.

Babiak, K. M. (2009). Criteria of effectiveness in multiple cross-sectoral interorganizational relationships. *Evaluation and Program Planning, 32*(1), 1–12.

Bartlett, H. M. (1970). *The common base of social work practice.* New York, NY: Putnam.

Battersby, M., Korff, M. V., Schaefer, J., Davis, C., Ludman, E., Greene, S. M., Parkerton, M., & Wagner, E. H. (2010). Twelve evidence-based principles for implementing self-management support in primary care. *The Joint Commission Journal on Quality and Patient Safety, 36*(12), 561–570.

Bodenheimer, T., & Abramowitz, S. (2010). *Helping patients help themselves: How to implement self-management support* (pp. 1–31). California Health Foundation. Retrieved from http://www.chcf.org/publications/2010/12/helping-patients-help-themselves

Boehm, W. W. (1954). The terminology of social casework: An attempt at theoretical clarification. *The Social Service Review, 28*(4), 381–391.

British Columbia Ministry of Health. (2011). *Self-management support: A health care intervention* (pp. 1–66). Vancouver, BC: Author.

Brown, L. D., & Stevens, B. (2006). Charge of the right brigade? Communities, coverage, and care for the uninsured. *Health Affairs, 25*(3), w150-w161.

Bryson, J. M., Crosby, B., & Stone, M. (2006). The design and implementation of cross-sector collaborations: Proposals from the literature. *Public Administration Review, 66*(6), 44–55.

Cesta, T. (2012, July). Case management insider: The role of case management in an era of healthcare—Part 1. *Hospital Case Management.* Retrieved September 16, 2013, from http://www .questushealth.com/wp-includes/cm%20articles/Role%20of%20CM%20in%20Era%20 of%20Health%20Reform%20P1.pdf

Clements, P., Chianca, T., & Sasaki, R. (2008). Reducing world poverty by improving evaluation of developmental aid. *American Journal of Evaluation, 29*(2), 195–214.

Cook, J. J., Michener, J. L., Lyn, M. M., Lobach, D. D., & Johnson, F. F. (2010). Community collaboration to improve care and reduce health disparities. *Health Affairs, 29*(5), 956–958. doi:10.1377/hlthaff.2010.0094

CSWE. (2013). CSWE hosted a White House briefing "Addressing the Social Determinants of Health in a New Era: The Role of Social Work Education." Retrieved September 16, 2013, from http://www.cswe.org/News/NewsArchives/69356.aspx

Dunlop, J., & Holosko, M. (2004). The story behind the story of collaborative networks-relationships do matter! *Journal of Health and Social Policy, 19*(3), 1–18.

Feit, M. D., & Holosko, M. (2013). *Distinguishing clinical from upper level management in social work.* London, UK: Taylor & Francis.

Fleming-Castaldy, R. P. (2010). Are satisfaction with and self-management of personal assistance services associated with the life satisfaction of persons with physical disabilities? *Disability and Rehabilitation, 33*(15/16), 1447–1459.

Foreman Kready, S. (2011). *Organizational culture and partnership process: A grounded theory study of community-campus partnerships.* Electronic manuscript, Virginia Commonwealth University, Richmond, VA.

Fusenig, E. (2012). The role of emergency room social worker: An exploratory study. *Master of Social Work Clinical. Research Papers.* Paper 26. Retrieved from http://sophia.stkate.edu/ msw_papers/26

Graddy, E., & Chen, B. (2006). Influences on the size and scope of networks for social delivery. *Journal of Public Administration Research and Theory, 16*(4), 533–552.

Hasenfeld, Y. (1983). *Human service organizations.* Englewood Cliffs, NJ: Prentice Hall.

Heller, P. (2006). The prospects of creating "fiscal space" for the health sector. *Health Policy and Planning, 21*(2), 75–79.

Hoge, M. A., Huey, L. Y., & O'Connell, M. J. (2004). Best practices in behavioral health workforce education and training. *Administration and Policy in Mental Health and Mental Health Services Research, 32*(2), 91–106.

Holman, H., & Lorig, K. (2000). Patients as partners in managing chronic disease. *British Medicine Journal, 320*(7320), 526–527. doi: 10.1136/bmj.320.7234.526

Holosko, M. J. (1997). Service user input: Fact or fiction? The evaluation of the trauma program. Department of Rehabilitation, Sault Ste. Marie, Ontario. *The Canadian Journal of Program Evaluation, 11*(2), 111–126.

Holosko, M. J. (2006). Why don't social workers make better child welfare workers than non-social workers? *Research on Social Work Practice, 16*(4), 426–430.

Holosko, M. J. (2009). Global realities of social policy: The devolution revolution. *Journal of Social Work in Public Health, 24*(3), 189–190.

Holosko, M. J. (2015). Neoliberalism, Globalization and Social Welfare. In K. Corcoran (Ed). *The Social Work Desk Reference* (3rd ed.). New York, NY: Oxford University Press.

Holosko, M. J., & Barner, J. (2014). Neoliberal globalization: Social welfare policy and institutions. In M. Vidal de Haymes, S. Haymes, & R. Miller (Eds.), *The Routledge handbook on poverty in the United States* (pp. 239–248). London, UK: Taylor & Francis.

Holosko, M. J., Bulcke, G., & Feit, M. D. (1997). Health care prevention: Real or rhetoric? *Journal of Health and Social Policy, 10*(1), 101–104.

Holosko, M. J., & Feit, M. D. (2006). Living in poverty in America today. *Journal of Health and Social Policy, 21*(1), 119–131.

Holosko, M. J., & Thyer, B. (2011). *A pocket glossary of research terms.* Thousand Oaks CA: Sage.

Hsieh, C. M. (2006). Using client satisfaction to improve case management services for the elderly. *Research on Social Work Practice, 16,* 605–612.

Human, S., & Provan, K. (2000). Legitimacy building in the evolution of small-firm multi-lateral networks: A comparative study of success and demise. *Administrative Science Quarterly, 45*(2), 327–365.

Jones, P. (2008). *Expanding the ecological consciousness of social work students: Education for sustainable practice.* Edith Cowan University Research Online. Retrieved from http://ro.ecu .edu.au/cgi/viewcontent.cgi?article=1026&context=ceducom

Kellogg, W. K. (2006). W. K. Kellogg Foundation program logic model. Retrieved from http:// www.wkkf.org/knowledge-center/resources/2006/02/wk-kellogg-foundation-logic-model-development-guide.aspx

Kendrick, M. J., Petty, R. E., Bezanson, L., & Jones, D. L. (2006). *Promoting self-direction and consumer control in home- and community-based service systems: Third of three papers on unlocking the code of effective systems change.* Houston, TX: Independent Living Research Utilization.

Kitwood, T. (1997). *Dementia reconsidered: The person comes first.* Buckingham: Open University Press.

Knitzer, J., & Cooper, J. (2006). Beyond integration: Challenges for children's mental health. *Health Affairs, 25*(3), 670–679.

Larner, W. (2005). Neoliberalism in (regional) theory and practice: The stronger communities action fund in New Zealand. *Geographical Research, 43*(1), 9–18.

Leske, S., Strodl, E., & Hou, X. (2012). Patient-practitioner relationships desired by overweight/ obese adults. *Patient Education and Counselling, 89*(2), 309–315.

Lubove, R. (1969). *The professional altruist: The emergence of social work as a career, 1880–1930.* New York, NY: Atheneum.

Lupton, R. D. (2011). *Toxic charity: How churches and charities hurt those they help (and how to reverse it).* New York, NY: Harper One.

MacDonald, M. B., Bally, J. M., Ferguson, L. M., Murray, B. L., Fowler-Kerry, S. E., & Anonson, J. M. (2010). Knowledge of the professional role of others: A key interprofessional competency. *Nurse Education in Practice, 10,* 238–242.

Martinez, E., & Garcia, A. (1997). *What is neoliberalism? A brief definition for activists.* CORP Watch: Holding Corporations Accountable. Retrieved July 15, 2013, from http://www .corpwatch.org/article.php?id=376

Minogue, V., Holt, B., Karban, K., Gelsthorpe, S., Firth, S., & Ramsay, T. (2009). Service user and career involvement in mental health education, training and research—A literature review. *Mental Health and Learning Disabilities Research and Practice, 6*(2), 211–227. ISSN 1743-6885.

Morgan, A., & Jones, D. (2009). Perceptions of service user and career involvement in health-care education and impact on students' knowledge and practice: A literature review. *Medical Teacher, 31*(2), 82–95.

Mullin, E. (2012, March 12). Health information exchanges still prove limited in data sharing: Study. *Dorland Health.* Retrieved from http://www.dorlandhealth.com/dorland-health-articles/ health-information-exchanges-still-prove-limited-in-data-sharing-study

NASW. (2013). *NASW standards for social work case management.* Retrieved October 7, 2013, from http://www.socialworkers.org/practice/naswstandards/CaseManagementStandards2013.pdf

Nilep, C. (2012, February 16). On socialism, liberalism, and neo-liberalism. *Society for Linguistic Anthropology.* Retrieved July 15, 2013, from http://linguisticanthropology.org/blog/2012/02/16/on-socialism-liberalism-and-neo-liberalism/

Parker, J. (2001). Interrogating person-centred dementia care in social work and social care practice. *Journal of Social Work, 1*(3), 329–345.

Pati, S., Keren, R., Alessandrini, E., & Schwarz, D. (2004). Generational differences in U.S. public spending, 1980–2000. *Health Affairs, 23*(5), 131–141.

Pires, S. (1996). *Characteristics of systems of care as systems reform initiatives.* Washington, DC: Human Service Collaborative.

Preston, C. (2010). Laid-off charity workers face tough market and career compromises. *Chronicle of Philanthropy, 22*(5), 14.

Provan, K., & Milward, H. (1995). A preliminary theory of interorganizational network effectiveness: A comparative study of four community mental health systems. *Administrative Science Quarterly, 40,* 1–33.

Ramsay, R. (n.d.). What is PIE (person-in-environment) and how does it relate to social work as a profession and its history? Retrieved from http://www.ucalgary.ca/sw/ramsay/

Reamer, F. G. (2013). Social work in a digital age: Ethical and risk management challenges. *Social Work, 58*(2), 163–172.

Rhodes, C. A. (2012). User involvement in health and social care education: A concept analysis. *Nurse Education Today, 32*(2), 185–189.

Rondero Hernandez, V. (2013). Generalist and advanced generalist practice. In T. Mizrahi & L. Davis (Eds.), *Encyclopedia of social work: 20th edition* (pp. 2: 260–268). New York, NY: Oxford University Press and the National Association of Social Workers.

Rose, S., & Moore, V. (1995). Case management. In R. L. Edwards (Editor-in-Chief), *Encyclopedia of social work* (19th ed., Vol. 1, pp. 335–340). Washington, DC: NASW Press.

Saari, C. (2002). *The environment and its role in psychosocial functioning and psychotherapy.* New York, NY: Columbia University Press.

Savaya, R., Gardner, F., & Stange, D. (2011). Stressful encounters with social work clients: A descriptive account based on critical incidents. *Social Work, 56*(1), 63–71.

Scholte, J. A. (2005). *The sources of neoliberal globalization.* United Nations Research Institute for Social Development, Programme Paper No. 8, 6E. 05-02689. Geneva, Switzerland.

Schriver, J. (2013). *Neoliberalism: A critical element of economic literacy for social workers.* Presentation. Baccalaureate Program Director's Conference. Myrtle Beach, SC.

Scott, R. (2013). 6 questions: The impact of "revolutionary" shared decision making. Case Management. Retrieved from http://www.dorlandhealth.com/Tags/Delivery%20Models

Segal, E. (2013). Beyond the pale of psychoanalysis: Relational theory and generalist social work practice. *Clinical Social Work Journal, 41*(4), 376–386.

Seligman, M. E. P., Maier, S. F., & Geer, J. (1968). The alleviation of learned helplessness in dogs. *Journal of Abnormal Psychology, 73,* 256–262.

Simmons, B. M. (2012). Evidence-based practice, person-in-environment, and clinical social work: Issues in practical concern. *Smith College Studies in Social Work, 82*(1), 3–18.

Singer, J. B., Gray, S. W., & Miehls, D. (2012). An educator's guide to the development of advanced practice competencies in clinical social work. *Journal of Teaching in Social Work, 32*(5), 451–470.

Society for Social Work Leadership in Health Care. (2014). Social work best practice healthcare case management standards. Retrieved from http://www.sswlhc.org/docs/swbest-practices .pdf

Starfield, B. (2011). Is patient-centered care the same as person-focused care? *The Permanente Journal, 15*(2), 63–69.

Stedman's Publishing: Stedman's medical dictionary for the health professions and nursing. (2012; 27th ed.). Riverlands, IL: Lippincott Williams & Wilkins.

SUNY Levin Institute. (2013). What is globalization? Retrieved July 15, 2013, from http://www .globalization101.org/what-is-globalization/

Sytch, M., Tatarynowicz, A., & Gulati, R. (2012). Toward a theory of extended contact: The incentives and opportunities for bridging across network communities. *Organization Science, 23*(6), 1658–1681.

West, E. (2014). Consumer subjectivity and U.S. health care reform. *Health Communication Journal, 29*(3), 299–308.

Whelan, C. (2011). Network dynamics and network effectiveness: A methodological framework for public sector networks in the field of national security. *Australian Journal of Public Administration, 70*(3), 275–286. http://onlinelibrary.wiley.com/doi/10.1111/j.1467-8500.2011.00735.x/ abstract

The History of Social Work Case Management

"There is one thing stronger than all the armies in the world, and that is an idea whose time has come."

—Victor Hugo

Brief History of Social Work: 1600–1900

Social work's history predates the profession's history. Its origins can be traced to the *Elizabethan Poor Laws of 1601*, where social welfare law and legislation were enacted in England to aid and define "deserving"—the sick, the poor, orphans, disabled, widows, and thrifty old persons (Lubove, 1965). Social legislation or policies targeted to vulnerable individuals has been one of the primary ways that social welfare provision has been defined in countries all over the world. As a nation's social, economic, and political realities change over time, so do their social policies, which provide the legislative scaffolding for all social welfare/care provision.

The institutions of care in England and Germany before the 1600s were greatly influenced by the church, and this linkage was solidified both explicitly and implicitly. In regard to the former for example, in 1313, Christianity was legalized by King Constantine, and the church was sanctioned to use donated funds to provide aid to the poor. Implicitly, Christian charitable attitudes and behaviors expected of richer members such as the re-distribution of wealth, helping those in need, etc., were deemed as part of being a Christian at that time.

As the Reformation Movement swept through Europe and the United Kingdom, cities and towns passed laws that encouraged secularism in the provision of social welfare. For example, in 1819, a Scottish mathematician Thomas Chalmers developed private philanthropies in Glasgow to meet the economic needs of the poor. And in 1833, German Chancellor Bismarck enacted the first national health insurance system.

On the heels of the Industrial Revolution between 1760 and 1840, American Social Welfare was birthed as a profession demarked by four significant events: 1) Jane Addams (the first U.S. woman to have won the Nobel Peace Prize) and Ellen Gates Starr, who worked in London in the alms-houses, opened Hull House in Chicago in 1889, considered to be the most influential social settlement house in the United States; 2) in 1898, the first school of social work established was called the New York School of Philanthropy that later became Columbia University School of Social Work; 3) also in 1898, Mary E. Richmond published a text describing our altruistic work in communities called *Friendly Visiting Among the Poor*; and 4) in 1900, educator Simon N. Patten coined the term *social worker* and applied it to so-called friendly visitors and settlement houses (Flores-Paso, 2014).

A Brief History of Social Work Case Management: 1900–Present Day

Any profession's history is shaped by many factors, events, changes, and influences, which are often interrelated. Figure 2.1 illustrates how three primary factors have influenced North American social work in general, and Social Work Case Management (SWCMG) in particular.

❖ **Figure 2.1 The Primary Influences That Shaped the Development of Social Work and SWCMG in North America (1900–Present)**

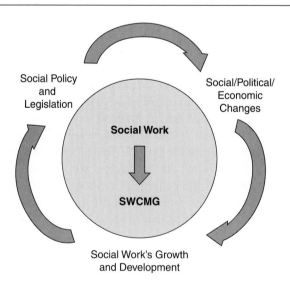

Given the prevalence and interrelatedness of these three factors in Figure 2.1, a brief overview of significant benchmarks within each will be discussed. Also, as the center of Figure 2.1 illustrates, the SWCMG evolved from the profession of social work, primarily from 1900 forward.

Social Policy and Legislation

One of my renowned professors at the University of Pittsburgh used to say repeatedly in class, "the only social policy we can consider—*is* federal legislation." As such, he explained that states, organizations, and communities were the authorities and implementation conduits for federal legislation, and social workers were the policy "figurer-outers" of how such policy was implemented on the street level—in their altruistic face-to-face work with clients. This "trickle-down policy thinking" in our profession has been a large part of the reason why historically social work has had very little influence in developing macro policy in the United States. However, it has had much more influence in how policy has been implemented at state and community levels (Holosko & Au, 1996).

The three braided domains of federal legislation, which is the context and scaffolding for how and where we work as a profession include 1) child welfare and adoption, 2) mental health, and 3) social welfare. Their respective timelines in the United States and major benchmarks are presented in Table 2.1, Charts A, B, and C.

The charts in Charts A, B, and C are but a brief snapshot of the most significant pieces of federal legislation that shaped social work, social welfare, and SWCMG.

The Profession's Growth and Development in SWCMG

The 20th century history of American SWCMG evolved from religious institutions → work house's → secular institutions → volunteers → settlement houses → "friendly (neighborhood or community) visitors" → caseworkers → social caseworkers → social workers → and eventually SWCMs. Historically, the indwelling and lifeblood of North American SWCMs was and still is in health care or health-related care organizations. Medical social service owes it origin to Dr. Richard Cabot, who in 1905 organized the first social service department in the outpatient unit of the Massachusetts General Hospital. It was "conceived by a physician who, in seeking the improvement of dispensary practice, found in the social worker a potent means for more accurate diagnosis and more effective treatment" (Canon, 1913, p. 15). As explained more fully by Mary Richmond (1917), "what Dr. Cabot had in mind in bringing social workers into the dispensary and later into its separate clinics was not a mixture of medical and social work but their chemical union" (p. 35).

Today, SWCMG has mutated in a variety of other non-health-care settings such as Worker's Compensation, child and family service agencies, legal settings, correctional settings, schools and other educational settings, and numerous business, financial, and commercial settings. Similar to the history of social workers in North America, SWCMs are often professionally trained BSWs or MSWs whose occupational adaptation to different emerging settings is one of the greatest strengths of both social work and SWCMs (Holosko, 2003).

❖ Table 2.1 Chart A. Federal Mental Health Legislation (1900–Present)

Year	Law	Description
1908	*Connecticut Society for Mental Hygiene*	Connecticut Society for Mental Hygiene was established by Clifford Beers and expanded, forming the National Committee for Mental Hygiene.
1910	*Mental Health America was formed.*	The National Mental Health Association, now known as Mental Health America, was responsible for helping children who are affected by mental illness. It created more than 100 child guidance clinics in the United States to prevent mental illness as well as treat children who are mentally ill.
1927	*Buck v. Bell*	The U.S. Supreme Court rules in *Buck v. Bell* that the forced sterilization of "defectives," including the mentally ill, is constitutional.
1929	P.L. 70-672	Established two federal "narcotics farms" and authorized a Narcotics Division.
1930	P.L. 71-357	Redesigned the PHS Narcotics Division to the Division of Mental Hygiene.
1935	*Social Security Act*	An act to provide for the general welfare by establishing a system of federal old-age benefits, and by enabling the several states to make more adequate provision for aged persons, blind persons, dependent and crippled children, maternal and child welfare, public health, and the administration of their unemployment compensation laws.
1939	P.L. 76-19	Transferred PHS from the Treasury Department to the Federal Security Agency.
1946	*The National Mental Health Act*, P.L. 79-487	Authorized the Surgeon General to improve the mental health of U.S. citizens through research into the causes, diagnosis, and treatment of psychiatric disorders.
1949	NIMH	NIMH was established.
1953	*Reorganization plan No. 1*	Assigned PHS to the newly created U.S. Department of Health, Education, and Welfare.
1954	*The Durham Rule*	Established by the U.S. Court of Appeals. It states that a person accused of a crime is not responsible if the criminal act "was the product of a mental disease or a mental defect." It was later rejected due to problems defining *mental disease* and *product*.
1955	*The Mental Health Study Act*, P.L. 84-182	Authorized NIMH to study and make recommendations on mental health and mental illness in the United States. Also authorized the creation of the Joint Commission on Mental Illness and Health.
1956	*The Alaska Mental Health Enabling Act*, P.L. 84-830	*The Alaska Mental Health Enabling Act* provided for territorial treatment facilities for mentally ill individuals in Alaska.

Year	Law	Description
1963	*The Mental Retardation Facilities and Community Mental Health Centers Construction Act*, P.L. 88-164	Provided for grants for assistance in the construction of community mental health centers nationwide.
1965	P.L. 89-105	Amendments to P.L. 88-164, provided for grants for the staffing of community mental health centers.
1966	*Narcotic Addict Rehabilitation Act of 1966*, P.L. 89-793	Launched a national program for long-term treatment and rehabilitation of narcotic addicts.
1966	*Lake v. Cameron*	U.S. Court of Appeals for the District of Columbia Circuit declares that patients in psychiatric hospitals have the right to receive treatment in the setting that is least restrictive.
1967	*Mental Health Amendments of 1967*, P.L. 90-31	Mental Health Amendments of 1967 separated NIMH from NIH and raised it to bureau status in PHS.
1968	NIMH	NIMH became a component of the newly created Health Services and Mental Health Administration.
1968	*The Alcoholic and Narcotic Addict Rehabilitation Amendments of 1968*, P.L. 90-574	Authorized funds for the construction and staffing of new facilities for the prevention of alcoholism and the treatment and rehabilitation of alcoholics.
1970	*Community Mental Health Centers Amendments of 1970*, P.L. 92-211	Authorized construction and staffing of centers for 3 more years, with priority on poverty areas.
1970	*Comprehensive Drug Abuse Prevention and Control Act of 1970*, P.L. 91-513	Expanded the National Drug Abuse Program by extending the services of federally funded community treatment centers to non-narcotic drug abusers, as well as addicts.
1970	*Comprehensive Alcohol Abuse and Alcoholism Prevention, Treatment, and Rehabilitation Act*, P.L. 91-616	Authorized the establishment of a National Institute on Alcohol Abuse and Alcoholism within NIMH.
1972	*Drug Abuse Office and Treatment Act of 1972*, P.L. 92-255	Provided that a National Institute on Drug Abuse be established within NIMH.
1973		NIMH rejoined NIH. NIMH later became a component of the Alcohol, Drug Abuse, and Mental Health Administration (ADAMHA).

(Continued)

❖ Table 2.1   (Continued)

Year	Law	Description
1974	P.L. 93-282	Authorized the establishment of ADAMHA.
1978	*The Community Mental Health Centers Extension Act of 1978,* P.L. 95-622	Enacted November 9, 1978 (P.L. 95-622). Re-codified the 1971 Act; reorganized and consolidated duties and functions of the NCI Director. It called for an expanded and intensified research program for the prevention of cancer caused by occupational or environmental exposure to carcinogens; expanded the mission of cancer centers to include basic research, prevention, and education; added several ex-officio members to the NCAB, reflecting the importance of environmental and occupation carcinogenesis research and required that five of the appointed members be knowledgeable in environmental carcinogenesis.
1979	*The Department of Education Organization Act,* P.L. 96-88	Created the Department of Education and renamed HEW the Department of Health and Human Services (HHS).
1980	*The Mental Health Systems Act,* P.L. 96-398	The Mental Health Systems Act reauthorized the community mental health centers program.
1981	*The Omnibus Reconciliation Act,* P.L. 97-35	Consolidated ADAMHA's treatment and rehabilitation programs into a single block grant that enabled each state to administer allocated funds.
1983	*Alcohol Abuse Amendments of 1983,* P.L. 98-24	Consolidated the current authorization for ADAMHA and the institutes into a new title V of the PHS act.
1984	*Alcohol Abuse, Drug Abuse, and Mental Health Amendments,* P.L. 98-509	Authorized funding for block grants for fiscal years 1985 through 1987, as well as extending the authorizations for federal activities in the areas of alcohol and drug abuse research, information dissemination, and development of new treatment methods.
1988	*The Fair Housing Amendments Act*	Prohibits housing discrimination against people with disabilities, including mental disabilities.
1990	*The Americans with Disabilities Act*	Prohibits discrimination against people with physical or mental disabilities.
1991	*PHS Act,* P.L. 99-550	Contained the requirement for State Comprehensive Mental Health Services Plan.
1992	*The ADAMHA Reorganization Act,* P.L. 102-321	Abolished ADAMHA, created the Substance Abuse and Mental Health Services Administration, and transferred NIMH research activities to NIH.

Year	Law	Description
2000	P.L. 106-310	The Act expands, intensifies, and coordinates activities of the NIH with respect to research on autism, including the establishment of not less than five centers of excellence that conduct basic and clinical research into autism. Also mandated that the Secretary, DHHS establish an Interagency Autism Coordinating Committee (IACC) to coordinate autism research and other efforts within the department.
2006	*The Combating Autism Act of 2006*, P.L. 109-416	Authorized expanded activities related to autism spectrum disorder (ASD) related research, surveillance, prevention, treatment, and education.
2010	*The Patient Protection and Affordable Care Act*, P.L. 111-148	Contains a section encouraging NIMH to continue relevant research, as well as a "Sense of the Congress" authorizing the Director of NIMH to conduct a longitudinal study of the relative mental health consequences for women of resolving a pregnancy.

❖ **Table 2.1   Chart B. Federal Child Welfare, Child Protection, and Adoption Legislations (1974–Present)**

Year	Law	Description
1974	*Child Abuse Prevention and Treatment Act (CAPTA)*, P.L. 93-247	Established the National Center on Child Abuse and Neglect, authorized funding for fiscal years 1974 through 1977 for demonstration projects on the prevention, identification, and treatment of child abuse and neglect.
1975	*Education of All Handicapped Children Act (EHA)*, P.L. 94-142	Required that all public schools that accepted federal funds provide equal access to education and one free meal a day for children with physical and mental disabilities. The act also required school districts to provide procedures so that parents can dispute decisions about their children's education.
1978	*Child Abuse Prevention and Treatment and Adoption Reform Act*, P.L. 95-266	Reauthorized through fiscal year 1981 and amended the *Child Abuse Prevention and Treatment Act;* funded the Adoption Opportunities program to facilitate the adoption of children with special needs.
1978	*Indian Child Welfare Act (ICWA)*, P.L. 95-608	Established standards for the placement of Indian child in foster or adoptive homes and to prevent the breakup of Indian families.
1980	*Adoption Assistance and Child Welfare Act*, P.L. 96-272	Authorized appropriations for adoption and foster care assistance to the states. It required states to provide adoption assistance to parents who adopt a child who is AFDC-eligible and is a child with special needs. For foster care assistance, states are required to make reasonable efforts to prevent placement or to reunify children with their families.

(Continued)

❖ Table 2.1   (Continued)

Year	Law	Description
1984	*Child Abuse Amendments,* P.L. 98-457	Required states to have procedures with protective systems to respond to the reporting of medical neglect, including instances of withholding medically indicated treatment from disabled infants with life-threatening conditions; directed HHS to develop regulations and to provide training and technical assistance needed by care providers to carry out the provisions of the act; required state-level programs to facilitate adoption opportunities for disabled infants with life-threatening conditions.
1988	*Child Abuse Prevention, Adoption, and Family Services Act,* P.L. 100-294	Established the Inter-Agency Task Force on Child Abuse and Neglect, with responsibility for programs and activities related to child abuse and neglect; broadened the scope of research to include investigative and judicial procedures applicable to child abuse cases and the national incidence of child abuse and neglect; established a national data collection system to include standardized data on false, unfounded, or unsubstantiated cases and the number of deaths due to child abuse and neglect; expanded the Adoption Opportunities program; to increase the number of minority children placed in adoptive families, with an emphasis on recruitment of and placement with minority families, and for families who have adopted special needs children; to increase the placement of foster care children legally free for adoption.
1992	*Child Abuse, Domestic Violence, Adoption, and Family Services Act,* P.L. 102-295	Revised provisions for research and assistance; provided for assisting states in supporting child abuse and neglect prevention activities through community-based child abuse and neglect prevention grants; required the operation of a National Resource Center for Special Needs Adoption.
1993	*Family Preservation and Support Services Program Act,* P.L. 103-66	Encouraged states to use funds to create a continuum of family-focused services for at-risk children and families; required states to engage in a comprehensive planning process to develop more responsive family support and preservation strategies; broadened the definition of family to include people needing services regardless of family configuration: biological, adoptive, foster, extended, or self-defined; defined services such as preservation services, support services to be provided by the states; provided grants to the highest court of each state to conduct assessments of the roles, responsibilities, and effectiveness of state courts in handling child welfare cases, and to implement changes deemed necessary as a result of the assessments.

Year	Law	Description
1994	*Multiethnic Placement Act (MEPA),* P.L. 103-382	Prohibited state agencies and other entities that receive federal funding and were involved in foster care or adoption placements from delaying, denying, or otherwise discriminating when making a foster care or adoption placement decision on the basis of the parent or child's race, color, or national origin.
1996	*The Interethnic Previsions of 1996 amends MEPA,* P.L. 104-188	Established the Title IV-E State Plan requirement that states and other entities that receive funds from the federal government and are involved in foster care or adoption placements may not deny any individual the opportunity to become a foster or adoptive parent and may not delay or deny a child's foster care or adoptive placement based upon the race, color, or national origin of the parent or the child.
1996	*Child Abuse Prevention and Treatment Amendments,* P.L. 104-235	Reauthorized CAPTA through FY 2001; abolished the National Center on Child Abuse and Neglect (NCCAN) and created the Office on Child Abuse and Neglect; required states to institute an expedited termination of parental rights process for abandoned infants or when the parent is responsible for the death or serious bodily injury of a child; set the minimum definition of child abuse to include death, serious physical or emotional injury, sexual abuse, or imminent risk of harm; recognized the right of parental exercise of religious beliefs concerning medical care.
1997	*Adoption and Safe Families Act,* P.L. 105-89	Reauthorized the Family Preservation and Support Services Program and renamed it the Safe and Stable Families Program; ensured safety for abused and neglected children; accelerated permanent placement by requiring states to initiate court proceedings to free a child for adoption once that child had been waiting in foster care for at least 15 of the most recent 22 months, unless there was an exception; promoted adoptions by rewarding states that increased adoptions with incentive funds.
1999	*Foster Care Independence Act,* P.L. 106-169	Revised the program of grants to states and expanded opportunities for independent living programs providing education, training, and employment services, and financial support for foster youth to prepare for living on their own; allowed funds to be used to pay for room and board for former foster youth age 18 to 21; mandated that state plans for foster care and adoption assistance include certification that prospective parents will be adequately prepared to provide for the needs of the child and that such preparation will continue, as necessary, after placement of the child; provided states with the option to extend Medicaid coverage to 18- to 21-year olds who have been emancipated from foster care.

(Continued)

❖ Table 2.1 (Continued)

Year	Law	Description
2000	*Child Abuse Prevention and Enforcement Act of 2000,* P.L. 106-177	Authorized the use of federal law enforcement funds by states to improve the criminal justice system in order to provide timely, accurate, and complete criminal history record information to child welfare agencies, organizations, and programs that are engaged in the assessment of activities related to the protection of children, including protection against child sexual abuse, and placement of children in foster care.
2000	*Intercountry Adoption Act,* P.L. 106-279	Established the U.S. Central Authority within the Department of State with general responsibility for U.S. implementation of the Convention and annual reports to Congress; allowed the State Department to enter into agreements with one or more qualified accrediting entities to provide for the accreditation of agencies (non-profit) and approval of persons (for-profit agencies and individuals) who seek to provide adoption services for adoptions covered by the Convention.
2002	*Promoting Safe and Stable Families Amendments of 2001,* P.L. 107-133	Amended Title IV-B, subpart 2 of the *Social Security Act;* added findings to illustrate the need for programs addressing families at risk for abuse and neglect and those adopting children from foster care; amended the definition of family preservation services to include infant safe haven programs; added strengthening parental relationships and promoting healthy marriages to the list of allowable activities.
2003	*Keeping Children and Family Safe Act,* P.L. 108-36	Reauthorized CAPTA through FY 2008; authorized an expanded continuing interdisciplinary and longitudinal research program; provided for an opportunity for public comment on research priorities; emphasized enhanced linkages between child protective service agencies and public health, mental health, and developmental disabilities agencies; mandated changes to state plan eligibility requirements for the CAPTA State grant, to address the needs of infants born and identified as being affected by prenatal drug exposure.
2003	*Adoption Promotion Act,* P.L. 108-145	Amended Title IV-E with respect to States eligible to receive Adoption Incentives payments to provide payments for special needs adoptions that are not older child adoptions and adoptions of older children (age 9 and older); modified requirements with respect to determination of numbers of special needs adoptions that are not older children as well as adoptions of older children; authorized the Secretary to impose specified penalties against a state for failure to provide necessary data to the Adoption and Foster Care Analysis and Reporting System (AFCARS).
2005	*Fair Access Foster Care Act,* P.L. 109-113	Amended section 472(b) of the *Social Security Act* (42 U.S.C. 672(b)) by striking the word nonprofit each place it appears.

Year	Law	Description
2006	*Deficit Reduction Act of 2005*, P.L. 109-171	Prohibited access to Medicaid to an individual who declares he or she is a U.S. citizen unless one type of specified documentary evidence of U.S. citizenship or nationality is presented (certain classes were exempt from this requirement); replaced incentive bonuses to states for a decrease in the illegitimacy rate with healthy marriage promotion and responsible fatherhood grants, and limited the use of funds for demonstration projects designed to test the effectiveness of Tribal governments or consortia in coordinating the provision of child welfare services to families at risk of child abuse or neglect and activities promoting responsible fatherhood.
2006	*Safe and Timely Interstate Placement of Foster Children Act*, P.L. 109-239	Required each Title IV-E State plan for foster care and adoption assistance to provide that the state shall have procedures for orderly and timely interstate placement of children, complete home studies requested by another state within a specified period, which is 60 days in most cases but up to 75 days if specified circumstances warrant an extension, and accept such studies received from another state within 14 days unless reliance on the report would be contrary to the child's welfare.
2006	*Adam Walsh Child Protection and Safety Act*, P.L. 109-248	Required 1) fingerprint-based checks of the national crime information databases (NCID) for prospective foster or adoptive parents and 2) checks of state child abuse and neglect registries in which the prospective foster or adoptive parents and any other adults living in the home have resided in the preceding 5 years; permitted states that prior to September 30, 2005, had opted out of the criminal background checks until October 1, 2008, to comply with the fingerprint-based background check requirement (after October 1, 2008, no state is exempt from those requirement); required states to comply with any request for a child abuse registry check that is received from another state.
2006	*Child and Family Services Improvement Act*, P.L. 109-288	Required each state plan for oversight and coordination of health care services for any child in foster care to include an outline of the monitoring and treatment of emotional trauma associated with a child's maltreatment and removal from home, protocols for the appropriate use and monitoring of psychotropic medications; required each state plan for child welfare services to describe activities to reduce the length of time children under age 5 are without a permanent family, activities to address the developmental needs of such children who receive benefits or services, the sources used to compile information on child maltreatment deaths that the state agency is required by federal law to report, as well as why the compilation does not include information on such deaths from specified state entities, if it does not, and how the state will include such information.

(Continued)

❖ **Table 2.1 (Continued)**

Year	Law	Description
2006	*Tax Relief and Health Care Act*, P.L. 109-432	Amended section 1903(x) of Title XIX of the *Social Security Act* (the Act) (42 U.S.C. § 1386b) by including all foster children assisted by Titles IV-B and IV-E of the Act and children receiving Title IV-E adoption assistance in the groups exempt from the requirement to present documentary evidence of citizenship or nationality if they declare themselves to be citizens or nationals of the United States; added a new provision to Title IV-E of the Act to require that State plans include procedures for verifying the citizenship or immigration status of children in foster care under state responsibility under Titles IV-B or IV-E; amended section 1123A of the Act (42 U.S.C. 1320a-2a) to include review of state conformity with this requirement in the Child and Family Services Reviews (CSFRs).
2008	*Fostering Connections to Success and Increasing Adoptions Act*, P.L. 110-351	Amended Title IV-E to permit states to claim federal reimbursement for part of the cost of providing kinship guardianship assistance to relatives who become legal guardians of children who have been in foster care.
2010	*Patient Protection and Affordable Care Act*, P.L. 111-148	Provisions relevant to child welfare practice include extended Medicaid coverage to former foster care children younger than age 26; Required state Children's Health Insurance Program (CHIP) plan, beginning January 1, 2014, to use modified gross income and household income to determine CHIP eligibility; required state to treat any child as a targeted low-income child eligible for CHIP who is determined to be ineligible for Medicaid as a result of the elimination of an income based on expense or type of income.
2010	*CAPTA Reauthorization Act*, P.L. 111-320	Amended the state plan eligibility provisions to require submission of a plan that will remain in effect for the duration of the state's participation in the program, with states required to periodically review and revise the plan to reflect any changes in state programs, provide notice to HHS of any substantive changes related to child abuse prevention that may affect the state's eligibility for the grant program, provide notice to HHS of any significant changes in how the state is using grant funds, prepare and submit to HHS an annual report.
2011	*Child and Family Services Improvement and Innovation Act*, P.L. 112-34	Required each state plan for oversight and coordination of health care services for any child in foster care to include an outline of the monitoring and treatment of emotional trauma associated with a child's maltreatment and removal from home, protocols for the appropriate use and monitoring of psychotropic medications; required each state plan for child welfare services to describe activities to reduce the length of time children under age 5 are without a permanent family, activities to address the

Year	Law	Description
		developmental needs of such children who receive benefits or services, the sources used to compile information on child maltreatment deaths that the state agency is required by federal law to report, as well as why the compilation does not include information on such deaths from specified state entities, if it does not, and how the state will include such information.

❖ Table 2.1   Chart C. History of Social Welfare Legislation (1900–Present)

Year	Law	Description
1935	*Social Security Act*	Amended federal legislation but initially provided social security old-age insurance, employment and unemployment insurance, and public assistance for needy, aged and blind, and physically handicapped. It enacted Aid to Families with Despondent Children (AFDC) in effect, up until 1966, which provided financial assistance to families who had no or low incomes.
1937	*Public Housing*	Provided for subsides to be paid from the U.S. government to local housing agencies in order to improve living conditions for low-income families.
1939	*Social Security Old-Age and Survivors Insurance*	A major amendment to the *Social Security Act* of 1935, it provided two new categories of benefits: 1) payments to the spouse and minor children (so-called dependents benefits), and 2) survivor benefits paid to the family in the event of the premature death of a covered worker. This change transformed social security from a retirement program for a worker into a family-based economic security program.
1946	*National School Lunch Program*	This program provided by cash support and USDA food distributed among schools participating in the lunch programs.
1950	*Aid to the Permanently and Totally Disabled (replaced by the SSI program)*	Aid to the Permanently and Totally Disabled (APTD) is cash assistance for individuals who are between the ages of 18 and 64 and who are physically or mentally disabled.
1956	*Social Security Disability Insurance*	Benefits were provided for severely disabled workers aged 50 and older. Additionally, benefits were provided for adult disabled children of deceased or retired workers.
1960	*Medical Assistance for the Aged (replaced by Medicaid)*	This amendment created Medicare and Medicaid. These programs established government-provided health insurance coverage for the elderly and poor individuals.
1964	*Food Stamp Program*	The original program provided for food-purchasing assistance for low- and no-income people living in the United States; currently known as SNAP, the Supplemental Nutrition Assistance Program.

(Continued)

❖ **Table 2.1** **(Continued)**

Year	Law	Description
1965	*Medicare and Medicaid Programs*	Federal Legislation guaranteed Medicare access to health insurance to American's 65 or older who have worked and paid into the system, younger people with disabilities, and other chronic illnesses. Medicaid is a government insurance program for persons of all ages whose income and resources are insufficient to pay for health care.
1966	*School Breakfast Program*	Provides federally subsidized breakfasts to children at schools and child care facilities in the United States.
1972	*Supplemental Security Income Program*	Amended the Social Security Act. This Federal legislation replaced the categorical federal–state programs for the needy, aged, blind, and disabled with the Federal Supplemental Security Income (SSI) Program.
1974	*Special Supplemental Food Program for Women, Infants and Children (WIC)*	Provided federal grants to states for supplemental foods, health care referrals, and nutrition education for low-income pregnant, breastfeeding, and non-breastfeeding postpartum women, and to infants and children up to age 5 who are found to be at nutritional risk.
1975	*Earned Income Tax Credit*	Provided a tax credit for low-income workers. It reduces the tax liability for individuals who make low wages and in some cases, provides a refund.
1996	*Personal Responsibility and Work Opportunity Reconciliation Act*	A major welfare reform initiative, which added a workforce development component to welfare legislation. It instituted Temporary Assistance for Needy Families (TANF), which became effective one year later. TANF provided cash assistance to indigent American families with dependent children and is administered by the U.S. Department of Health and Human Services.

The development of social work's history had often been characterized by the identification of certain milestones or benchmarks (Holosko, 2003; "Milestones in the Development of Social Work," 1995). The ones selected here and presented in Table 2.2 are ones that pertain mainly to SWCMG in particular:

As indicated in these significant milestones, it was our initial practice in hospitals described in the watershed 1916 text by Mary Richmond titled *Social Diagnosis,* that gave SWCMG its legitimacy, professional identity, and prominence in not only assisting with patient-centered care, but also being appreciated and recognized for having a distinct skillset that complemented medicine and nursing. This legacy is still the raison d'être for SWCMG, who not only ply their craft in health care settings uniquely, but also beyond health care organizations.

❖ Table 2.2 **Milestones in the Development of Social Work and Social Welfare (1900–Present)**

Year	Milestones
1905	First social services department to help patients with social problems associated with their illnesses was created by Dr. Richard Cabot at the Massachusetts General Hospital in Boston. The success of this program led to more than 100 hospitals hiring social workers in the following decade.
1907	The start of psychiatric social work begins as social workers are hired at the Massachusetts General Hospital to work with patients that are considered mentally ill.
1914	The title Psychiatric Social Worker was used for the first time in the social services department at the Boston Psychopathic Hospital.
1915	Abraham Flexner addresses the National Conference on Social Welfare (NCSW), stating that social work has not yet qualified as a profession. Flexner cited reasons of its membership not having a great deal of individual responsibility and lacking a written body of knowledge and educationally communicable techniques.
1917	Mary Richmond published *Social Diagnosis* in 1917 (New York, NY: Russell Sage Foundation). This text was used to combat Flexner's 1915 report by social workers to argue for the qualification of the profession. It was considered the first text to legitimize and identity the role of social workers in hospital settings as being complementary to medicine and nursing.
1917	The National Social Workers Exchange, later known as the American Association of Social Workers (AASW) was established. This was the first organization for social workers, and its primary purpose was to select applicants for social work jobs.
1918	The first specialization within the social work field was created when the American Association of Hospital Social Workers (AAHSW) was formed. In 1934, the association was renamed the Association of Medical Social Workers (AAMSW).
1918	The director of medical social work at Massachusetts General Hospital, Ida M. Cannon, defines the principles of medical social work. An award named for Cannon has been given to a national figure in health care social worker since 1971.
1918	The first training program for psychiatric social workers was established at Smith College in Northampton, Massachusetts.
1919	The existing 17 American and Canadian schools of social work to create united standards for training students and professional education form the Association of Training Schools for Professional Social Work. They would later undergo a name change to become the American Association of Schools of Social Work (AASSW), which merges with the National Association of School of Social Administration (NASSA) to create the Council on Social Work Education (CSWE).
1926	With the social work profession being comprised of increasingly more caseworkers and clinical practitioners, the American Association of Psychiatric Social Workers (AAPSW) was formed.

(Continued)

❖ **Table 2.2 (Continued)**

Year	Milestones
1928	The Milford Conference was held by social workers to discuss if social work was a consolidated profession with similar knowledge and skills or a discordant group of specialties. The conference concludes that social work was a unified profession. The findings of the Milford Conference are reported in the *Social Case Work: Generic and Specific* (New York, NY: American Association of Social Workers) in 1929.
1936	To embattle the social worker employment shortages, the National Association of Schools of Social Administration (NASSA) was established. NASSA later merged with the American Association of Schools of Social Work (AASSW) to become the Council on Social Work Education (CSWE) in 1952.
1953	President Eisenhower creates the Department of Health, Education, and Welfare (HEW), including a cabinet position. The HEW was later renamed to the Department of Health and Human Services (HHS).
1961	In response to the growing population and its longer lifespans, the White House Conference on Aging was held to develop a plan for caring for the nation's elderly population. The conference's findings later led to the *Older Americans Act* of 1965.
1963	In response to the Joint Commission on Mental Illness and Health's findings, President Kennedy signs the *Community Mental Health Centers Act* into law. The act provides funding for the creation and development of mental health centers, training programs, and outpatient treatment programs.
1965	Building on the efforts of previous programs, Medicare, Medicaid, the *Older Americans Act of 1965*, and the *Elementary and Secondary Education Act of 1965* were passed by congress.
1969	The National Association of Social Workers (NASW) allows social workers with qualified bachelor's degrees to obtain membership, an honor that was previously only available to social workers with MSW's. The NASW also approved separate licensing procedures at the state level.
1971	The National Federation of Societies for Clinical Social Work (NFSCSW) was founded for the purpose of organizing a national voice for clinical social workers.
1983	The National Association of Social Workers (NASW), in order to develop and implement a peer evaluation process between social workers in order to facilitate accountability and quality control according to government and third-party funding standards, founded the National Peer Review Advisory Committee.
1983	As a result of the Curriculum Policy Statement was sued by the Council on Social Work Education (CSWE), a Bachelor of Social Work education was now considered the first level of professional social work education.
1991	The Academy of Certified Baccalaureate Social Workers (ACBSW) was founded to certify BSW students professionally.
1994	The National Association of Social Workers (NASW) publishes the Person-in-Environment (PIE) system in order to make the classification and coding of psychosocial, health, and environmental functioning possible by social workers.

Task-Centered Case Management (TCCMG)

"I hear and I forget. I see and I remember. I do and I understand."

—Confucius

Task-Centered Case Management

One of the features of this text recommended by SAGE Publications was to define a unique *social work* (SW) model that could be used in case management (CMG) today. After scouring much of the practice-related literature to achieve this goal, a few things became apparent. First, many BSW and MSW social workers are doing CMG jobs as well as non-social workers. The second was that social work has a long tradition with client-centered practice, as previously mentioned in Chapters 1 and 2. Having had the pleasure of personally knowing William Reid and his legacy work in presenting one of the more practical and empirically validated models of social work task-centered practice, I was reminded of its applicability to both social work and CMG. With the blessing of William's partner, "Ricky Ann Fortune," at SUNY Albany, I took his model and essentially tweaked and contemporized it for this chapter.

Why Social Work Should Adopt Task-Centered Case Management (TCCMG)?

Despite the fact that Reid's model was developed some 45 years ago and has been used in over 20 countries of the world since then (A. Fortune, personal communication, 2015) as mentioned earlier, it was not only visionary in its day, but it is surprisingly still relevant and appropriate for use in today's current reality. What has changed and will inevitably change again, when the *U.S. Affordable Care Act* (2010) unfolds more fully (as indicated in Chapter 2) is the reality of how health and human services offer care to their clients and family systems (Katzen & Morgan, 2014). Chapter 1 outlined several trends shaping social work practice globally, nationally, and locally. What was noted then was that as societies evolve, new and different priorities and new and different policies become enacted (like the *Affordable Care Act*), which, in turn, shape how CMG is currently practiced.

There are also more socio-demographic shifts occurring all over the world such as more and more individuals are living longer than ever before, there are more single-parent families, more displaced immigrant populations, more hunger, more poverty, more incarcerated people, more persons with mental and emotional health problems, more addicted individuals, more unemployment, more homelessness, more disenfranchised minority groups, etc. Although we tend to perceive these issues often as being only "in third world" or other developing countries far, far away from our native shores and land, each and every one of them is apparent in the landscape of North America's socio-demographic reality.

Additionally, as indicated in Chapter 1, every day in America, more and more people need more and more services, and there is less and less money to treat and serve this growing cohort. Waiting lists, more stringent eligibility criteria, fewer resources, more compressed time frames for treatment, more limited restrictions for fee-for-services, more urban-centered and concentrated treatment, and more complex systems of care are the stark realities in which CMs in general, and task-centered case managers (TCCMs) in particular, practice their daily craft.

TCCMG is an empirically field-tested social work model that not only presents an effective and prescriptive step-wise approach to CMG practice as noted, but it is one that is also contextualized by important wrap-around factors or variables that consider the environment more realistically, and take into account its ever-changing landscape. As such, TCCMG fits hand-in-glove within the environments where it is practiced, and therefore transcends the numerous and different practice settings in which it can be effectively used.

Figure 3.1 identifies an 8-step model illustrating the TCCMG approach. As indicated, it is not as linear as the step-wise illustration conveys because client systems, problems, resources, availability of service, support systems, etc., constantly change for clients in systems of care that CMs deal with. For example, in Steps 5 through 7, this re-assessment and flexibility is required as issues change with the client in care and the treatment of their problems.

Figure 3.2 presents five wrap-around pillars anchoring TCCMG, using Reid and Epstein's (1972) original ones, and two of which were added to contemporize its current utility.

1. *Core Anchoring Values*—Reid contended that our values anchor practice and that empirical data verify practice. But, the first domino in this chain of events is that anchoring values must be echoed and magnified in *each and every client–worker transaction*. The three he mentioned were autonomy, self-determinism, and advocacy. In regard to the former, it is important that TCCMs continue to safeguard the rights for clients to *always* express their voices in each step of the treatment process. Thus, TCCMs need to actively seek client voices—even when they seem withdrawn, or present as incapable to do so

❖ **Figure 3.1**   Steps in Reid's Task-Centered Social Work Case Management (TCCMG) Model

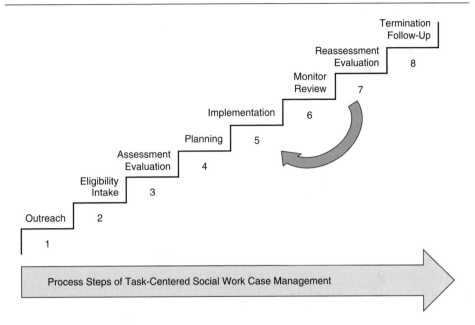

❖ **Figure 3.2**   Task-Centered Case Management Model

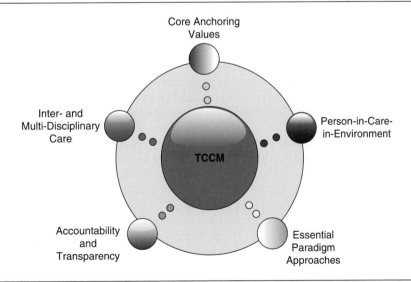

Source: Adapted from Reid, W. J., & Epstein, L. (Eds.). (1972). Task-centered casework. New York: Columbia University Press.

themselves. Reaching for their voice means more autonomy and choice, as by tabling their issues or concerns in the helping process, they are able to continue to make more informed choices for themselves as their treatment process unfolds.

The second value, self-determinism, means that the client is now required to direct the full range of treatment that he or she receives, in partnership with their TCCM. Thus, options, choices, limitations, concerns, assessments, and re-assessments of the services and issues that arise during the course of their treatment journey are determined in large part by the client and their resources. The final core value he noted, advocacy, involves a shifting of the TCCM advocating *for* the client (the more traditional approach), to engaging the client in learning how *to advocate for himself or herself.* This, as noted above, ties in to the two former values and becomes the beginning step of empowerment for clients, who often believe that they have been detached and disempowered by their own illnesses, problems, family members, friends, resources, and/or treatment or helping systems.

2. *Person-in-Care-in-Environment (PICIE)*—As indicated in Chapters 1 and 2, the environment that hosts the community-of-care for clients in their systems of care requires far more outreach, collaboration, interactions, and transactions than ever before. My, not Reid's, extended re-frame on this is what is referred to as PICIE. In this regard, astute TCCMs perceive of themselves as ostensibly having "three main clients": one is the client, the second is their community, and third is their support systems. Each year, in any given system of care, service providers come and go, eligibility criteria change, referral and admission criteria change, insurance providers change, forms and protocols change, and contacts/email address/phone numbers change. The TCCM, therefore, needs to be apprised of such changes, or he or she cannot effectively navigate or coordinate care for their clients. For many TCCM's today, their "second client," the community, often takes up more time to stay abreast of than does their "first client," the client themselves, ergo the term PICIE. I believe that as the *Affordable Care Act* unfolds (see Chapter 2), given that social work's historic main strengths are knowing and understanding the community, PICIE will become the dominant paradigm and new "industry standard" for all social workers practicing TCCMG.

3. *Essential Paradigm Approaches*—Paradigm approaches are not values themselves, but they are anchored in social work values. After reading numerous articles, books, manuals, accrediting reports, agency reports, etc., for background to writing this text, I concluded that three predominant or essential paradigm approaches need to be practiced by all TCCMs. Indeed, others could and should be used as needed, but these continued to prevail as being essential in today's CMG reality. First, as mentioned more extensively in Chapter 1, clients *are now required to become full partners* in the entire TCCMG process. This shifting of responsibility for all care decisions, treatment options, and issues that arise in treatment, begins at the first contact meeting with the client and TCCM. At this time, TCCMs shift the therapeutic relationship from one of an authority position to one of a collaborative partnership. This first paradigm approach has now become "the norm" in today's CMG practice, and will continue to be the norm in the future of CMG.

Second, from the late 1970s onward, social work adopted the strengths-based perspective as a paradigm for all clients and client systems. This notion transcends and can be applied to all social work practice from macro to meso to micro. Often, TCCMs are required to assess not only the problems/issues/needs/and concerns of clients to help plan for their care, but their agency protocols also require full assessments of capacities, activities, assets, strengths, mobility, and physical and mental capability, etc. These required detailed data are used to interface with the tabled "presenting problems" of clients in care, to foster a more complete and comprehensive strengths planning approach. Table 3.1 presents 12 principles of strengths-based approaches. Often we mention the importance of strengths-based perspectives, but provide no examples of it. Table 3.1 is intended to offset this issue.

The third dominant paradigm essential to TCCMG practice today is system navigation. Since the TCCM's second client is the community and the third client is the support system, as mentioned above, TCCM's must routinely share knowledge about treatment options, barriers, challenges, etc., with clients, and their support systems to assist clients in negotiating their own course of treatment. For some clients, this is their first major illness requiring such extended care or self-management of their own care, and for some of these, getting their heads wrapped around to the daunting systems, paperwork, eligibility issues and providers, in their community-of-care is an overwhelming experience in and of itself. TCCMs must always shepherd this process by being constantly focused on tasks, goals, objectives, and outcomes, which helps anxious clients with their new problem of "system navigation-itis." Staying the course of the treatment process, mirroring core values to clients, and having them be empowered to make choices for themselves through their treatment journey, all assist in reducing the aforementioned affliction.

❖ **Table 3.1**   Twelve Principles of the Strengths-Based Perspective Model* Used by SWCMs

---

1. A conscious effort to incorporate a positive and optimistic view of the client and his or her capacity needs to drive the model.

2. The focus is on individual strengths and assets, not on deficits or pathology.

3. The community is viewed as a potential gold mine of resources that needs to be tapped.

4. The helping process requires it be anchored in a rigorous standard of core client individuation and self-determination values at all times.

5. A development of a relationship between the client and SWCM is essential.

6. The community needs constant outreach and relationship building to ensure effective client and system navigation with available service providers.

7. All protocols, record keeping, and client tracking materials should adequately address and note client strengths and assets.

8. Realistic benchmarks for achievement of outputs and outcomes require strengths re-framing.

9. All barriers/concerns/obstacles are re-framed as challenges.

10. Assets need to be harvested in all client/worker transactions, even if clients do not see them as assets.

11. The constant instillation and reinforcement of hope is essential.

12. Seeking and valuing client voice and decision-making ability in all instances.

Note: Based on the work of Modrcin, Rapp, and Chamberlain (1985).

4. *Accountability and Transparency*—In Figure 3.1, the TCCM extends the notion of accountability and transparency from simply client ↔ worker to a multi-systemic one, requiring ongoing transactions as indicated in Figure 3.3 between numerous interrelated stakeholders.

Figure 3.3 illustrates a synergistic triangle wrapped around by different types of ongoing supports. The triangle moves the basic didactic and linear communication model of "sender ↔ receiver" into a more multi-level and multi-systemic communication process constantly being shared (minimally) between clients, providers, and TCCMs. This information is not only essential and required (by agencies) for monitoring services, but in TCCMG it is meaningfully incorporated in Steps 3 to 7 (see Figure 3.1), that uses such data for assessment/re-assessment, and planning/re-planning accountability purposes. Thus, not only are agencies, providers, and client accountability promoted simultaneously, but ongoing transparency in the treatment process becomes normal "part and parcel" of the TCCMG approach.

Also illustrated in Figure 3.3 is the context within which the client/provider/TCCM communication triangle resides. It is nested in and wrapped around by ongoing re-assessments and utilization of informal supports, formal supports, and resources. Over the course of a client's care provision, these contexts may change, and different stakeholders may move in and out of them accordingly, but their interrelated synergy to the "accountability triangle" in Figure 3.3 are essential to making TCCMG work. For instance, increased resources could result in additional formal care supports not used before, which could in turn reduce the attendant care by some family members or friends in the informal care system. Figure 3.3 re-emphasizes the importance of the previously mentioned PICIE and its "three-client" system, namely the client, community, and support systems (as noted above).

5. *Interdisciplinary and Multidisciplinary Care*—Reid's model was eclipsed by the necessity for TCCMs today to work with various professionals in interdisciplinary teams to promote holistic client care. This reality is not only a necessity for TCCMG, but is deemed

❖ **Figure 3.3**   The Accountability and Transparency in Today's TCCMG

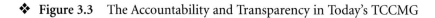

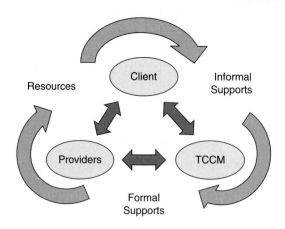

likely to be more apparent on the horizon in the United States. For instance, the *National Academies of Practice* (NAP, 2011) developed a specialty report to address this issue titled "Toward Interdisciplinary Team Development." In it, they stated:

National health care reform in the U.S. provides the opportunity when the concept of 'interdisciplinary teams' must move from being an interesting idea to a practical necessity. Inter-professional team practice, which is common in geriatrics, home, hospice, rehabilitation, and some aspects of mental health, is rarely found in other areas of health delivery. Teams have the potential to become the cutting edge management tool in the private practice settings, managed care, group practices, and integrated health care systems. (p. 6)

Since the definition of teamwork simply means two people in different disciplines or more working together in some fashion, interdisciplinary teams that TCCMs work in come in differing forms. Boon, Verhoet, O'Hara, and Finley (2004) described seven hierarchical levels of team functioning, which included:

1. *Independent health care practitioners:* Those who work in a common setting

2. *Consultative team:* A traditional medical referral model

3. *Collaborative team:* Independent practitioners sharing information

4. *Coordinated team:* A formalized structure in which members share records and communicate about specific patients

5. *A multidisciplinary team:* Multiple different disciplines, each practitioner making independent decisions, with a team leader appointed to integrate the various decisions.

6. *Interdisciplinary team:* A multidisciplinary group that makes group decisions, usually based on a consensus model, face-to-face meetings, and collateral contact information

7. *Integrative care team:* A non-hierarchical blending of conventional medicine and complementary and alternative health care (p. 16)

Regardless of where TCCMs practice on this hierarchy, they become acutely aware of (a) how to collaborate with different disciplines, (b) how to talk and communicate with different disciplines, (c) how to blur their roles effectively with others and to respect the professional boundaries of other professions, and (d) how to delineate clearly and confidently what unique social work skills you bring to the "teamwork table" as a TCCM. So now we finally have a field-tested and uniquely social work CMG model for practice—thank you, Dr. Reid!

Motivational Interviewing: A Practice Framework for Implementing the TCCMG Model

"People will forget what you said. People will forget what you did. But, they will never forget—how you made them feel."

—Maya Angelou

This profound and well known quotation written by Nobel Laureate Maya Angelou exemplifies not just what TCCMs do, but what they actually care about. These are the emotions, pains, concerns, anxieties, losses, confusion, ambivalence, and uncertainties that many clients experience during all client–worker interactions. Taken together, and as echoed above, these are the actual feelings of our clients. Our Code of Ethics (2008) mandates that professional social workers must anchor all client–worker transactions in core values that promote the human conditions of genuineness, respect, autonomy, and honesty. Thus, our client–centered work, as mentioned earlier, is not only value driven, but when implemented, it is caring driven as well. The braiding of values with human caring extends the definition of social work that Lubove (1965) historically referred to as "the professional altruist." As such, our well known values guide and anchor our client-centered work; the caring for the well-being of our clients is how we juxtapose and operationalize these values in all relational approaches, models, or frameworks used in practice. It is the intersection of values, social work skills, and caring that becomes the essence of what effective TCCM practice is really all about.

The first TCCMG model that social workers could use to effectively practice CMG was presented earlier in this chapter. The discussion herein presents *how* to practice TCCMG, and it is recommended that the approach used in this regard is William R. Miller's "Motivational Interviewing" (Miller & Rollnick, 1991; 2002; 2013).

What is Motivational Interviewing (MI)?

First, MI is not a theory, although it is primarily based on the person-centered theory of Carl Rogers (1951; 1959), which promoted self-actualization and increased client congruence with both one's self and others. It is also somewhat based on Cognitive Behavioral Theory (Beck, 1979; Ellis & Grieger, 1977; Meichenbaum, 1977; Shaw, 1977) whose goal is changed thinking, identification of beliefs, and awareness of thoughts. It is also partially based on Solution-Focused Therapy (Berg, 1994; de Shazer, 1988) aimed to identify problems and action steps to solve them. Taken together, the common techniques used in these three foundational theoretical approaches include client-driven solutions to problems; their effectiveness for use in both short- and long-term time frames, their use of active counselor listening; the client–counselor transparency; collaboration and enabling clients to act; and, their overt focus on eventual changed thinking and/or perspectives initiated by clients.

The non-psychotherapeutic MI approach developed by William R. Miller in the 1980s (Arkowitz, Miller, & Rollnick, 2015; Miller & Rollnick, 1991, 2002, 2013; Rollnick, Miller, & Butler, 2008; Steinberg, & Miller, 2015) has both lay and professional definitions. The former or so-called elevator definition by Miller is "a collaborative conversational style for strengthening a person's own motivation and commitment to change" (Miller, 2014). The practitioner definition also articulated by Miller in this same reference is "motivational interviewing is a person-centered counseling style for addressing the common problem of ambivalence to change. Essentially, this is a practice framework that structures conversations to help clients talk about positive change" (Miller, 2014).

Similar to Reid's TCCMG model mentioned earlier, MI has much empirical data that have directed and informed its development over the years. From Miller's early work to his most recent, MI has always been empirically studied in methods using case data, quasi-experimental data, randomized clinical trials (RCTs), multi-site RCTs, and meta-analyses in over 2,200 studies. Further, MI books have been translated into 22 languages worldwide; over 3,000 professionals in at least 47 different languages have been trained in MI; over 1,500 publications about MI doubles every 3 years; it has been referenced (up until 2013) over 50,000 times; and entire nations and states have developed best practices and have implemented MI in recommended practice protocols for helping individuals (Miller, 2014). Miller's legacy and early work was in the area of addictions (where I received my training) and today, addictions is still its main field of practice and research. However, it has evolved in a variety of other fields including mental health, corrections, education, health care, social services, child welfare, community settings, and dentistry. All of these areas have shown the practice framework to be empirically efficacious (Miller, 2014).

MI and Social Work

The historical origins and DNA of social work and MI have an excellent "goodness-of-fit" for a number of reasons. First, MI is a positive and human growth technique that is client-centered and client, not worker, driven. Both MI and social work are effectively practiced in short- (1 to 2 hours) and long-term (1 to 3 year) time frames. Both emphasize the core practice relational dimensions of genuineness, empathy, collaborative partnership relationships, reflective listening, non-judgmental approaches, the promotion of strengths-based perspectives, trust building, and promoting clients to talk more, converse, and reflect more than counselors in sessions. In short, these dimensions resonate with our core social work values of service to humanity, social justice, human dignity and worth, the importance of human relationships, integrity, and competence (Code of Ethics, 2008).

A Brief Overview of MI

Since this sub-section presents only a very brief overview of MI for SWCMs to use in TCCMG, only the main features of this practice framework will be presented here. So, first, what is unique to MI? MI is entirely focused on promoting client change—first and foremost. In MI, counselors facilitate clients to arrive at a place in client–counselor conversations where they can engage in what MI refers to as "change talk." During change talk, clients first begin by talking about their arguments for wanting change, referred to as their commitment to change.

Evolving to "Change Talk"

The ability to transform one's awareness of their problem and having clients then take ownership of their problem and engage them in "change talk" about their problem is a challenge for MI counselors. There are some key strategies offered to promoting eventual "change talk" in MI. Eight of these, which involve counselor skills, include the following, which are often labeled collectively as the "Spirit of MI":

1. Anchoring all counselor–client conversations in empathy

2. Promoting a collaborative relationship in conversations with clients

3. Promoting the feeling that clients are partners in their helping process

4. Evoking ideas, opinions, reasons to change, and client confidence to enact change

5. The use of active and reflective listening extensively in all client conversations

6. Resolving the omnipresent ambivalence that individuals have to make change

7. Supporting client autonomy and personal control in all conversations

8. Promoting ongoing commitment to an eventual positive resolve by the instillation of hope (Glovsky, 2009)

Using O.A.R.S. to Effect "Change Talk"

How counselors communicate the above noted counseling strategies is through the use of the acronym O.A.R.S. This includes the use of:

1. *O*pen-ended questions—The goal in using such questions is to understand meaning, rather than to collect facts. By using *how* and *what* questions, rather than *why* questions, open-ended, non-judgmental conversations eventually evolve. Some examples include the following: "tell me more about . . . ."; "could you help me better understand more about...?"; "what have you tried before?"; and "how was that for you when you tried it?"; etc.

2. *A*ffirmations—Counselors need to affirm and reaffirm the past and existing strengths and abilities of their clients to support their personal self-efficacy. For example, "You mentioned you were a positive person—how might your positive outlook help you deal better with your illness?" or "You have really tried hard to find a place to live. I believe your persistence in seeking housing will eventually be successful once we find a different strategy to achieve your goal."

3. *R*eflections—Counselors promote and encourage responses in conversations with their clients in MI, not reactions to them. All responses are reflections of real and perceived problems and, more importantly, real and perceived steps a client must take to embrace "change talk." Termed as Action Reflections, you reflect what the person says in the ways that suggest a potential future action toward behavior change (Resnicow & McMaster, 2012). Action Reflections are ways to bridge and move conversations toward a specific action step for change. The more such reflections are used in MI, they reinforce a focus on client feelings, rolling with resistance, and acknowledging ambivalence (Resnicow, McMaster, & Rollnick, 2012). Some examples include statements such as: "you seem to be thinking and saying that you might be able to quit drinking," "I'm not sure, but XYZ might be an option for you," or "there have been a range of options you have touched upon including . . ." (Resnicow et al., 2012).

4. *S*ummaries—The final counseling communication skill to evoke "change talk" involves counselors interspersing short summaries in client conversations. As such, summarizing periodically allows clients to hear that you are actively listening to them as you pull together themes, patterns, congruencies/incongruencies, reflections, and ideas. Miller and Rollnick (2012) described this process as "picking flowers and presenting them back to the client in a nice bouquet." The counselor essentially collects statements from the conversations and "connects the dots" by incorporating them and motivating for eventual client readiness for "change talk." For example,

You have told me a lot about why you like using marijuana. It helps you relax, and it is easier for you to have fun with your friends. You also said that you have gotten into a lot of trouble because dope is illegal, and it has started to cost you a lot of money. You are not sure you want to stop smoking marijuana right now but you are wondering what it is actually costing you overall. (Naar-King & Suarez, 2011, p. 38)

Commitment to "Change Talk"

Prior to the final and culminating step in getting to "change talk," a commitment to change *by the client* must evolve in the conversation. This involves the evoking of "commitment language" by the clients. As shown empirically in studies of MI, the stronger the statements of commitment by clients in conversations, the stronger the likelihood for change (Naar-King, & Suarez, 2011). The main difference between MI and a more directive counseling approach is that the MI counselor waits patiently for commitment language in the conversation before a plan for change can be developed. So what does "commitment language" look like? On a 5-point Likert type scale with 1 being "lowest commitment" and 5 being "highest commitment" here are a few phrases as examples:

A. "I mean to" → 2. "I favor" → 3. "I look forward to" → 4. "I am devoted to" → 5. "I guarantee"

B. "I hope to" → 2. "I aim to" → 3. "I expect to" → 4. "I am prepared to" → 5. "I give you my word" (p. 65)

As such, these points on the continuum, transition the client to a conversational place from "no change talk" to "ambivalence about change" (the main barrier for change), to "sustained talk," to "commitment to change talk," to "actual change talk." When clients arrive at this point in the conversations they frequently and readily use their own "change talk language." Change talk is often heard in five categories that counselors may use to elicit change talk using the acronym *D.A.R.N.-C* (Australian Heart Foundation, 2012).

❖ **Table 3.2**   D.A.R.N.-C. Five Categories of Change Talk and Questions Counselors Use to Evoke Conversations

Change Talk in Motivational Interviewing (MI) Using D.A.R.N.-C.	
Categories	Suggested Counselor Questions
1. **D**esire	Why would you make this change?
2. **A**bility	How would you do it if you decided?
3. **R**eason	What are the three best reasons to do this?
4. **N**eed	How important is it to you and why?
5. **C**ommitment	What will your first step now be?

Note: Reference Glovsky (2009).

After affirming some such change talk and D.A.R.N.-C., motivations are voiced and confidence and commitment to change strengthens to taking an action step. This invokes developing a specific behavioral change plan that the client has initiated, agrees to, and is willing to implement and be accountable for. In regard to the latter point, the client is encouraged to be accountable to herself or himself first and then the counselor and others second. MI advocates here that a *S. M. A. R. T.* plan is used at this point. This means that the plan is *S*pecific, *M*easurable, *A*chievable, *R*elevant, and *T*ime-Framed. It is recommended that the plan is feasible, discrete, and task oriented, which conceptually and theoretically links MI back to the recommended TCCMG model described earlier.

This completes this sub-section that advocates strongly for linking MI and TCCMG for social work practice. Their relevance to one another, their alignment to a social work frame of reference, and their strong value-based orientation make them the recommended goodness-of-fit for effective CMG practice in a variety of settings. The uniqueness of MI and the fact that it is not heavily theory laden in addition to it being empirically effective continues to reinforce this practice approach as being what it is actually not, rather than what it actually is. Miller and Rollnick (2009) summarized this perspective in the following way. This verbatim summary, in their own words, hopefully will assist CMs using this approach with TCCMG to use it in the way it was intended and operationalized.

- MI is not based on the transtheoretical model—the stages of change. They are two discrete models, and neither one requires the other.
- MI is not a way to trick people to get them to do what they do not want to do.
- MI is not a technique, it is more complex and better understood as a communication method.
- MI is not the decision balance; this has been over-utilized and misperceived as MI methodology.
- MI does not require assessment feedback; this design is specific to MET.
- MI is not a form of cognitive-behavior therapy, nothing is installed; rather, MI elicits from people what is really there.
- MI is not *just* client-centered counseling, MI departs be being goal oriented and having intentional direction toward change.
- MI is not easy, it involves a complex set of skills that are used flexibly.
- MI is not what you are doing, learning MI requires training, supervised practice, and feedback.
- MI in not a panacea, it is not meant to be a school of psychotherapy, rather it is a particular tool for addressing a specific problem. (p. 96)

Finally, you can download a free application on your Apple or Android phone called Change Talk. As we of this generation know—if you have a phone app—you must really have something worthwhile!

The Underbelly of TCCM: The Uniqueness of How Social Work CMs Practice

Finally, social workers using the TCCMG model use practice wisdom in not only implementing the previous steps described in this chapter, but they understand that the real essence of their work is focused on making the model work. TCCMG is driven by three aims that occur simultaneously. One is the task at hand, the second is the client-centered relationship, with not only the client but his or her support system, and the third is the community system of care. Understanding how to braid these systems in a process to tie them to specific planning steps and outcomes is indeed a challenging, but not an insurmountable, task for experienced SWs using this model. An old Chinese adage that embraces this is: "If you take care of the work first—everything else will take care of itself." Thus, it is the task that always drives the TCCMG process in all three braided areas noted.

In accredited BSW and MSW North American curricula, students are taught knowledge and skills about both micro practice (face-to-face with individuals, small groups, and families) and, also macro practice (either indirectly, or face-to-face with larger groups, systems, organizations, and communities). The disproportionate majority of students who graduate from these programs (about 80%) select micro or direct practice, which historically has been the area of practice that social work has been primarily identified with (see Chapter 2). However, as mentioned earlier about always having "one eye on the client" and "one eye on the community of care," TCCMG necessitates the adroit and constant blending of micro and macro practice. Indeed, many TCCMs would deem that micro and macro practice as currently taught in SW education is a false practice dichotomy, as both skills are essential for effective CMG work.

However, the real "back story" behind effective TCCMG is using a set of therapeutic skills that are not really taught in the classroom, but are essentially learned on-the-job. These not only underpin the TCCM model, but demark our professional approach to practice in this area as being decidedly unique from other cognate disciplines who practice as partners with us. These are collectively referred to, as indicated in the above sub-title, as the real underbelly of TCCMG. Each will be briefly and candidly described herein.

1. *The Instillation of Hope*—With each and every client or client system transaction and contact, TCCMs consciously seek to instill and re-frame hope. They do this by continually clarifying, demystifying, de-medicalizing, de-labeling, and de-complexifying the care management tasks in the various client interactions that arise. Indeed, when TCCMs offer empathy, genuineness, and care information about the steps used in the previously described TCCMG model, they remind their clients, both subtly and often more assertively, that whatever happens during this care journey, there is always hope for them.

2. *Creating Space*—TCCMs proactively work to create space in the many nuanced and complex systems of care that cause stress and anxiety to their clients. They do this so that clients and their support systems can be truly heard. A metaphor will be used here to describe this more vividly. A TCCM carries both the picnic basket and blanket to the beach with their client and support system alongside of them. She or he then asks where their blanket should be placed on the very crowded and noisy beach. When their spot is selected, the client and their support systems physically sit down, on their newly claimed space, to talk about the process steps to be achieved in their managed care journey. As such, the client and her or his support system seem now to be more physically and mentally comforted and less anxious, and more likely to be at ease for "having the necessary conversations" they need to have as they gaze more peacefully at the ocean together.

3. *Humanness/Kindness*—The word often used cavalierly to describe social workers is *compassionate*. However, a quick dictionary check of the actual synonyms for this favorite

moniker indicates that they are not so favorable as they convey dependency and help-lessness. Those include the likes of pity, sympathy, solitude, mercy, leniency, and charity. However, being humane and kind have no such non-affirming synonyms or connota-tions. Social work TCCMs, therefore, who work in systems fraught with uncertainty, ambiguity, and much client anxiety, continue to inject liberal doses of humane caring and kindness to all of their clients. This, by default, engenders trust, communication, and honesty—anyway one looks at this process and relationship.

4. *Humility*—Many clients desire TCCMs to be the "experts" in their care management process. Ironically, a good number of clients also defer their voice or care options to their social work CM "experts." Skilled TCCMs constantly engage the client to act and mirror humility back to their clients in a conscious counter-transference way, so that the client recognizes them "*not* as the expert." But the TCCM is a social worker who is a full partner in their care management, with a decided knowledge and skillset, and is someone who will always help them with the care issues and situations as they arise.

5. *Relational-Practice Focus*—Establishing a relationship with clients and client systems in often very short and compressed time frames is a challenging, but not impossible, task. Small communication gestures such as engendering pleasantness, offering sin-cerity, establishing good eye-contact, and always "staying with the client," in which-ever peaks and valleys the journey holds, is anchored in a decided relational focus. This focus transcends the client–worker system and evolves to the client–worker–sup-port system-service provider and system-fiscal accountability system, all of which require important effective relational dimensions to successfully negotiate their care management.

6. *Flexibility*—TCCMs live in work environments that require great measures of personal and professional flexibility, despite the fact that much of the bureaucracy delimited eligibility and treatment options appear rather inflexible. Simple things such as filling out forms in different ways that suit the client and not the worker, adjusting criteria on a continuum for timely decision making, modifying short- and long-term treatment goals based on the changing status of the client or care arrangements, and ensuring that such flexibility is role-modeled to both the client and the client system is the norm for effective CMG in TCCMG.

7. *Embracing Culture*—Given the projected sociodemographic population trends in North America, inevitably more and more different cultures will end up on the future caseloads of TCCMs. Today's notions of cultural sensitivity have really moved beyond the "Level 1" thinking of simply "tolerating others" to understanding how to work effectively *with* others. Such Level 2 thinking requires knowledge and understanding of cultural mores and customs, communication patterns, and understanding the critical importance of language as being the most important cultural variable that influences all others. Indeed, embracing culture in more meaningful ways will be the norm for the future of TCCMG, rather than the exception.

8. *Vigilant Monitoring*—Effective social work TCCMs are constantly prompting, cueing, updating, assessing, re-assessing, coordinating, and collaborating with their clients, their support systems, and service providers. Unfortunately, despite our technologi-cal revolution, computers do not do this task themselves, clients may forget to do this, and service providers are not often contracted to do this. Thus, it is incumbent upon a TCCM to exercise tactful, constant, and fully accountable vigilant monitoring of the entire group of stakeholders in the clients' overall care management.

9. *Time-Clock Management*—Although this term is normally associated with athletic coaching, it is essential that TCCMs constantly understand the "day-to-day time issues" that arise with their client cases. In some CMG systems, when workers log on to their computers to complete required assessment tasks to negotiate with service providers for care, they are "on the clock" to complete this work within a time frame such as 24–36 hours, ergo the term *time-clock management*—rather than just *time management.* In other instances, waiting list information, care provider information, medication, bed availability, etc., change by moments or minutes, ergo the term *time-clock management* once again.

10. *Tolerating Ambiguity and Contradictions*—Skillful TCCMs realize that tolerating ambiguity/bureaucracy/uncertainty and the contradictions of organizations, is "part and parcel" of doing their job. It is not just about "figuring things out as they go"—but it involves the TCCM to model a constant comfortability about all situations as they unfold in the process—anticipating and dealing with things as they arise. Indeed, this comes with experience, patience, tolerance, and large measures of practice wisdom used judiciously at both macro and micro levels. When our cognate partnering disciplines offer a compliment to competent social work TCCMs, they often say "she gets it," and/or "gets it quickly."

11. *Getting the "Client's Story Out"*—A very wise social worker once said this to me, "If you really think about what we [social workers] do well, it is we get our clients to tell their stories." Indeed, this is what TCCMs do very well, and they do it in sincere and respectful ways. Making anxious and/or troubled clients feel at ease and safe enough to converse openly and honestly, to tell their stories about their situations and problems, is truly a skill that social work "brings to the table." We can also do it in a very cost effective manner.

12. *Barrier Identification*—It is difficult in many of the transactions we have with clients and client systems to remove the pervasive structural and systemic barriers that exist within them. However, as a full partner in system navigation with their client, skilled TCCMs assist in identifying barriers and helping clients to negotiate them. This is quite different than negotiating the barrier *for the client*, which borders on a violation of our Code of Ethics to protect client autonomy, and her or his decision making, at all costs.

13. *Active vs. Reflective Listening*—The notion of active listening tends get a bad rap as a bonified technique that can be used effectively in counseling situations. Without question, reflective listening is certainly more desirable. However, TCCMs work in bureaucracies driven extensively by paperwork, forms, laws, rules, regulations, and ever-changing policies. They work with clients who are medicated, anxious, overwhelmed, have hearing and visual impairment, have cognitive distress, emotional distress, and economic hardships limiting their ability to develop much of a conversational repertoire. The rather glib view that active listening just "parrots back" and repeats what was said by an individual is often a useful technique that TCCMs use with such clients, and also ensures that verification of the material being discussed is presented in the most accurate way possible to receive eligible services. Our relational DNA in social work is patient centered, and it has been shown to yield more positive outcomes when reflective listening is used. However, this ideal has to be re-framed in concreteness and the reality that the paperwork necessary to move the client forward to receive services may be better served by using more active listening in some cases.

14. *Getting Unstuck With Negativity*—Social and behavioral scientists have shown that when people experience negativity and loss, it is more difficult for them to unlearn

how to allow such negativity to personally impact them. Many clients on the caseloads of TCCMs are not just mired in their overwhelming situation that exacerbates their anxieties and problems, but they tend to become emotionally debilitated by being in this negative situation. Skilled TCCMs try to use techniques that help clients first to learn how to communicate more positively about their situation, and then assist them to "grab on" to whatever positive strengths this situation presents, in order for them to try to move forward. Unfortunately, some of these clients actually evolve in continuums of learned helplessness, to learned hopelessness, to emotional negativity-paralysis. It is challenging for TCCMs to assist individuals who are spiraling down this negativity slide, to prop them up with whatever semblance of hope that may anchor them in an opposite positive direction.

15. *Enabling Client Change*—We have come to finally dispel the communication myth that providing education about a problem will change a person's behavior. Experienced TCCMs realize that it is not just education and information, *but how you present it*— which is the real key to effectively communicating with clients. Such information has to be framed minimally in the following ways: a) it must be tangible, b) it must be honest, c) it must be forthright, d) it must be personalized, e) it must be socially interactional, f) it must address how to convey how issues of loss have occurred to patients and their families, and g) it must be audience specific.

16. *Health Literacy*—According to Kanj and Mitic (2009), health literacy refers to the degree to which people are able to access, understand, appraise, and communicate information to engage with the demands of different health contexts in order to promote and maintain good health across the life-course. Research has shown that health literacy is important, and good health literacy results in both more positive outcomes and cost savings. TCCMs acknowledge that before patients can be empowered to advocate for themselves, they must at least meet the basic level of functional health literacy. This involves skills that allow an individual to read consent forms, medicine labels, health care information, and to understand written and oral information offered by physicians, nurses, pharmacists, social workers, or other health care professionals; and to act on directions by taking medication correctly, adhering to self-care at home, and keeping scheduled appointments (Kanj & Mitic, 2009).

Concluding Remarks

This chapter presents a bona fide social work CMG model originally developed in 1972 by W. Reid. It was built, field-tested, and utilized by social workers for social workers and their client systems. The model was visionary in its time and its contemporary approach to task-centered case management (TCCMG) is as relevant today as it was some years ago. It has been tweaked, adapted, and contemporized its use for social workers in today's CMG reality. It is hoped that all SWCMs practicing today in North America will see fit to refer to themselves as TCCMs from hereon in, given the appropriateness of this model to today's reality of how CM's practice in the variety and range of health and human services in their communities of care.

❖

REFERENCES

Arkowitz, H., Miller, W. R., & Rollnick, S. (Eds.) (2015). *Motivational interviewing in the treatment of psychological problems* (2nd ed.). New York, NY: Guilford Press.

Australian Heart Foundation. (2012). Motivational interviewing: Clients arguing for change—Introducing DARN-C [Video file]. Retrieved from https://www.youtube.com/watch?v=Pwu99NIGiXU

Beck, A. (1979). *Cognitive therapy and the emotional disorders.* New York, NY: Penguin Books.

Berg, I. K. (1994). *Family-based services: A solution-focused approach.* New York, NY: W. W. Norton.

Boon, H., Verhoet, M., O'Hara, D., & Finley, B. (2004). From parallel practice to integrative healthcare: A conceptual framework. *BMC Health Services Research, 4,* 15–19. http://www.biomedicalcentral.com/1472-6963/4/15

Code of Ethics, National Association of Social Workers (2008). Retrieved online from https://www.socialworkers.org/pubs/code/code.asp

de Shazer, S. (1988). *Keys to solution in brief therapy.* New York, NY: W. W. Norton.

Ellis, A., & Grieger, R. (1977). Handbook of rational-emotive therapy. New York, NY: Springer.

Glovsky, E. (2009). Motivational interviewing—Listening for change talk. Retrieved from http://www.recoverytoday.net/archive/19-june/45-motivational-interviewing-listening-for-change-talk

Kanj, M., & Mitic, W. (2009). Promoting health and development: Closing the implementation gap. Nairobi, Kenya.

Katzen, M., & Morgan, M. (2014). *Affordable Care Act opportunities for community health workers: How Medicaid preventive services, Medicaid health homes and state innovation models are including community health workers.* Center for Health Law and Policy Innovations, Harvard Law School.

Lubove, R. (1965). *The professional altruist: The emergence of social work as a career, 1880–1930.* Cambridge, MA: Harvard University Press.

Meichenbaum, D. (1977). *Cognitive behavior modification: An integrative approach.* New York, NY: Plenum Press.

Miller, W. R. (2014). *Motivational interviewing and quantum change 2014* [Video file]. Retrieved from https://www.youtube.com/watch?v=2yvuem-QYCo

Miller, W. R., & Rollnick, S. (1991). *Motivational interviewing: Preparing people to change addictive behavior.* New York, NY: Guilford Press.

Miller, W. R., & Rollnick, S. (2002). *Motivational interviewing: Preparing people for change* (2nd ed.). New York, NY: Guilford Press.

Miller, W. R., & Rollnick, S. (2013). *Motivational interviewing: Helping people change* (3rd ed.). New York, NY: Guilford Press.

Naar-King, S., & Suarez, M. (2011). *Motivational interviewing with adolescents and young adults.* New York, NY: The Guilford Press.

National Academies of Practice (2001). *Toward interdisciplinary team development: A policy paper of the National Academies of Practice.* Accessed November 1, 2014, from www.NAPractice.org

Reid, W. J., & Epstein, L. (Eds.). (1972). *Task-centered casework.* New York, NY: Columbia University Press.

Resnicow, K., & McMaster, F. (2012). Motivational interviewing: Moving from why to how with autonomy support. *Journal of Behavioral Nutrition and Physical Activity, 9*(19), 1–9.

Resnicow, K., McMaster, F., & Rollnick, S. (2012). Action reflections: A client-centered technique to bridge the WHY-HOW transition in motivational interviewing. *Journal of Behavioral Cognitive Psychotherapy, 40*(4), 474–480.

Rogers, C. (1951). *Client-centered Therapy: Its current practice, implications and theory.* London, UK: Constable.

Rogers, C. (1959). A theory of therapy, personality and interpersonal relationships as developed in the client-centered framework. In (ed.) S. Koch, *Psychology: A Study of a Science. Vol. 3: Formulations of the Person and the Social Context.* New York, NY: McGraw Hill.

Rollnick, S., Miller, W. R., & Butler, C. (2008). *Motivational interviewing in health care: Helping patients change behavior.* New York, NY: Guilford Press.

Shaw, B. F. (1977). Comparison of cognitive therapy and behavior therapy in the treatment of depression. *Journal of Consulting and Clinical Psychology, 45*(4), 543–551.

Steinberg, M., & Miller, W. R. (2015). *Motivational interviewing in diabetes care.* New York, NY: Guilford Press.

4

Social Work Case Management

Practice Certification and Licensure

"The best vision is insight."

—Malcolm Forbes

I n researching the topic of case management (CMG) in general, and social work case management (SWCMG) in particular for this text, a few things became apparent, which were underscored in the previous chapters. These were the following: 1) CMG is a field that social work is evolving into and gaining professional legitimacy daily—and this process is being accelerated with the passage of the *Affordable Care Act of 2010;* 2) as indicated in Chapter 3, the Task-Centered Case Management (TCCMG) model provides an empirically field-tested framework for SWCMG; 3) nursing clearly dominates the field of North American CMG and will continue to do so in the future; and 4) individuals who do CMG tasks and/or call themselves case managers (CMs) varies considerably. The latter of these will be discussed initially in this chapter.

Who are CMs and What Do They Do?

CMs in North America currently work in a variety of public, profit, and non-profit sectors including but not limited to mental health care, additions, long-term care, aging, HIV/AIDS, occupational services, legal services, patient record information services, child and welfare family services, and immigrant and refugee services (Case Management Society of America, 2015).

The U.S. commission for case manager certification offers a well-regarded definition for this differentially interpreted term:

"Case Management" is a collaborative process that assesses, plans, implements, coordinates, monitors and evaluates the options and services required to meet the client's health and human service needs. It is characterized by advocacy, communication, and resource management and promotes quality and cost-effective interventions and outcomes. (Commission for Case Manager Certification, n.d., p. 3)

Of the areas of CMG practice above, health care is clearly projected to be the largest area of growth. According to employment projections, published by the U.S. Bureau of Labor Statistics (2014), "occupations and industries related to health care are projected to add the most new jobs nationally between 2012–2022. Total employment is projected to increase 10.8% or 15.6 million in the next decade." The main domains of current and projected health care employment ranked in descending order of priority include:

1. General Medical and Surgical Hospitals

2. Home Health Care Services

3. Individual and Family Health Services

4. Nursing Care Facilities (Skilled Nursing Facilities)

5. Outpatient Care Facilities (U.S. Bureau of Labor Statistics, 2014)

As a result, SWs practicing in health care and SWs who are labeled as CMs (which I refer to as SWCMs), the current trend today, will provide routine SW services in these settings such as screening/assessment/discharge/and support for individuals, families, and groups coping with acute, chronic, and/or terminal illness. The focus of their work will include the tasks of advising individuals, family caregivers, providing patient education, and offering brief counseling, and making referrals for services. SWCMs will continue to be involved in activities that are either attached to a specific health care unit such as mental health, oncology, gerontology, etc., or a task function of the particular unit, for example, assessment, discharge planning, etc. Here, SWCMs will focus more on providing CM and care coordination, community and system navigation, assessment and negotiation of insurance eligibility, integration of formal and informal community supports, more in-depth or unique patient assessments, that is, capacity or capability, and offer targeted interventions designed to promote patient and family stability, wellness, and health, the prevention of further illness or disease, the promotion of independent living, the monitoring of outcomes, and advocacy to address barriers to health care systems (U.S. Bureau of Labor Statistics, 2014).

What Other Licensed Professionals Practice CM or Support SWCMs?

SWCMs routinely find themselves working with other health care professionals who are either CMs themselves, such as nurses, or work collaboratively with them in providing SWCM services, for example, physicians. In the previous chapter, it was noted that interdisciplinary teams are the lifeblood of our current and future health care systems of care. It is therefore incumbent upon SWCMs to embrace the concept of "role blurring." In such a reality, interdisciplinary professionals share an understanding of their common roles and responsibilities, such as developing treatment plans for their patients, and also share common language and knowledge to work together, for example, medical terminology. As such, each of these team member disciplines works more efficiently and seamlessly in bringing to the table their own discipline-specific knowledge and education, as well as their necessary role-blurring knowledge.

Presented in a summary chart below are the various partners who normally assist us in our SWCM jobs, all of whom are licensed professionals. The Bureau of Labor Statistics (2013) projected that in the next decade, fewer individuals will be permitted to work in health care who do not have minimally an undergraduate university degree and who are not licensed to practice. Licensure for practice ensures that there is a minimum of not only a baccalaureate degree in this list of professionals, but that all are individuals who have passed a minimum set of qualifications via a written examination and who are members of a sanctioned professional licensing body that has a code of ethics (COE) and requires its members to attend ongoing professional continuing education.

❖ **Table 4.1**   Social Work (SW) Case Management Cognate Disciplines

Professions	Educational Requirements
Nurses	
a. BSN	4-yr. university degree
b. MNS	12- to 24-mo. graduate degree
c. RN	2-yr. associates degree in tech./comm. college
d. LPN	2-yr. associates degree in tech./comm. college
Physicians	
a. PA	3-yr. graduate degree
b. MD	4-yr. graduate degree, plus residency
c. GP	4-yr. graduate degree, plus residency
Pharmacists	
a. Pharmaceutical technician	2-yr. associates degree in tech./comm. college
b. Pharmacists	3- to 4-yr. graduate degree, and clinical residency
Psychologists	
a. MA/MS	2- to 3-yr. graduate degree
b. PsyD	4- to 6-yr. graduate degree
c. PhD	5- to 7-yr. graduate degree, plus residency

(Continued)

❖ Table 4.1 (Continued)

Professions	Educational Requirements
Lawyers	
a. LLB	3- to 4-yr. undergraduate degree
b. LLM	12- to 24-mo. graduate degree
c. JD	3-yr. graduate degree
Phys. and Occup. Therapists	
a. MPT	2- to 3-yr. graduate degree, clinical field work required
b. MSPT	2- to 3-yr. graduate degree, clinical field work required
c. DPT	3- to 4-yr. graduate degree
d. OT	2- to 3-yr. graduate degree, clinical field work required
Chiropractors	
a. Chiropractic Technician	2-yr. associates degree in tech./comm. college
b. M.Sc. Ciro.	12- to 24-mo. graduate degree
c. DC	4-yr. graduate degree, plus supervised clinical work
Counselors/Therapists	
a. MA/MS	2-yr. graduate degree
b. BSW	4-yr. university degree
c. MSW	12- to 24-mo. graduate degree
d. LMSW/LCSW	12- to 24-mo. graduate degree plus state licensure
e. LPC	12- to 24-mo. graduate degree plus state licensure
f. MACC	12- to 24-mo. graduate degree
g. LMFT	12- to 24-mo. graduate degree plus state licensure
Speech and Language Pathologist/Audiologists	
a. BS	4-yr. university degree
b. MS	12- to 24-mo. graduate degree

Health and Human Service Workers Who Are Considered Case Managers

Table 4.2 indicates the respective websites and codes of ethics of these selected careers, all of whom frequently refer to themselves as health care case managers.

❖ **Table 4.2** Health Case Management (CM) Professions and Corresponding Code of Ethics Websites

Professions	Corresponding Code of Ethics
Nurses	
a. BSN	ANA—http://www.nursingworld.org/codeofethics
b. MNS	ANA—http://www.nursingworld.org/codeofethics
c. RN	ANA—http://www.nursingworld.org/codeofethics
d. LPN	ANA—http://www.nursingworld.org/codeofethics
Physicians	
a. PA	AAPA—https://www.aapa.org/WorkArea/DownloadAsset.aspx?id=815
b. Psychiatry (MD)	APA—http://www.psychiatry.org/practice/ethics
c. GP	AMA—http://www.ama-assn.org/ama/pub/physician-resources/medical-ethics/code-medical-ethics.page
d. MD	AMA—American Medical Association—http://www.ama-assn.org/ama/pub/physician-resources/medical-ethics/code-medical-ethics.page or the American Board of Physicians Specialties—http://www.abpsus.org/code-of-ethics ** If working internationally must abide by the ethics set forth by the World Medical Association—http://www.wma.net/en/30publications/10policies/c8/
Pharmacists	
a. Pharmaceutical technician	APA—http://www.pharmacist.com/code-ethics
b. Pharmacists	APA—http://www.pharmacist.com/code-ethics
Psychologists	
a. MA/MS	APA—http://apa.ore/topics/ethics/index.aspx
b. PsyD	APA—http://apa.org/topics/ethics/index.aspx
c. PhD	APA—http://apa.org/topics/ethics/index.aspx
Lawyers	
a. LLB	ABA—http://www.americanbar.org/groups/professional_responsibility/publications/model_rules_of_professional_conduct/model_rules_of_professional_conduct_table_of_contents.html
b. LLM	ABA—http://www.americanbar.org/groups/professional_responsibility/publications/model_rules_of_professional_conduct/model_rules_of_professional_conduct_table_of_contents.html
c. JD	ABA—http://www.americanbar.org/groups/professional_responsibility/publications/model_rules_of_professional_conduct/model_rules_of_professional_conduct_table_of_contents.html

(Continued)

❖ Table 4.2 (Continued)

Professions	Corresponding Code of Ethics
Physical and Occupational Therapists	
a. MPT	APTA—http://www.apta.org/Ethics/Core/
b. MSPT	APTA—http://www.apta.org/Ethics/Core/
c. DPT	APTA—http://www.apta.org/Ethics/Core/
d. OT	AOTA—https://www.aota.org/media/Corporate/Files/AboutAOTA/OfficialDocs/Ethics/Code%20and%20Ethics%20Standards%202010.pdf
Chiropractors	
a. Chiropractic Technician	ACA—http://www.acatoday.org/content_css.cfm?CID=719
	ICA—http://www.chiropractic.org/ethics
b. M.Sc Chiro.	ACA—http://www.acatoday.org/content_css.cfm?CID=719
	ICA—http://www.chiropractic.org/ethics
c. DC	ACA—http://www.acatoday.org/content_css.cfm?CID=719
	ICA —http://www.chiropractic.org/ethics
Counselors/Therapists	
a. MA/MS	
b. BSW	NASW—http://www.socialworkers.org/pubs/code/default.asp
c. MSW	NASW—http://www.socialworkers.org/pubs/code/default.asp
d. LMSW/LCSW	NASW—http://www.socialworkers.org/pubs/code/default.asp
e. LPC	ACA—http://www.counseling.org/resources/aca-code-of-ethics.pdf
f. MACC	AACC—http://aacc.net/files/AACC%20Code%20of%20Ethics%20%20Master%20Document.pdf
g. LMFT	AAMFT—https://www.aamft.org/iMIS15/AAMFT/Content/legal_ethics/code_of_ethics.aspx
Speech and Language Pathologist/audiologists	
a. BS	ASLHA—http://www.asha.org/Code-of-Ethics/
b. MS	ASLHA—http://www.asha.org/Code-of-Ethics/

Selected Social Work Licensing Agencies

In North America, there are many licensing boards that provide certification and licensure to case managers. In some instances, it is required for employment as a CM, or professionals working as CMs may choose to be licensed, and it is not a condition of employment. The majority of these licensing agencies provide a CM credential, for nurses, however, some permit social work and other professions to sit for CM examinations required for certification. Below is a list of selected licensing boards that *permit* social workers to take national certification examinations. These were the main boards located in web searches, in Spring 2015, on the Internet. This is not to say that other state or certification boards do not exist.

1. ***American Case Management Association*** provides the Accredited Case Manager (ACM) licensure to individuals seeking employment in hospital/health care settings. This license is offered to individuals who have previous education in nursing, and/or social work. All applicants must have at least 2 years of full-time experience in Health Care Delivery System Case Management, or 4,160 work hours in Health Care Delivery System Case Management. If one holds both an RN, and/or SW license, they must indicate which exam they wish to take and provide the relevant eligibility documentation. A Registered Nurse (RN) applicant must have a valid and current nursing license, and must provide a nursing license number, state/locale, and expiration date. Social work applicants must have a BSW or MSW degree from an accredited school of social work, or possess a valid social work license. Social work applicants must provide copies of the degree(s) obtained, name of school, and year of completion, or current social work license number, state/locale, and expiration date. All candidates must take a written exam consisting of two case management components. The first contains core case management questions that test one's knowledge, skills, and abilities about work in a hospital/ health system. The second sub-section is made up of separate discipline-specific clinical case simulations. Sample questions and further information about this certification can be found in the handbook on the agency website: https://www.acmaweb.org/acm/.

2. ***The Commission for Case Manager Certification*** provides the Certified Case Manager (CCM) certification to case managers from Multiple Setting Case Managers; and nursing and social work are again both eligible. The CCM examination given by the Commission for certification is practice based, which means that all of the questions on it are based around knowledge that an experienced case manager should possess and understand. The examination has a total of $N = 180$ multiple-choice questions. It is administered in one written sitting with no time allotted for breaks. Applicants have a total of 3 hours to complete the content portion of the test. To be eligible for this particular examination, all applicants must hold a current, active, and unrestricted licensure or certification in a health or human service field. This field must be within the scope of CM practice, which allows professionals to conduct assessments independently. Applicants may have a BSW or MSW degree in social work, a nursing degree, and other health and human services related degree backgrounds that promote physical, psychosocial, and vocational well-being of the clients being served. All applicants must also satisfy a minimum of 12 to 24 months of CM employment experience. For further information, examination materials and the link to register for CM examination workshops are noted on the Commission for Case Management Certification's webpage at http://ccmcertification.org/.

3. ***The NASW Credentialing Center*** is the only national major licensing agency solely responsible for providing professional social work case management certification. It certifies individuals who have either a BSW or an MSW degree to be eligible for one of their two certification's offered. BSW level social workers are eligible to take the

examination for the Certified Social Work Case Manager (C-SWCM), and MSWs are eligible for the Certified Advanced Social Work Case Manager (C-ASWCM) examination. Applicants for either must have obtained degrees from an accredited university. BSW candidates must be able to provide documentation of at least 3 years and 4,500 hours of paid, supervised, post-BSW professional experience in an organization or agency that provides case management services to be eligible. BSW applicants also need to provide documentation that they have a current state BSW-level license or an ASWB BSW-level exam passing score, or 20 contact hours of relevant continuing professional education. MSW applicants must be able to provide documentation of at least 2 years (equivalent of 3,000 hours) of paid, supervised, post-MSW case management experience. They must also document that they hold a current state MSW-level license or an ASWB MSW-level exam passing score to be eligible for the examination. For more information on the examination, the application, and for preparatory materials, visit https://www.socialworkers.org/credentials/specialty/c-swcm.asp. Applicants can also contact the credentialing center via e-mail at credentialing@naswdc.org.

4. *National Academy of Certified Care Managers* provides the Certified Care Manager (CCM) certification to multiple setting case managers including those who work in fields related to care management such as social work, counseling, nursing, psychology, gerontology, rehabilitation, public health, or human services. In this particular licensing agency there are three criteria levels that applicants may fall into, in order to be eligible to take the certification examination. Criteria 1 are those individuals who have a master's degree in a field related to care and 2 years paid, full-time, supervised (at least 50 hrs/year) care management experience. Criteria 2 are for those individuals who have a bachelor's degree in a field related to care management, or those who have a bachelor's degree and a university-based certificate in care management. In addition, these individuals must have 2 years paid, full-time, supervised (at least 50 hrs/yr) care management experience and 1 year paid, full-time direct experience with clients in areas such as social work, nursing, mental health/counseling, or care management. Criteria 3 are those individuals who have an associates' degree in a field related to care management, or a bachelors or higher degree in an unrelated field, or those who have an RN diploma. These individuals must also have 3 years paid, full-time, supervised (at least 50 hrs/yr) care management experience and 2 years paid, full-time direct experience with clients in work such as social work, nursing, mental health/counseling, or care management. Care management experience consists of a post-eligibility degree and must include all of the following core CM functions: screening, face-to-face assessment, care plan development, coordination and implementation; ongoing monitoring of client situation and the care plan, periodic formal re-assessment, discharge from CM, documentation of all care management functions, and quality evaluation activities. Consultation/supervision in this case is defined as individual, group or peer review of performance, use of clinical skills and core care manager functions. The exam has 200 multiple choice questions including some case scenarios with questions related to the situation. The CCM examination is given twice a year, during the months of April and October. It is administered Monday through Saturday, excluding holidays. Applications for the April exam window can be submitted starting December 1, and no later than February 15. Applications for the October exam window can be submitted starting June 1 and no later than August 15. For more information, visit the National Academy of Certified Care Managers website at http://www.naccm.net/.

5. ***The American Institute of Outcomes Health Care Management (AIOCM)*** provides Case Manager Certification (CMC) designation to all health care professionals. Eligibility requirements are represented on the membership application form that can be found on the AIOCM website. There is a standard membership and a portfolio review membership process offered to applicants who meet the appropriate criteria. Both application processes require individuals to pass the AIOCM examination. For more information, visit the AIOCM website at http://www.aiocm.com/#membership or contact them at info@aiocm.com.

6. ***The Center for Case Management*** lists three broad categories for eligibility for the Case Management Administration Certification (CMAC). Meeting one criterion among the three broad sub-sections is considered sufficient for examination eligibility. The first category is the General Criteria for eligibility. Under this sub-section, one can have a master's degree and 1 year of experience in case management administration, or a master's degree and 3 years of experience as a case manager; or, a bachelor's degree and 3 years of experience in case management administration, or a bachelor's degree and 5 years of experience as a case manager.

7. If you do not meet any of these criteria, the next category is the Equivalent Certification Criteria, which allows for active certification from one or more of the following organizations as sufficient eligibility to obtain a case management certification. These criteria include an A-CCC from the National Board of Certification in Continuity of Care; ACM from the American Case Management Association; CRRN from the rehabilitation Nursing Certification board; CCM from the Commission for Case Manager Certification; CDMS from the Certification of Disability Management Specialists Commission; SWCM (Certified Social Work Case Manager) and C-ASWCM (Certified Advanced Social Work Case Manager) from the National Association of Social Workers; and an RN, C (Modular Certification in Nursing Case Management) from the American Nurses Credentialing Center. Their third broad category is specific to faculty. Faculty who are in academic settings teaching graduate level courses that pertain to case management will be permitted to take the certification exam. The length of their experience in teaching CM-related content must be at least a minimum of 2 consecutive academic semester's within a 24-month period or 2 academic semesters within a 24-month period.

For more information related to nursing-specific CM agencies and various other certifications available to CMs, see the Case Management Society of America website at http://www.cmsa.org/Individual/Education/AccreditationCertification/Certification/tabid/261/Default.aspx. This resource provides information related to the certification, the primary career focus areas of the certification, and the specific licensing agency that provides the certification in addition to the licensing agency's contact information.

Practice Domains for Examination Licensure

Since this is a text written by and for social workers, and the model used has been developed and field tested for social workers, it is important that the starting point for understanding the various components of practice roles and responsibilities for social workers is framed by the National Association of Social Work (NASW) *Standards for Social Work Case Management* (2015). The NASW presents 12 standards by which case managers should practice, that dovetail with their accredited BSW and MSW degrees, Code of Ethics (COE), and *NASW Indicators for the Achievement of the NASW Standards for Cultural Competence in Social Work Practice.* I recently called the NASW directly in March 2015 to ask if formal certification testing had been developed as of this date. Their answer was no, but described in Number 3, Section IV above are the licensure requirements and their respective time frames. The educational expectation for licensure is that professionals are competent in the following 12 standards.

1. Ethics and Values

2. Qualifications

3. Knowledge

4. Cultural and Linguistic Competence

5. Assessment

6. Service Planning, Implementation, and Monitoring

7. Advocacy and Leadership

8. Interdisciplinary and Inter-organizational Collaboration

9. Practice Evaluation and Improvement

10. Record Keeping

11. Workload Sustainability

12. Professional Development and Competence

Given what has been mentioned repeatedly in this text about the potential growth of case management in the nation, it would appear that the NASW should soon begin more formal testing with an examination process for social workers in the future. If not, I feel that our BSW/MSW students' professional persona would become engulfed by other licensure and certification boards and/or health and human service organizations. In summary here, these 12 standards frame up many of the expected practice roles and responsibilities and testing and licensure requirements of the five other licensing boards mentioned above. The other source document that is not a licensing or testing board for certification is the Case Management Society of America *Standards of Practice for Case Management* (2010). They list both standards of care in addition to extensive documentation of how each standard should be demonstrated. Their 15 standards of care are the following:

1. Client Selection Process for Case Management

2. Standard Client Assessment

3. Problem/Opportunity Identification

4. Planning

5. Monitoring

6. Outcomes

7. Termination of Case Management Services

8. Facilitation, Coordination, and Collaboration

9. Qualifications for Case Managers

10. Legal

11. Ethics

12. Advocacy

13. Cultural Competency

14. Resources Management and Stewardship

15. Research and Research Utilization (www.cmsa.org)

Taken together, these standards set the framework and expected competing areas for all case managers practicing in all different settings in the United States.

The American Case Management Association listed above has core areas with varying numbers of questions on the following domains:

1. Screening and Assessment (11 questions)

2. Planning (25)

3. Care Coordination and Intervention (32)

4. Evaluation (22), plus 20 questions added for pre-testing

The Commission for Case Manager Certification domains for certification include:

1. Psychosocial Aspects

2. Healthcare Re-imbursement

3. Rehabilitation

4. Healthcare Management and Delivery

5. Principles of Practice

6. Case Management Concepts

The National Academy of Certified Care Managers that provides the CCM has five competency standards:

1. Assess and Identify Client Strengths, Needs, Concerns, and Preferences

2. Establish Goals and a Plan of Care

3. Implement Care Plan

4. Manage and Monitor the Ongoing Provision of and Need for Care

5. Ensure Professional Practice

The American Institute of Outcomes Health Care Management requires certification in four areas, which include:

1. General information

2. Professional experience

3. Education in the specific area

4. Ethical requirements

Their examination includes knowledge in the specific area of certification that includes:

1. Clinical

2. Customer service

3. Management/Supervision

4. Quality/Performance Improvement

5. Legal/Risk Aspects

6. Working with Payer Organizations

7. UM/CM/DP/DM

8. Clinical Chart Audit

9. Working With Employer Organizations

10. Working With Provider Organizations

11. Working With Community Resources

12. Resources Management

13. Financial Management

14. Business Management

Lastly, the Center for Case Management, which provides certification examination for case management administrators have seven domains for testing that include:

1. Identification of At-Risk Populations

2. Assessment of Clinical System Components

3. Development of Strategies to Manage Populations

4. Leadership for Change

5. Market Assessment and Strategic Planning

6. Human Resource Management

7. Program Evaluation through Outcomes Measurement

As indicated above, social work has lagged far behind other case management disciplines requiring certification and licensure for practice in America. Given a) how the *ACA* (2012) is rapidly unfolding; b) how social work's role is emerging in this community-centric model and gaining traction daily (Hawk, Ricci, Huber, & Myers, 2015; Pettus & Holosko, 2015); and c) how issues of service user rights, eligibility for service, care provision, quality assurance, service availability, and provider liability are being tabled in this movement-a-foot, the profession needs to stop their foot dragging for education, training, and examination-based licensure. Hopefully, this information may provide an advocacy source for these essential requirements.

❖

REFERENCES

American Case Management Association. (2015). ACM certification exam. Retrieved from https://www.acmaweb.org/acm/

The American Institute of Outcomes in Healthcare Management (AIOCM). (2015). *Membership.* Retrieved from http://www.aiocm.com/

Bureau of Labor Statistics. (2013). Employment projections: 2012–2022 summary. Retrieved from http://www.bls.gov/news.release/ecopro.nr0.htm

Bureau of Labor Statistics. (2014). Occupational employment and wages, May 2013: 21-1022 healthcare social workers. Retrieved from http://www.bls.gov/oes/current/oes211022.htm

Case Management Society of America. (2010). Retrieved from http://www.cmsa.org/portals/o/pdf/embersonly/standardsofpractice.pdf

Case Management Society of America. (2015). Where do case managers work? Retrieved from http://www.cmsa.org/findacasemanager/wheredocasemanagerswork/tabid/277/defalt.aspx

The Center for Case Management. (2015). Case management administrator certified. Retrieved from http://www.cfcm.com/wordpress1/cmac/

Commission for Case Manager Certification. (2015). CCM exam. Retrieved from http://ccmcertification.org/

Commission for Case Manager Certification (CCMC). (n.d.). Definition of case management. Mt. Laurel, NJ: Author. Retrieved November 13, 2010, from http://ccmcertification.org/about-us/about-case-management/definition-an

Hawk, M., Ricci, E., Huber, G., & Myers. (2015). Opportunities for social workers in the patient centered medical home. *Social Work in Public Health, 30,* 175–184.

The NASW Credentialing Center. (2015). The Certified Social Work Case Manager (C-SWCM). Retrieved from: https://www.socialworkers.org/credentials/specialty/c-swcm.asp

NASW Standards for Social Work Case Management. (2015). Retrieved May 1, 2015, from http://www.socialworkers.org/practice/naswstandards/CaseManagementStandards2013.pdf

National Academy of Certified Care Managers. (2015). *Certification.* Retrieved from http://www.naccm.net/

Pettus, J., & Holosko, M. (2015, April 10). *Traditional social work practice transformed to case management under the Affordable Care Act (2010).* Presented at the Interprofessional Health Care Summit, Savannah, GA.

Part II

Social Work Case Management in Selected North American and Chinese Settings: The Frontlines of Practice

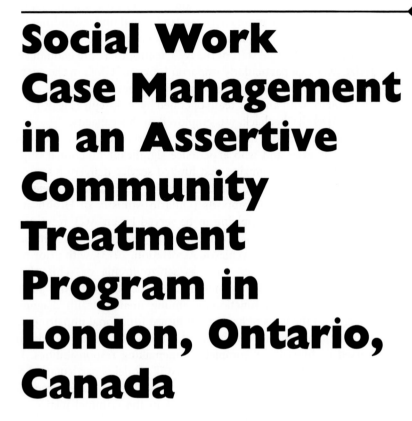

5

Social Work Case Management in an Assertive Community Treatment Program in London, Ontario, Canada

Derek Chechack and Judith M. Dunlop

The Clientele

The provision of case management (CMG) in mental health care has long been regarded as the preferred mode of service delivery in Canada. One particularly intensive form of CMG, known as assertive community treatment (ACT), has been demonstrating its clinical value since the 1970s, following the widespread de-institutionalization of psychiatric inpatients (Test, 1979). At its foundation, CMG refers to the coordination of community services by a single professional who is responsible for assessing a client's needs, developing and implementing appropriate care plans based on this assessment, and then evaluating the care plan through ongoing follow-up. In some instances, case managers (CMs) are also responsible for transitioning clients to other services when they move, or no longer meet program or diagnostic criteria. While there are some differences between traditional understandings of CMG and the ACT model, such as coordinating external services versus providing them in-house (i.e., by other professional staff of the ACT team), there are enough similarities to characterize ACT as a particularly important form of CMG in the current North American service delivery context. This chapter describes the experience of working as a service coordinator with an ACT team operated by St. Joseph's Health Care London. The first author, Derek Chechack, was employed in this capacity.

ACT is a model that primarily supports individuals with serious and persistent mental illnesses and who experience significant functional impairments because of their illnesses. Recognizing that limited service delivery resources are commonplace today, current program standards advise ACT teams to select clients who are "in the greatest need" of supports (Ontario Ministry of Health and Long-Term Care, 2004, p. 6). Clients applying to be served by an ACT team are required to have a diagnosed mental illness according to the *Diagnostic and Statistical Manual of Mental Disorders* (American Psychiatric Association, 2013), with priority given to individuals with psychotic illnesses, such as schizophrenia or schizoaffective disorders and bipolar disorders. These illnesses are associated with the greatest disease burdens and impairment in functioning among mental health diagnoses. Clients are also selected on the basis of having significant functional impairment, such as an inability to maintain housing, employment, obtain child care, avoid dangers or hazards to herself or himself, or complete homemaking responsibilities. Because these clients are typically high-service users, the ACT model is particularly beneficial for this subpopulation, as they are also at an increased risk to have comorbid health conditions, substance use disorders, involvement in the criminal justice system, and difficulty using traditional outpatient services. Overall, the ACT service recognizes the chronic nature of these mental illnesses and encourages ongoing support with illness or symptom management, employment, socialization, and ultimately maintaining community residence, and/or independent living.

Clients in our agency are typically not discharged, owing to the history of ACT being a lifelong service. However, this is slowly starting to change with the emphasis on transitioning to community agencies. Therefore a typical client can receive services in our agency for many years and atypical clients tend to only receive services for up to a year. Because community resources almost universally operate at lower cost than institutionalized care, ACT is a cost-effective and highly successful approach to providing hospital-quality care in the community (Slade, McCarthy, Valenstein, Visnic, & Dixon, 2013). The ACT model also reduces the prospect of duplicating services, which can occur when multiple service providers operate independently of each other to support the client. Although all ACT clients are supported by a psychiatrist, a service coordinator in our hospital is also assigned to perform the traditional case manager (CM) role. This structure is particularly valuable for clients with complex needs, as their service coordinators can develop an intricate knowledge of their strengths, deficits, and required needs for successful community-based illness management. Additionally, such coordinated care has become more important in recent years, as clients' needs have become more complex. Among other factors, this occurs because of an aging population, poverty and legislative restrictions, insufficient community resources, and the frequent overlapping of mental health and health care needs.

Practice Roles and Responsibilities

CMG is simultaneously both a professional and organizational endeavor. While any number of regulated professionals can serve as CMs, effective service delivery also requires a commitment by their employing organizations to provide resources that promote CMG activities. According to the National Case Management Network of Canada (2009), there are five guiding principles of CMG: 1) It supports client rights; 2) it is purposeful; 3) it is collaborative; 4) it supports accountability; and, 5) it strives for cultural competency. The role of the ACT service coordinator (CM) in our hospital can be described according to these five guiding principles.

First, CMG is a collaborative approach that should solicit client input as much as possible in each step of the process of client engagement. Although some authors like Dennis and Monahan (1996) and Gomory (2002) invited a lively debate about whether the ACT model is better described as coercive than collaborative, in practice, ACT principles can operate within our overarching recovery-oriented program philosophy that balances its intensive purpose with service users' rights. The CM, as the primary clinician working with the service user, can begin to develop rapport with the client in order to maximize voluntary participation in the program. Critical social work skills at this stage inform the basis of the therapeutic relationship, especially with clients with psychosis who may be naturally skeptical and suspicious of others, due to the illness itself. Closely related to the second principle noted, when clients' identified needs and willingness to receive services coincide with the program's available resource offerings, the ACT model becomes inherently less coercive and more purposeful, with regard to overall illness management. Canadian ACT teams (like ours) typically offer, in addition to psychiatry and nursing services, vocational rehabilitation, therapeutic recreation, social work, occupational therapy, substance abuse counseling, and peer support. The CM, while continuing to develop the working relationship, can use her or his social work assessment skills to formulate a treatment plan to address the interpersonal and social impediments owing to the client's illness.

Third, CMG is a collaborative process, not just between service users and providers, but among social service agencies in the so-called community-of-care. Flexibility and accommodation are particularly important, since ACT clients may be involved with multiple providers to address their complex needs, and their unique life goals should be captured by individualized service or treatment plans. Similarly, when working with people who have psychotic or bipolar illnesses, client motivation and interest can vary tremendously, in many instances from one day to another. Social work assessment and re-assessment skills continue to be critical, as does current knowledge of the medical basis for these conditions, so as not to personalize the client's wavering commitment to or participation in the service delivery process. An annual awareness of existing and emerging community resources and programming will also help clients find the best fit for their illness management plans. For instance, peer support and professional interventions have traditionally been dichotomized; however, a service user may find the comradery and relational qualities of a peer support program to ideally meet their recovery goals. Here, the CM can be a key resource to establish these important connections.

In terms of supporting accountability, our CMs are expected to be responsible for their actions and decisions in regard to the overall service coordination of their primary clients. Service coordination with ACT clients requires timely responsiveness to ever-changing abilities and changing needs. Goal attainment and direction can vary according to clinical presentation, and a regular treatment planning review can promote the team's accountability to the clients' health care objectives. The ACT team also promotes accountability through the responsible stewardship of available publicly funded resources, in terms of having consistent and reliable eligibility guidelines and ethical service delivery practices.

Lastly, from a diversity perspective, culturally sensitive CMs participate in an ongoing process of increasing self-awareness to ensure that service recipients are treated with genuine concern, respect, and appreciation for their unique identities. Although diversity is often thought of in terms of racial and ethnic differences, it is equally important to recognize other social and economic differences, the influence of gender and class, and sexual orientation. Our CMs are encouraged to learn principles of cross-cultural communication, strengths-based assessments, and how to integrate divergent perspectives about illness, disability, or dysfunction. Practitioners are trained and required to work collaboratively to ensure that these perceptions, which often vary by culture and may clash with the clinician's own understanding, are not a barrier or impediment to the delivery and service user's receipt of proper health care.

Role Development Potential

Social workers, as both members of our interdisciplinary ACT teams and primary service coordinators for ACT clients, can contribute to the team's overall delivery of quality health care through role development in three areas. First, we are deemed the experts in the social determinants of health, the environmental or contextual factors that influence the health of individuals and populations. These include income and social status, the availability of social support networks, level of education, working conditions in employment settings, the physical state of surrounding environments, personal health practices and coping skills, healthy child development, gender, and culture (Public Health Agency of Canada, 2015). In practice, social workers are ideally suited to situate these factors within their knowledge of the person-in-environment (PIE) perspective in order to effect positive change in a client's life. Although some factors are more difficult to positively improve on than others, such as income or financial status, awareness of community resources and access to members of the in-house interdisciplinary team can promote positive change with regard to several other determinants.

Second, social work CMs possess a cogent understanding of family dynamics and conflict resolution skills, which can be invaluable to supporting a client who is newly diagnosed and living at home, or living in an enmeshed or otherwise conflictual home environment. There is a fine line with some service users that divides positive interpersonal relationships and rejuvenating solitude. Too much stimulation can be overwhelming and contribute to symptom manifestation, while on the flip side, too much solitude can lead to isolation that is detrimental and negatively associated with both physical and mental health outcomes. The social work CM can support clients to develop and emphasize pro-social relationships, while also articulating the boundaries necessary to promote her or his optimal symptom control. With newly diagnosed clients, there is the added responsibility of providing simply communicated culturally informed psychoeducation to family members about illness management, particularly in high-conflict settings.

Social work CMs can also increase their role potential more by fully embracing the recovery philosophy which conceptually overlaps with many practice standards and ethical codes. As noted in the introduction, the recovery model or philosophy is the dominant service delivery model today, which contrasts with the historically biomedical model and top-down approach to psychiatric treatment. In a 2006 practice snapshot, the U.S. National Association of Social workers described how the mental health recovery model is congruent with core social work values and ethics. Specifically, the client's self-deterministic right to accept or reject treatment and the overarching concepts of strengths and empowerment are overlapping tenets. As the NASW (2006) noted, helping clients achieve their own health care goals through increased decision-making abilities will ultimately encourage their independence and level of initiative. This outcome is "consistent with the values of the social work profession, which is committed to the empowerment and self-determination for all populations, particularly those who are traditionally disenfranchised" (NASW, 2006, para. 2).

Within both BSW and more so MSW social work education in Canada, the role of linker, broker, resource developer, and more recently system navigator is highly valued and considered professional competencies for professional social workers. Historically, the role of linker has been incorporated into all levels of intervention and considered a key function of social workers that approach practice with a PIE perspective. Despite social work's focus on the importance of skills such as resource development, linking, engagement, and inter-organizational collaboration, there is little application of these skills to a CMG specific curriculum, which I (the first author) studied in before assuming this position.

Social workers involved in CMG practice utilize knowledge and skills in areas of 1) assessing individual and family dynamics; 2) assessing and re-assessing the relationship between person and environment; 3) analyzing how social, psychological, political, and economic factors impact individual and family functioning; 4) acquiring knowledge of relevant agency and governmental policies and legislation that affect service delivery; and 5) developing an extensive knowledge of community resources that are available in local and regional areas (Summers, 2001). Although there are several levels of CMG that may occur within many Canadian agencies and communities, resource coordination is often the focus of social work CMG practice. CMG responsibilities such as assessment, planning, linking, monitoring, and evaluation are required practice skills for CMG (National Council of Social Service, 2004). Although CMG is not therapeutic intervention, but the managing of potential referrals for clinical services, social workers must possess both clinical assessment skills and administrative skills. The skills needed to carry out interorganizational coordination are grounded in organizational and community development models that function to coordinate services and ensure continuity of service.

We believe that the advanced generalist practice (AGP) model used in both Canada and parts of the United States could be strengthened at the MSW level to include a specific CMG qualification with a focus minimally on the CMG functions of assessment, planning, intervention, monitoring, and evaluation. While these functional responsibilities are covered in multiple graduate level classes in individual and family therapy, community social work practice, and administrative practice, they are usually taught in compartments. The lack of integration of these practice models into a specific CMG qualification or specialty is a critical area for future curriculum development for CMG practice. Generally, there has been little recognition of the professional expertise required to carry out the CMG role and thus at a graduate level, social work has failed to incorporate the managerial aspects of CMG in Canada.

As such, there are two differential aspects of CMG: 1) clinical assessment and intervention knowledge, skills and experience with clinical intervention models, and their evidence-based outcomes; and, 2) managerial expertise that requires both administrative and community development leadership skills. This is where the basic understanding of the role bifurcates and leads to failure to follow through and actually effect change. This is a MSW level skill that needs to be a specialist position, drawing on the undergraduate and graduate experience with increasing competency in clinical assessment, intervention, and evaluation. Thus, the CM role moves into specialist territory where the clinical knowledge and skill is coupled with administrative knowledge and skill to create leadership positions for CMs at community levels (Guransky, Harvey, & Kennedy, 2003). Unfortunately, the current Canadian conceptualization of CMG as administrative practice has not been generally incorporated into graduate social work either at the community or organizational practice level. There is recognition, however, that "training in multidisciplinary skills is essential for case managers" (Guransky et al., 2003, p. 171).

The AGP work practice model in graduate social work education, in which I (the first author) was trained, incorporates a framework that addresses levels of intervention, namely, 1) individual, 2) family, 3) group, 4) community, and 5) organization, and works at these intervention levels using a 5-step process model of 1) engagement, 2) assessment, 3) intervention, 4) evaluation, and 5) follow-up. This model contains all of the necessary knowledge and skills needed to be an effective CM and effective social change agent. However, this goodness-of-fit is often unrecognized because an organizing framework for CMG is still missing in social work (M. Holosko, personal communication, June 2015).

CMG is essentially a leadership position that requires competency in community and administrative practice in order to manage complex interorganizational relationships and service user/provider relationships. Perhaps more importantly, social work values and ethics that underscore the strengths-perspective with clients provide the essential foundational principles that drive social work CMG; or if you will, creates social work client advocacy within CMG systems in local communities. This set of social work knowledge and skills coupled with a value base of client self-determination offers social workers the ability to advocate for clients to take leadership roles in planning services, which are relevant to their quality of life. The more recent focus on service user/provider planning processes highlights the importance of service user voice and participation in planning for health and human services (Dunlop & Holosko, in press). We perceive that what is currently missing for social workers in CMG positions is the acceptance of CMG as a managerial position. What seems to be also missing is the *recognition* that CMG knowledge and skills are solidly grounded in community social work practice. Collaboration as a community and administrative practice skill requires encouraging, motivating, and building trust among service providers, and between service providers and service users in order to achieve change at the individual, family, and community service system levels. One of social work's most well-known community social work scholars, Jack Rothman, perhaps said it best when he identified that bringing together components of social work practice into a "new configuration represents something unique" (Rothman & Sager, 1998, p. 15). Moxley (1997) had the final word on this when he stated that the "aim or purpose of CMG should always be client-centered and the CM is the "steward of the perspectives and desires of consumers" (p. 6).

Concluding Remarks

Working both inside the employing organization to look at the best available intervention for the client, the CM has to be skillful in managing external environmental relations in order to bring diverse disciplines and organizations into a cohesive CMG planning process. The community and administrative practice skill of managing external environmental relations positively impacts the entire CMG process and benefits the client because of the CM's ability to facilitate inter-agency relations and manage the timing, delivery, and evaluation of human services. In addition, excellent organizational skills are required to ensure that all members of the CMG team including the client and family are provided with relevant documentation, lead times for meetings, and copies of decisions made at previous CMG meetings. The monitoring of the delivery of the CMG services and their effectiveness also requires high level diplomacy and leadership skills in order to effect the collaboration between service providers that is required in effective CMG practice.

Social work values and ethics, rooted in the belief of the inherent dignity and worth of every individual, position social work CMs as the best possible advocates for individual clients and for service system change. However, this cannot be done without the necessary knowledge and skills for CMG practice. While these skills are taught in social work, they are not comprehensively organized into a CMG practice model. They exist, they are learned, and then they are practiced in isolation from each other without this necessary organizing framework. It is important to acknowledge that there is considerable debate within the literature about whether CMG is a profession within itself, or if it is a specialization within an existing profession (Guransky et al., 2003). Recognizing there is no consensus on this issue and that the question has critical implications for social work education, the position taken here is to support CMG as a social work MSW level specialization. That said, it will take acceptance of CMG as a managerial skill for social work to take its rightful place in a leadership role. The increasing interest in service user participation in research, education, and planning for human services supports social work CMG, which emphasizes working with clients to meet their identified needs and working with the community to bring about necessary changes in the service delivery system. Social work needs to bring to the forefront the managerial competencies that comprise a professional graduate social work degree. The managerial dimension of social work CMG needs to be addressed by social work educators to put an end to the "suggestions that case managers may be better trained through undertaking public administration and business management courses" (Gursansky et al., 2003, p. 159).

Case Example

Shawn is a 35-year-old man with a diagnosis of paranoid schizophrenia who is supported by our ACT team. He lives independently thanks to the support of the ACT model, but it has taken many years for him to get to this point. In his 20s, Shawn began experiencing typical symptoms of schizophrenia, including hallucinations, delusions, and distressing thoughts. With no prior psychiatric history, he would make frequent emergency room visits, often reporting that he was being followed or hearing voices. Although frightened by his symptoms, he was suspicious of the medical staff and refused psychotropic medication for many years. His level of insight was such that he was aware of his illness and able to consent to treatment, and as there was no evidence that he was an imminent danger to himself or others, he could not be hospitalized or forced into treatment against his will. He would live with family and friends, but his quality of life was poor and he was extremely isolated. He was reluctant to leave his home out of concern that he was being watched, and found the hallucinations and suspiciousness of others too distracting to maintain employment. After several years of continued clinical deterioration and more frequent emergency room visits, he was referred to the ACT team psychiatrist for an assessment.

After years of struggling with increasingly distressing symptoms, Shawn came to the ACT team with a willingness to accept treatment. He was still suspicious of others, but the positive symptoms of the illness, namely auditory hallucinations, had become so distressing that they overwhelmed him. He was assigned a social worker as his CM, a vocational rehabilitation counselor, and a mental health nurse. He began a course of antipsychotic medication, which provided relief from his positive symptoms, and met with each team member weekly to ensure medication compliance (especially during the initial titration when side-effects can be most prominent), and began to build relationships with his care providers.

As Shawn and his CM met during the first few weeks of his involvement with the team, they collaboratively developed a treatment plan that identified goals that they would work toward. He desired independent living and at least casual employment, and was tired of "couch surfing." They agreed that a supportive residence would offer an appropriate transition to eventual independence, allowing Shawn to increase his independent living skills, demonstrate medication compliance, and become more comfortable and familiar with the larger community. The CM completed this referral, along with a referral to a consumer-operated center that offers recreation, leisure, and peer socialization opportunities.

In his role as the CM, the social worker working with Shawn promoted client-centered treatment planning in accordance with the recovery model of mental health practice. The CM also acted as a resource for Shawn's family, providing psychoeducation and resource linking where appropriate. The CM provided Shawn with a reliable and consistent source of professional support, ensuring that his treatment plan was collaboratively modified depending on his changing life and treatment goals, symptom presentation and severity, and social factors. They met weekly to maintain trust and rapport, and to promote accountability in accordance with the ACT framework that offered intensive follow-up.

❖

REFERENCES

American Psychiatric Association. (2013). *Diagnostic and statistical manual of mental disorders* (5th ed.). Washington, DC: Author.

Dennis, D. L., & Monahan, J. (Eds.). (1996). *Coercion and aggressive community treatment*. New York, NY: Plenum Press.

Dunlop, J., & Holosko, M. (In press). *Increasing service user participation in local planning: A "how to" manual for macro practitioners*. Chicago, IL: Lyceum.

Gomory, T. (2002). The origins of coercion in "Assertive Community Treatment" (ACT): A review of early publications from the "Special Treatment Unit" (STU) of Mendota State Hospital. *Ethical Human Sciences and Services, 4*(1), 3–16. Retrieved from http://www.springerpub.com/ethical-human-psychology-and-psychiatry.html

Guransky, D., Harvey, J., & Kennedy, R. (2003). *Case Management: Policy, practice and professional business*. New York, NY: Columbia University Press.

Moxley, D. P. (1997). *Case Management by design: Reflections on principles and practices*. Chicago, IL: Nelson-Hall.

National Association of Social Workers. (2006). *NASW practice snapshot: The mental health recovery model*. Retrieved from https://www.socialworkers.org/practice/behavioral_health/0206snapshot.asp

National Case Management Network of Canada. (2009). *Canadian standards of practice for case management*. Toronto, ON: Author.

National Council of Social Service. (2004). *CM service: A guide for service providers* (NCSS Serial No. 026/SDD15/NOV04). Retrieved from https://www.ncss.gov.sg/

Ontario Ministry of Health and Long-Term Care. (2004, October). *Ontario program standards for ACT teams* (2nd ed.). Retrieved from http://www.health.gov.on.ca/en/common/legislation/priv_legislation/

Public Health Agency of Canada. (2015). Social determinants of health. Retrieved from http://cbpp-pcpe.phac-aspc.gc.ca/public-health-topics/social-determinants-of-health/

Rothman, J., & Sager, J. (1998). *CM: Integrating individual and community practice* (2nd ed.). Needham Heights, MA: Allyn & Bacon.

Slade, E. P., McCarthy, J. F., Valenstein, M., Visnic, S., & Dixon, L. B. (2013). Cost savings from assertive community treatment services in an era of declining psychiatric inpatient use. *Health Services Research, 48*(1), 195–217. doi:10.1111/j.1475-6773.2012.01420.x

Summers, N. (2001). *Fundamentals of CM practice: Exercises and readings.* Toronto, ON: Nelson Thomson Learning.

Test, M. A. (1979). Continuity of care in community treatment. *New Directions for Mental Health Services, 1979*(2), 15–23. doi:10.1002/yd.23319790203

ANCILLARIES

Internet Resources for Additional Reading

Ontario Ministry of Health and Long-Term Care. (2004, October). *Ontario program standards for ACT teams* (2nd ed.). Retrieved from http://www.health.gov.on.ca/

Ontario Ministry of Health and Long-Term Care. (2005, May). *Intensive CM service standards for mental health services and supports.* Retrieved from http://www.lco-cdo.org/en/disabilities-final-report-endnotes. Hard Copy References for Additional Reading.

Kanenberg, R. L. (2003). *CM handbook for clinicians.* Eau Claire, WI: PESI Healthcare.

Manoleas, P. (Ed.). (2000). *The cross-cultural practice of clinical CM in mental health.* New York, NY: Routledge.

National CM Network of Canada. (2009). *Canadian standards of practice for CM.* Toronto, ON: Author.

Powell, S. K., & Tahan, H. A. (2008). *CMSA core curriculum for CM* (2nd ed.). Baltimore, MD: Lippincott Williams & Wilkins.

Hard Copy References for Additional Reading

Kanenberg, R. L. (2003). *Case management handbook for clinicians.* Eau Claire, WI: PESI Healthcare.

Manoleas, P. (Ed.). (2000). *The cross-cultural practice of clinical case management in mental health.* New York, NY: Routledge.

National Case Management Network of Canada. (2009). *Canadian standards of practice for case management.* Toronto, ON: Author.

Powell, S. K., & Tahan, H. A. (2008). *CMSA core curriculum for case management* (2nd ed.). Baltimore, MD: Lippincott Williams & Wilkins.

Case Management With Homeless Veterans

Brent Temple

The Clientele

I work in the social work department of one of our nation's many Veterans Affairs Medical Centers (VAMC) as a case manager (CM) in the HUD-VASH program, which is a national partnership between Housing and Urban Development (HUD) and Veterans Affairs Supportive Housing (VASH). HUD-VASH CMs serve veterans who face homelessness by assisting them in finding housing and then providing them with supportive case management (CMG). It is clearly a "Housing First" model wherein housing is established prior to addressing any other biopsychosocial needs.

Through this partnership, HUD provides Section 8 housing vouchers, namely guaranteed rental supports to qualifying individuals, and the VA provides CMG services. Our mission is based on the goal set in 2009 of "ending veteran homelessness by 2015" (U.S. Department of Veterans Affairs, n.d.). While that may strike some as more of an aspiration than an achievable goal, recent news reports have lately declared success in ending homelessness among veterans in some larger U.S. communities (Lawrence, 2015). In order to make sense of that declaration, one needs to understand that homelessness is not a "problem that stays solved," and so what we really mean is something like this—"for every new veteran facing homelessness, we have tools at the ready to rapidly re-house them."

Our program serves veterans of our Armed Forces who are eligible and registered for VA health care services, and eligible for the Section 8 voucher. The primary eligibility for the voucher is financial, that is, the recipient must have a "very low" annual income—this is in fact a technical term used by HUD to determine a bench-mark percentage below the poverty line. It includes both family size and income. HUD calculates the voucher on a case-by-case basis to ensure that the recipient pays no more than 30%–40% of their total household income on rent and utilities. The voucher excludes applicants who make more than the maximum income annually and registered sex offenders whose adjudicated terms exclude them from publicly supported housing.

For the most part, my clients, veterans who face homelessness, face the same structural realities as those in the general population: macro-economic problems and political realities leading to low income and social instability, unresolved per-sonal issues leading to troubled relational patterns in adulthood, and individual skills deficits, unique to each person, making stability a uniquely difficult goal to retain.

My clients have the dubious benefit of belonging to two sub-groups who are vul-nerable in America. For instance, because they are veterans, people tend to assume that post-traumatic stress disorder (PTSD) is the primary cause of their social difficulties. But, because they face homelessness, people tend to perceive mental health and addic-tive disorders to be the primary factors contributing to their homelessness. Although PTSD, mental illness, and addictive disorders are indeed important in my work, I have learned that it's always best to take each individual "where they are at" at that moment. Thus, I am much better able to collaborate and partner with my clients in planning how to achieve stable housing by meeting them "where they are now," regardless of their diagnosis or my professional expectations (Lee, Tyler, & Wright, 2010).

Demographically, my clients are men and women, families and singles, from multiple racial and ethnic backgrounds. Most are males over the age of 55; some are in their 30s, and very few are in their 20s. What they all share is that they are veterans, and they are all in pretty bad shape, financially. Many have families that they can turn to in helping them get through the voucher process. For those who have no assistance from their families, or no resources of their own to bring to this process, we rely heavily on the local community network of resources that exists to support such people in need.

Both the VA and HUD must track demographic data during the intake process and throughout CMG services. This information is used to guide the program nation-ally and locally, to design new solutions to problems, and to report on the successes of the program to our funding sources and oversight. The HUD-VASH CM aids in this data collection process as a part of our required documentation responsibilities. Demographic data are highly significant in the "big picture," but demographics do little to influence my work on the "front-line" in any way other than this; I try to stay highly attuned to how my client demographic profile (by which I mean perceived white "privilege") matches and contrasts with that of my client's, so that I more inten-tionally meet them where they truly are, rather than importing any cultural biases into their lives. I honestly believe this sentiment to be clearly in line with the "patient-first" mission of the VAMC where I serve.

Practice Roles and Responsibilities

Each HUD-VASH office, just like each VAMC, is unique. We each respond to the needs of individuals whom we reach out to serve. We each have a unique geographic location where we practice our craft, with different social service infrastructures, different attitudes toward homelessness, different housing availability and landlords, and different HUD offices with which to carry out our community partnerships.

In my office, our initial work with clients invites their personal narratives and assesses their needs on several levels, at once. First, we assess the veteran's stated needs and also what needs may be lacking from their narrative. We are also listening for clinical clues about eligibility for the pending HUD-VASH voucher. If they are not eligible, we link them immediately with our many local community partners to assist them in meeting their identified needs. Thus, we actively appraise and consider what resources are at our disposal, to offer assistance, while staging that important first contact with the client. If a veteran is deemed eligible for the voucher, then we begin the first step in the HUD-VASH voucher process. That process (simplified) is described briefly below.

HUD-VASH Voucher Process Steps

Step 1

1. *Referral.* A HUD-VASH CM becomes aware of a veteran who may need assistance with finding and maintaining stable and adequate housing. Referrals typically come from community partners, VAMC staff who ask screening questions, self-referral, and from CMs ongoing outreach into the local community.

2. *Assessment.* The CM then schedules a meeting with the veteran, at a location where he or she and the CM can both be comfortable, and offers a preliminary assessment for application to the HUD-VASH program.

3. *Staffing and triage.* If the CM determines that the veteran is eligible, the HUD-VASH team staffs the case to confirm eligibility, confirm voucher availability, and to ensure that the application does not conflict with another application.

There is also a hierarchy of needs that comes into play here. For instance, veterans with children/dependents, female veterans, chronically homeless veterans, veterans with disabilities, and veterans of recent military combat postings all have priority when conflict exists in offering a voucher. Obviously, resources are not omnipresent at any given time, as sometimes all of the office's vouchers are spoken for. At these times, other resources are brought to bear to find the veteran housing. Vouchers become available again when a veteran successfully stabilizes and "earns out" of the program (i.e., earns more money than the threshold; the voucher recipient has 6 months to maintain that status before losing the voucher), or when the HUD office generates more vouchers. A veteran can also lose the voucher due to failure to follow the rules, but this is not common in my area of practice. Eagerness to remain in stable housing and CMG are both effective stabilizing factors. The culminating Step 2 in this process then unfolds.

Step 2

1. *Application.* When it's clear that the voucher will be offered to the veteran in need, the CM requests the application from HUD, schedules a time to complete it with the veteran, and assists, as needed, in compiling all required personal identification and financial documents to submit with the application.

2. *Briefing.* The CM acts as a liaison between the veteran and HUD (as needed) to schedule a "briefing," where the veteran is oriented to all of the rules pertaining to the Section 8 voucher. Each voucher is tailored to each veteran's unique family and financial situation and is given to her or him at this briefing. We then determine a "ballpark figure," of what rent amount will be approved under the voucher and use that to seek out housing.

3. *Locating housing.* The CM then assists (as needed) while the veteran seeks and secures an agreement with a landlord who will accept her or him as a tenant and the voucher as part of the rental payment. Here, the HUD representative determines the amount of the rent and utilities costs that the veteran must pay monthly, not to exceed 30%–40%; HUD prefers 30%, but allows a maximum of 40% to allow some "wiggle room" in securing appropriate housing. The voucher makes up the difference of the rent. So the amount that the voucher pays toward rent is unique to each client and residence. However, it cannot be precisely calculated prior to the voucher holder choosing a residence. Also, the voucher can only cover rent up to a certain amount, so one of the major challenges for the developing CM–client partnership is finding housing that fits the veteran's needs at or below a certain price point.

4. *Utility management.* Having secured a deal with a landlord, arrangements must be made to establish utility service in the tenant's name as per HUD rules. The voucher does not cover deposits, so the veteran must bring those resources to the table or work with the CM and the community to find them.

5. *Inspections, contracts, and move-ins.* Next, a series of two inspections follows wherein the HUD representative checks to make sure that the residence is compliant with current zoning and safety regulations. During this first inspection, the HUD representative makes a list of changes needed to the property before it will pass inspection. By the second inspection, the veteran must have the utilities turned on in their name, and the landlord must have completed all noted repairs. When all is complete, the landlord, HUD, and the veteran each sign the lease and the contract. The veteran who was previously surviving homelessness just a few short weeks ago is now given the keys and a lease to their new residence. This is a lovely moment indeed, but it's one that often occurs in an apartment with a distinct echo!

6. *Furnishings.* That really happens because there's no furniture in their new residence! So the veteran and the CM go back into the community and arrange for furniture donations. We actively partner with local service agencies, churches, and the community at large to accept donations of beds, couches, tables and chairs, recliners, televisions, and kitchenware. It is a matter of routine for us to load the agency van full to the top with such donated and appreciated goods and deliver it to a veteran who we know needs it

immediately in their residence. Once move-in and furnishing is complete, CMG can now begin.

It is important to note here that the process described in Step 2, Items 1–6 above, is neither short nor easy, but lends itself to developing a stable and continued rapport between the client and the CM. We actually spend days with each voucher recipient prior to move-in, handling all of their documents and responding to all the challenges and barriers unique to each individual's situation.

7. *Housing plan.* Building on this rapport, we collaboratively write a housing plan that is basically a treatment plan focusing on housing stability. Varying in intensity, and based on the needs and abilities of the client, we help the new resident focus on how they came to face homelessness, and more importantly what can be done to prevent them from facing it again in their future.

8. *Wrap-around service linkages.* The seventh step means medical, mental health, addictive disorder treatments, etc., so we arrange these through the VAMC or our other community partners. If financial stability is more so the focus here, then we assist as needed in clarifying what public, VA, and military benefits are available for the client, and what employment opportunities exist that the veteran wishes to pursue. If legal issues present a possible barrier to the veteran's housing stability, such clients are quickly linked with VAMC services to provide legal representation formally through the court system.

9. *Documentation.* Each encounter with a veteran is carefully documented in their medical record. We follow the industry standard of "same-day documentation," to ensure that all follow-up service providers have access to potentially timely and important information when they access the veteran's record.

10. *Suicide risk assessments.* Unfortunately, our veterans are over-represented in the U.S. population for both suicide attempts and completions. Thus, every member of the VA, social work and otherwise, takes on, by default, the responsibility of preventing veteran suicide. We offer ongoing risk assessments and access to mental health counseling. HUD-VASH CMs, because of the client rapport already built into this process described above are in excellent positions to offer face-to-face crisis management.

Social work skills. I must confess that I was not a vigilant student of social work practice methods during my MSW studies. Social work students tend to already have the instinct for their altruistic work, and I knew that I was just going to have to learn to do what was asked of me when I got this job. I immediately felt that the "borrowed vocabulary" of social work lacked real-world applicability. To me, our MSW course language of "rapport" and "joining," "strengths" and "self-determination" felt rather contrived and constraining. It seemed that way in the classroom, but I believe in retrospect that I missed the point then; as the language we use to describe our interventions with clients can be cliché, but only until we transcend it in real-world practice.

Clinical skills. Using fancy helping/altruistic language or not, when I'm working with a new client, I'm actually making space for them to do something that most of us find extremely difficult to do—they are asking for help from a complete stranger. In order to do this, I use value neutral and active therapeutic client-centered language, unconditional positive regard, reflective language/mirroring, active listening, de-escalation, praise, re-framing, genuine empathy, and so on. If I'm helping an established client face a challenge, then I'm going to rely on the rapport that we've already built. That gives me room to add to the list of client-centered jargon above. I then may deflect, re-direct, challenge, confront, set boundaries, empower, cheerlead, and/or coach.

Whatever I'm doing, I'm *always* trying to meet the client where they are at, considering all social and environmental systems that influence the client, determine what I am being asked to do (if I'm confused about that I ask, "what do you want me to do right now?"), and I'm always trying to be genuine and compassionate to where I am, at the present moment. If I'm tired, stressed, or distracted—I usually do little to hide it. I just say very honestly and clearly that it's me having that experience and not the client.

A valuable client-CM interactional insight I would like to share is that the clients you are going to serve are probably more sensitive to other people's emotions than other people we will ever meet. They may not always interpret those emotions accurately, or respond to them in effective ways, but they likely sense other people's emotions with extraordinary and uncanny sensitivity. CMs are thus urged to get to the point and speak your mind honestly and forthrightly because it is the rule, not the exception. In each instance and each client interaction, I am always reminded that genuineness always works.

Self-care. I have learned in this position that the importance of self-care cannot be overstated. This was something not stressed as it should be in my MSW curriculum. The way you define it is up to you, however. My candid advice is, be honest and explore what works for you. If you weep on the long drive home from your job, drive carefully and weep honestly. If you blast heavy metal music all the way to work in the morning and all the way home at night, roll your window up and crank it. I used to come home from work and spend 30 minutes in bed shaking, faking my body into feeling like it was convulsing. That worked fine when I needed it.

This may be unwelcomed news to some students or CMs, but be careful with your drinking. Further, eat healthy food, exercise, turn off your version of TV, and go to sleep at night. My last thoughts on self-care are that I did not really learn about boundaries and finances until I was out on the job. Both are critical aspects of one's self-care. Setting appropriate boundaries between work and home is very important. For instance, if you are on-call, then be on-call. If you are not, turn your phone off and teach yourself and your clients about healthy boundary-keeping skills. And to whatever extent possible, insist on making a living wage in your noble and important work (Skinner, 2015).

Social justice. To my way of thinking, issues of social justice feel like a battery, a thermometer, and a compass at my work. This links back to self-care. For instance, I realize that my personal battery is low when I notice that I'm not frustrated *on my clients' behalf.* One example is when I feel emotional self-protection setting in; it is always with someone who's lying to me. When that happens, empathy requires that I appreciate the pressures that lead people to seek the resources I manage, using the tools they have at hand. I may not understand those pressures or value those tools, but I really don't have to. I only have to understand what my mission is and notice whether or not I'm capable of doing it. So my frustration at being lied to is my thermometer, telling me to personally re-focus on what really matters (not my feelings). The frustration is my compass needle and it's supposed to point at such pressures that lead to the behavior. When I get that right, I can actually love and admire clients who literally cannot trust me yet. I'd like to offer this suggestion to help you gauge your own sense of personal social justice frustration. Again, if that's not your thing, don't do it. Some people have been hurt by anger and prefer not to engage in it. That's a good path and, if you're on it, why not skip ahead and re-frame it as a re-affirmation of social justice and advocacy for all clients, regardless of how they present to you or anyone else.

Main challenges and barriers. One of the major benefits working for HUD-VASH is that our mission is very clear: house veterans facing homelessness. Ironically, to achieve this, our resources at this time in our nation's history are currently vast and effective (U.S. Department of Veterans Affairs, n.d.). One explanation for this is that our sub-population is very narrow: veterans who face homelessness. In that sense, there are no large barriers to achieve our goal, compared to my colleagues who confront homelessness in the resource depleted local non-profit sector.

However, I do work in a government organizational setting that is steeped in bureaucracy and red tape that is the reality of my work. It is something all CMs must learn to cope with and negotiate, and not succumb to it. Prior to this, I was privileged to work for private agencies also under strict state regulation. These experiences have taught me some important things about the value and challenges of bureaucracy. And it's not all bad!

Not all of us are born to immediately appreciate the value of compliance, rules, and regulations. Many of us want to learn by experience, make up rules as we need them, and just get the job done, however we can. But larger systems such as mine cannot tolerate this approach at all. I believe that the mission of any successful organization depends on the right balance of exploring new possibilities and being anchored in what works. Further, the larger the agency, the more difficult it is to isolate and promote what works. Ironically, I have come to believe that bureaucracy is the "best imperfect solution" to that reality.

An organization that spans the government of the nation requires a fairly large amount of required annual training, re-certification, protocols/procedures and their updates, and a vast quantity of e-mail. In my privileged serving of veterans, our bureaucratic body, by its very nature, functions as a barrier or constraint in a few ways. On the one hand, I could probably spend all day every day out in the field, promoting my program, finding veterans to assist, and serving the goals of my mission. In this way, documentation, trainings, communication with administration, etc., limit my relative effectiveness. On the other hand, if I treated my job like a run-away truck without brakes, I would cease to be effective rather quickly. The fact that I am required to "rein it in," do all my paperwork, stay current on my trainings, and answer all e-mails, creates space in the day that allows me to process what I've accomplished and makes sure that I am always aligned with the goals of my agency. This in turn allows me to highlight where our department has succeeded (which leads to future funding), and allows the department to focus on areas we can all work on to increase our collective effectiveness.

Role Development Potential

Federal service offers continuing and various ongoing growth opportunities for all employees who want it. Jobs are posted internally and advertised by management to ensure that all workers are encouraged to make career changes when they desire to. Pay scales are based on reasonable living standards and benefit packages are usually generous and competitive. Career enhancement trainings, many combined with CEUs, are available, as are tuition reimbursement and textbook support programs for increasing worker skills and ongoing education. My management team actively reaches out within my department to encourage us to focus on long-term career goals including pursuing leadership positions within government service. Indeed, this is a refreshing and employee-caring feature of our employment.

Educational job preparation. The MSW degree, and the invaluable internships that went with it, gave me 2 critical years to professionally and personally mature. I came in to the degree, as you likely did too, with much altruism and passion. The MSW degree gave me time to temper these attributes and helped me to become more educationally focused, and it gave me a safe space to be wrong and ill equipped. Then, I was sent out into the real world knowing ostensibly nothing about what I ended up actually doing in practice.

I left school understanding how to speak boldly to issues that mattered, even when I did not have all the facts. I left with a résumé that accounted for more than just sitting idle in class. I left with the confidence that I had survived and thrived in situations where seasoned professionals needed guidance with how to care for easily abused and neglected human beings, and I offered that guidance. Maybe what I appreciated most about the MSW is the time we were afforded to learn about privilege. Privilege is another of those barometric notions that is absolutely critical to sustaining a caring human-centered practice, wherever we end up working. So honestly, did the degree teach me how to do my work? No it did not. But the folks who hired me out of school had a strong sense of what they were getting when they saw my degree. I'm still learning daily now (as you will), how to do what I do.

Educationally speaking, I would add required courses in economics, macro and micro; American political and economic history to demonstrate the distinctions between our various political movements over time; and a crash course in law to the MSW curriculum. I also wish that there were more time for electives outside of the degree, so that MSWs could bring other interests to bear in their work (e.g., art, music). I would add business classes with accounting, budgeting, and all that other commerce stuff that we social workers traditionally ignore. We need this information to run our non-profits, and we need it to teach our clients fiscal responsibility.

When I started working as a therapist right out of school (totally unrelated to my Management of Nonprofits [MANPO] degree sub-specialty), the only lesson I really wished I had learned more about was how to write clinical notes more efficiently. As I spent my first year on-the-job writing ungainly novellas, attempting to describe my detailed interventions with various clients. Slowly pecking away with two fingers while trying to compose my thoughts into a clinical narrative, I spent more time that year writing than I did billing for it. For me, this was an awful experience. In my first year, I forced myself to type properly, to think about notes while engaged with clients, and to learn the shorthand jargon that would thrill an auditor.

The concept of systems is a primary educational issue that social work claims ownership of, and it comes up continually in my work. My work is partly clinical, in that I require a clinician's emotional dexterity to build trust with my clients. The work is also largely administrative, in that each and every one of my clients requires a knowledge of my work environment, and most of them require practical guidance in walking through the many steps of our process. The work is also macro-practice, in that my colleagues and I must maintain a well-organized practice within a vibrant and ever changing external organizational environment. In each of these examples, the work is based on a constant view of all systems that intersect and influence our client-practice. Thus, I learned to blend elements of micro, mezzo, and macro practice to be effective, which was not really taught to me effectively in graduate school.

Also, I strongly encourage all students of social work to reach into the "way back machine" and learn about Transactional Analysis. This is an overblown title for a simple theoretical framework that demonstrates how effectively, or ineffectively, to relate with people. It may be summed up in the question, "Do you walk in front of your client or do you walk beside them?" I believe it is essential to our cherished client-centered work, so please take a look at it, if you can.

Concluding Remarks

As mentioned above, social workers need to bring passion and resolve for never-ending service and an assertive sense of justice to all their clients and client systems. And here's the good news: Practicing social work actually increases that! Also burn-out is very real, and you will experience it, but it does not last long once you learn how to re-charge your self-care batteries (mentioned earlier in the chapter).

Finally, social workers bring a wonderful lack of specialty to the therapeutic table. Some folks refer to this as being a "generalist," but I think that's a distasteful term. During my first years on the job, I frequently had to step back professionally and learn the jargon of other specialties (i.e., clinical psychology, marriage and family therapy, licensed counseling; and they were all well worth learning from)—before I could engage collaboratively in my staff meetings. But by the time I tuned my ear to their unique jargon, it became my jargon, and I did not owe anyone for it, and I could take it or leave it!

Our profession's malleability and lack of specialty leads to an openness and transparency of practice that lets us move in the right direction at the right time without ever needing to run to the bookshelf, to make sure we're being true to our craft (Holosko & Feit, 2004). But, our work is more important than that—as our clients need us working with them, not arguing about nonsense, and our will to get the job done is well served by our non-specific practice. I say let others worry about whether social work is a profession or not, or if we rise to the level of a lofty science. It really doesn't matter. What matters to me is helping veterans in need get housed every day I go to work. Now, what matters to you?

Case Example

Robert is a 55-year-old black male who served in the Army for 2 years as a truck driver during the mid-1970s. He is not eligible for "service connected" benefits or pension because he served in peace-time and was not permanently injured while on duty. He did complete his tour of duty, discharged honorably, and he meets the income limit for services, so he is eligible for VA health care.

Robert grew up in the southern United States and has multiple family members in the area where he lives and receives CMG from the HUD-VASH program. He was referred to HUD-VASH by the veterans' benefits office: a state level office that handles records, disability claims, pension, burial, and survivor benefits for all veterans. He was homeless when I met him and, although he stays in touch with his children and their mother, he cannot stay with any of them for long without running into significant conflict. In the past, that has included kicking each other out of housing, and on one occasion of the veteran being stabbed in the ribs with a kitchen knife.

Robert was already known to the HUD-VASH team. Once I was established in my new position, my colleague gave me Robert's telephone number and asked me to follow up with him about a housing voucher. Then my colleague said something like, "Oh wait, what day is this? He might not be able to talk for a few days. You can try texting him if he doesn't pick up the phone. We'll look for him at the library later, too."

We were nearing the end of the month, and Robert was out of pre-paid minutes for his phone. He didn't respond to my voice mail, but we scheduled a meeting at the library by text messages. It took Robert and I several conversations by phone and in person for us to tune in to each other's communication style. I think we both thought the other was intellectually challenged at first because we didn't seem to share any linguistic "short hand." But after a rough start, Robert and I eventually developed a solid rapport and mutual respect. I practiced a firmly consistent focus on my mission of helping him gain housing, showing up when I said I would, owning my personal mistakes, and always focusing on the job. He has a practiced attitude of rather pleasant acceptance, he greets adversity with a startlingly fierce, and equally brief, frustration (we're talking about 10 to 30 seconds of surprise and anger to significant challenges) before he takes a deep breath, he puts a smile on his face, and exudes understanding and generosity toward whomever/whatever has forced him to change his plans.

While seeking housing under the voucher we faced these challenges: Robert was working at a local restaurant whose employment practices are inappropriate; Robert never missed work; always reported when called in; was paid minimum wage; but was never once offered more time than 28 hours per week. The manager would call and insist that Robert come in to cover for someone on his time off, or keep him late to work another shift. But the manager would then reduce his hours later to keep from appearing to have a full-time employee. Robert averaged about $200 per week.

After Robert and I got to know each other better, he shared with me that he had applied for SSI benefits. He was on temporary SSI, for a probationary period, but his benefit was reduced to around $150 dollars per month due to his work income. Robert elected to leave his position at the restaurant and report a lower income to Social

Security. We spoke frankly about this choice and I drove him to Social Security to find out what he could expect in terms of income and wait times. We learned that he could quit the job and have about the same income through SSI, but he would have to wait 2 months before the payment would change. It was late in May, and Robert chose to reduce his income to $150 per month until August.

That meant that even with the voucher, it would be difficult to apply for housing successfully because he'd have no funds to move in. It also meant that the amount that the voucher would pay would be lower (due to the algorithm used to calculate the payment for each voucher). That was our first major hurdle—the voucher was calculated for Robert to a number that was roughly 10% less than the lower-end average for affordable housing in my service area. Where I serve clients, if you give me a voucher for $500/monthly rent, I can easily get the job done. Robert's voucher was more in the neighborhood of $450; so he couldn't use the voucher to move into a place that charged more.

Robert established a plan to stay with friends or outdoors, until his August SSI check came in with enough to pay rental deposits and establish his utilities. In the 2 months while we waited, we applied to various churches and support organizations to build up a donation package that we could use to pay his way indoors. However, very little of that effort paid off for Robert. Our work included a 2-hour session in the library filling out paperwork for a third-party grant that pays deposits for veterans.

The third-party grant did end up paying his deposits. I set up an opportunity for the grant manager to meet the veteran while she was in the community on another assignment. That introduction allowed her to put a face on the man I had been describing to her and may have made the follow-through more successful.

Another challenge was finding a place that would rent to Robert. There is a short list of properties in our area that will accept the amount of rent that his voucher would allow (i.e., again, it's different for each recipient based on many factors). We toured a place and Robert was enthusiastic. Everything looked great, and we had money on the table—not all of it refundable, but then, his background check came back with a bad check from 15 years ago—and the deal was over. He was devastated (for about 45 seconds), and I truly didn't know where to go next. We decided to try across town where I'd succeeded before. I elicited funding for the application from a local veterans' outreach charity fund, and we drove across town. I didn't recognize anyone in the office, and they knew nothing about the Sect. 8 voucher. The place had been bought and sold since the last time I was there. They refused to rent to anyone who didn't bring 2.5 times the rental amount in monthly income. They were deaf to my argument that the Sect. 8 voucher ensured that the veteran would indeed eventually have sufficient financial means. Robert bounced back from that setback in less than 1 minute. When we finally found a place he could move to, the inspection didn't pass at first, so he had to stay outdoors for 3 days more than he had planned on. "I'm good," he said on that occasion, and he moved in to an empty apartment 3 days later.

Since moving in, he has suffered a drug and alcohol relapse once that I was aware of. He called me early one morning sounding severely down and pleaded with me to come get him from a rough neighborhood. I checked that he was not in immediate danger, not a danger to himself or from others, and agreed to get to him as soon as I could. He was standing where he said he'd be and looking very sad when I got there 45 minutes later. He climbed in my agency van, filling it instantly with powerful body odor, and begged me not to be mad at him.

I got him to his house and directed him to have a hot shower. An hour later, he was in better spirits. We had been discussing relapse and addiction, trying to establish a plan to protect his future from an uncertain disease (addiction). He started practicing the skills he learned in rehab: owning his powerlessness, speaking his shame out loud, etc. We drove to Social Security (as previously scheduled) where he received his permanent SSI benefit. His future was not as certain as his infectiously positive attitude.

Our next immediate challenge was how to cover his portion of the rent and how to pay his utilities. His monthly income literally went up in smoke in a local drug house in about 24 hours. Our next, and much more difficult, challenge will be to establish a protocol that is congruent with his needs and psychosocial readiness to reduce the threat of relapse in his future.

Ironically, his inspiringly positive and resilient attitude feels like a barrier to his success from this side of his relapse. He is skilled at making people comfortable (his CM included), and he has a truly a unique ability to embrace honest and painful truths. However, it is also a shield that may lead him to expect, and insist on, bad things happening to him.

REFERENCES

Holosko, M., & Feit, M. D. (2004). *Social work practice with the elderly*. Toronto, ON: Canadian Scholars' Press.

Lawrence, Q. (2015, August 4). *The US declared war on veteran homelessness—and it actually could win* (NPR, Producer). Retrieved from http://www.npr.org/2015/08/04/427419718/the-u-s-declared-war-on-veteran-homelessness-and-it-actually-could-win

Lee, A. B., Tyler, K. A., & Wright, J. D. (2010). The new homelessness revisited. *Annual Review of Sociology, 36*, 501–521. doi: 10.1146/annurev-soc-070308-115940

Skinner, J. (2015). Social work practice and personal self-care. *Social Workers' Desk Reference, 3*, 130–143. New York, NY: Oxford University Press.

U.S. Department of Veterans Affairs. (n.d.). Homeless veterans: About the initiative. Retrieved from http://www.va.gov/homeless/about_the_initiative.asp

---

ANCILLARIES

Internet Resources for Additional Reading

1. Health Care Eligibility. Retrieved from www.va.gov/healthbenefits

2. Homeless Veterans. Retrieved from www.va.gov/homeless

3. Case Management Society of America. Retrieved www.cmsa.org

4. American Case Management Association. Retrieved from www.acmaweb.org

Hard Copy References for Additional Reading

Berne, E. (1996). *Games people play*. New York, NY: Ballantine Books

Frankel, A. J., & Gelman, S. R. (2011). *Case management: An introduction to concepts and skills* (3rd ed.). Chicago, IL: Lyceum Books.

Gambrill, E. (2014). Social work education and avoidable ignorance. *Journal of Social Work, 50*(3), 391–413.

Hassan, A., & Kintzle, S. (2015). Military social work in the community. *Social Workers' Desk Reference*. New York, NY: Oxford University Press.

U.S. Department of Veterans Affairs. (2014). Federal benefits for veterans, dependents and survivors. Retrieved from http://www.va.gov/opa/publications/benefits_book.asp

❖ JOB DESCRIPTION

USA Jobs Search of HUD-VASH

Duties

The Senior Social Worker (HUD-VASH) is responsible for the assessment, identification, facilitation, and referral to appropriate medical and psychiatric services to those veterans identified as appropriate for the HUD-VASH program. The social worker evaluates the veteran's situation, abilities, and capabilities, and arrives at a reasoned conclusion including an assessment of vulnerability and prioritization for admission. The social worker assesses at-risk factors and develops a preliminary plan, involving the veteran and family or significant others, and performs an insightful assessment of serious and complicated cases involving psychiatric illness that may also include catastrophic medical condition, dementia, traumatic brain injuries, and other high-risk diagnoses. As part of a comprehensive psychosocial assessment, the social worker interviews the veteran and their family members or significant others to establish facts about the veteran's situation, presenting problems and their causes, and the impact of such problems on the veterans functioning and health. The social worker reviews all data, subjective and objective, and makes a clinical assessment identifying needs and strengths. Based on the psychosocial assessment, the social worker uses professional judgment and advanced practice skills to make a psychosocial diagnosis.

The social worker provides referrals to VA medical and mental health inpatient and outpatient treatment programs and to other VA services including VA benefits, as well as community-based social services and other non-VA entitlement programs. If appropriate, the social worker provides referrals or consults, or in some cases direct admission of the Veterans prior to HUD-VASH participation, for other VA programs including community-based residential treatment such as Grant and Per Diem (GPD) Programs and Compensated Work Therapy (CWT), etc.

The social worker establishes procedures and coordinates the screening and admission process for the HUD-VASH program by developing and maintaining criteria that recognizes program eligibility, prioritization for program acceptance, and requirements of the PHAs. Effectively uses professional skill, objectivity, and insight. Uses advanced clinical training, insight, and experience to interpret data and to identify viable treatment options, including assessment for eligibility and clinical appropriateness of a HUD/VASH program admissions or subsequent discharge. The social worker coordinates the screening and admission multidisciplinary team and provides primary input for program candidates. Assesses high-risk factors, acuity, and need for services. Makes appropriate referral to community-based agencies, CBOCs and VA Southern Nevada–based services.

Work Schedule: 8:00 am to 4:30 pm

Qualifications Required

Basic Requirements

Citizenship. Be a citizen of the United States. Non-citizens may be appointed when it is not possible to recruit qualified citizens in accordance with VA Policy.

Education. Have a master's degree in social work from a school of social work fully accredited by the Council on Social Work Education (CSWE). A doctoral degree in social work may not be substituted for the master's degree in social work.

Licensure. Persons hired or reassigned to social worker positions in VHA must be licensed or certified by a state to independently practice social work at the master's degree level.

English Language Proficiency. Social workers must be proficient in spoken and written English in accordance with VA Handbook 5005, Part II, chapter 3, section A, paragraph 3j.

Preferred Experience

At least 1 (one) year experience in case management with the homeless patient population.

At least 1 (one) year experience in case management and coordinating patient care in a community setting.

10

In-Patient Psychiatric Case Management

Janice Caldwell and Mark W. Flanagan

The Clientele

The first author, Janice Caldwell, is employed as a geriatric social work case manager (CM) in a 250-bed capacity in-patient psychiatric hospital that includes the following units; child and adolescent, adult, substance abuse, stabilization, and geriatric. The majority of clientele seen by the first author are older adults, aged 60 years and above. There are slightly more female patients at the hospital (roughly 60%) than male patients. This hospital in Southeastern United States serves an equal number of white and black patients, each making up 49% of the clientele, respectively. Only 2% of the populations are a variety of other ethnic groups.

The hospital treats a significant number of patients with schizophrenia, as schizoaffective disorders make up about 40% of the clientele. About 40% present with substance use disorders, which often is co-morbid with another mental illness. Additionally, roughly 20% of the clientele consists of persons with bipolar disorder, major depressive disorder, or dementia. About 40% of the population is currently experiencing or has experienced a psychotic breakdown, resulting in their inability to make safe decisions for themselves and/or those around them. At the in-patient hospital, psychotic breakdowns are seen most commonly among schizophrenia-related illness, substance use disorders, bipolar disorder, and major depressive disorders.

A typical patient. A typical patient we see is diagnosed with schizophrenia/psychotic breakdown, who has not taken medication in several months. He is no longer able to care for himself and currently lives alone in the community. He has monthly income of approximately $800.00 from Social Security Disability Insurance (SSDI) with no savings, but he has Medicare or Medicaid insurance. His family and/or support group want him to be "safe," but they are unable to physically and/or financially care for him. Therefore, the patient needs to be placed in a suitable, supportive living environment. He does not want to live anywhere other than home, and the family currently does not have legal guardianship of him. A family member may have financial or medical Power of Attorney (PoA). He is likely able to eat, use the toilet, groom himself, and walk independently. Therefore, he does not meet nursing home criteria eligibility. If his treating physician in the community believes the patient is no longer able to live independently, and the patient is still resistant to a Personal Care Home (PCH), the CM begins discussing the emergency legal guardianship option with family member(s) for placement purposes upon discharge. The best case scenario is when such a patient is stabilized and is able to return home, with family support and home health care (that Medicare pays for, if the patient meets criteria). Such a patient may be seen in the hospital for 1 to 2 weeks.

Atypical patient. This patient came to the in-patient hospital with no cash, no insurance (including Medicare/Medicaid), an uncontrolled schizophrenia diagnosis, and no family financial support. The CM engaged an outside benefits coordinator (paid for by the family), who obtained emergency Medicare for her. She was placed in a nursing home, as she met the dementia criteria along with diagnosis of schizophrenia. Such atypical patients may be seen for 1 week until placement is obtained for client.

Practice Roles and Responsibilities

The main responsibilities of an in-patient psychiatric CM are as follows:

1. *Meet patient on the day of admission and gather pertinent logistical information.*

   This includes minimally: family contact details, where the patient was living prior to admission, where the patient is planning to go upon discharge, and how the patient will get to a potential discharge location. It is important to facilitate positive rapport with the patient as much as possible, as placement in an in-patient setting can be very traumatic, scary, and unsettling. The more the CM can connect personally with the patient from the onset, the easier it will be to offer other, essential CMG tasks.

2. *Contact family member(s) to inform them of the patient's admission to hospital.*

   Gather background information from the patient and family members in order to complete the comprehensive biopsychosocial assessment. Such information includes minimally, a required history of the presenting problem, developmental history (if available), family history, intimate relationship history, employment and education history, use of alcohol and other drugs, medical history, mental health history, significant events, cultural background, religious/spiritual information, strengths, environmental stressors, and current mental status.

3. *If needed, begin working as soon as possible with the patient on placement options.*

Because most patients only have limited insurance that covers short-term stays (typically 1–2 weeks), in most cases, it is crucial to immediately start working on where they will go once they are discharged.

4. *Coordinate all outpatient resources.*

Another very important CMG task is to ensure that patients have high-quality mental health care, including psychotropic medication provision, once they leave the in-patient setting. The CM spends a lot of time searching for psychiatrists near the locale the person will be placed and contacting the psychiatrist's office to set up an appointment for the patient. If the patient needs supportive health services because they have significant chronic mental or physical impairments, the CM will coordinate home health care for their residential placement.

5. *Initialize treatment plans, informed by biopsychosocial assessments, and review the plan carefully with the patients.*

An important part of this CMG task is to establish goals in full collaboration with the patient. It is necessary to do this as much as possible, to better understand what the patient wants for their mental health – in the short and long term. Often, this is challenging as patients with severe depression or unstable psychotic symptoms may not be fully capable of properly advocating for themselves. Nonetheless, even in these cases, the CM should create a unique plan based on what he or she believes the patient would want for their health, rather than based on what is "usually done," or is "most convenient." This plan is reviewed and revised every 7 days, in conjunction with the patient and their treating physician, as long as the patient is in the in-patient setting.

6. *Set up sessions with patients and their families.*

This is done to ensure that the patient and her or his family (or other close supportive person/group) are on the "same page" before the patient is discharged. This ensures timely continuity of care, and that the family knows what to expect when the patient returns home. It is also necessary to complete a "safety plan" with the patient prior to discharge to improve the likelihood the patient will not harm herself or himself or others in the immediate period following discharge, should an unexpected stressor occur for the patient while he or she is still in a vulnerable state.

7. *On the day of discharge, ensure the patient has a follow-up outpatient appointment with a psychiatrist within 30 days.*

This is true if the patient is returning home or going to a personal care home, rather than another in-patient setting.

8. *Facilitate daily process groups with patients in the hospital unit on a rotating basis.*

These process groups are extremely important for the patient as they allow patients to see other patients at various stages of recovery. For example, a newly admitted major depressive patient with suicidal ideation may gain hope by seeing another depressive patient, who has begun working through her or his issues in a meaningful way. There are many types of groups, each with different kinds of clientele, so CMs engage a variety of issues, contexts, and dynamics by facilitating such daily process groups.

Social work skills utilized. *Always meet the patient where he or she is at that moment!* This is perhaps the most critical skill necessary for effective in-patient psychiatric CMG. Sometimes a patient will be frightened, extremely agitated, or simply non-responsive. In normal situations, all of these realities can be very distressful. However, as a social work CM, your job is to empathize with the patient, accept her or him as she or he is currently presenting, and construct concrete plans to move the patient from their current situation to situations that are progressively better. Ultimately, an idealized "best" situation may not be possible, and social work CMs should focus on making defined, measurable improvements, no matter how small, to the patient's circumstances, based on a shared vision between the CM and patient system.

Educate the patient (and/or family) about discharge options. During this step, there is substantial emphasis on placement options that are feasible financially for the patient and her or his family. It is often shocking for family members to learn how much long-term treatment actually costs and how little insurance is usually covered. The CM must have a significant level of skill to find appropriate resources and work with the family to negotiate an agreement on an eventual placement.

Utilize systems theory to conceptualize threats and resources in the patient's environment—once they are discharged. This step is vital and perhaps the most complex. The skilled CM must be able to understand how a patient may interact with her or his environment, including social systems, in order to optimize the likelihood of patient recovery and long-term success. The CM must then make concerted efforts in order to contact and learn more about all available services in the community in order to relay this information to the patient and her or his family. The CM must also communicate potential threats in the environment including substance availability, lack of access to transportation, and potentially negative social influences, in order to create realistic resiliency plans for the patient and her or his family.

Challenges/barriers. *Lack of long-term care facilities for the chronically mentally ill patients.* A recent case example of an elderly patient seen at the hospital with severe mental illness demonstrates the challenges created by the absence of extended-stay mental health centers. This patient was admitted with a diagnosis of schizophrenia (symptoms began manifesting in 2011). He was terminated from his job that same year, and he was on his wife's health insurance, as he had no insurance of his own. He and his spouse lost their home in 2014 and were living with the patient's sister. The patient's wife became seriously ill in 2015, and her sister began taking care of her, however she could not care for the patient. He had a sister he did not keep in close contact with, except for a few phone calls over the past few years. The patient came to the hospital with schizophrenia and trauma-induced dementia, and was assessed as not able to live independently by the physician. The patient is in his early 60s and is physically capable of managing activities of daily living (ADL), such as using the rest room, grooming, eating, and walking independently. However, he no longer remembers that he is married and is not verbally acute.

The patient remains chronically ill and is not able to manage his medications independently. Because he lacks social and financial support, he is in need of supportive care from an organization. However, all long-term mental health facilities were eliminated in our state between 1960 and 1980. Although other facilities were supposed to be replaced with community-based mental health services, such a transition never occurred (Szasz, 2007). So, while the elimination of long-term in-patient hospitals was initially seen as positive as it stopped long-standing patient maltreatment, we are now seeing huge gaps in mental health care that negatively affect patients like the one presented here.

Our perception is that this patient's condition will likely deteriorate, as his illness will not be effectively managed, and he may end up coming to our facility again or being admitted to an emergency room for acute psychosis. Such realities create difficult daily challenges for psychiatric CMs, as the burden falls on us to link the patient to what little services may be offered in her or his community. Psychiatric CMs can play a vital role in advocacy to increase state funding for community psychiatric services, as many CMs have firsthand experience in witnessing the profound consequential negative effects of ineffective mental health state policy.

Lack of affordable placement options. Many patients receive approximately $800.00–$1,000.00 SSDI. However, the least expensive post-discharge placement option, personal care homes (PCHs), generally charge $1,200.00 per month. A PCH provides meals, transportation to doctors' appointments, and access to outside activities. The cost for Assisted Living Facilities (ALF)—a more intensive supportive living service with onsite medical monitoring, regular meals, and onsite activities—begins at $2,500.00 per month, for independent living, and increases with increasing levels of service required. Most patients needing a locked memory-care unit, one of the more intensive support services, will pay a minimum of $3,000.00 per month. Many patients at our hospital have low socio-economic statuses and cannot afford PCHs, and most cannot afford ALFs.

Lack of outpatient services to allow the patient to "age-in-place." As one can surmise, the primary challenge faced by all psychiatric CMs is the lack of community resources for vulnerable populations who lack resources of their own. Older adults have an enhanced need for psychiatric support and non-medical care in the community, because mental health issues tend to become exacerbated as they grow older (Eden, Maslow, Le, & Blazer, 2012). Medicare will pay for "some" home health care, if a patient meets stringent eligibility criteria. However, this home health care is relatively very limited and includes visits to a maximum of three per week, for approximately one hour each day, only for medical purposes. Adult day care centers cost on average $80.00 per day, and non-medical caretakers cost an average of $19.00 per hour. Most patients and their families we see simply do not have this income available to them. Further, Medicare or Medicaid do not pay for non-medical caretakers. However, there is an exception under a specific Medicaid program, where a family member *may* become a paid caretaker, but again the patient must meet the medical criteria.

Role Development Potential

As a new CM at the hospital, there is a tremendous opportunity for me (Janice Caldwell) to enhance my professional career. After a year at work, I am still learning about available resources for my geriatric patients, and I see more patients with complex and unique problems than I have ever seen before, weekly. In addition, I have weekly supervision with colleagues who work with different populations (adults, children, and adolescents, people with mainly substance abuse problems), so I learn from the clinical issues they present as well. I have also learned that I probably never will "know it all"—as there is always a new issue to be addressed daily.

My MSW education grounded me in essential theory for my social work career. However, as a CM, I have to say that I do not usually consciously think about which theory I'm going to use to work with a particular patient. Rather, I continue to focus on meeting the patients where they are at that moment, recognizing that the patient in the hospital is not isolated in the care he or she receives, and that the family system is equally affected by the patient's overall illness and care. Our family sessions with each patient are based on systems theory, as we recognize the supportive and buffering roles a family system plays for a patient's recovery, in an environment filled with numerous stressors and threats. However, the most theory-based part of my job is when I am conducting groups.

When I facilitate groups with the geriatric patients, I tend to rely mostly on ego-integrity theory, in keeping with Erikson's (1959) developmental theory of ego integrity versus despair. Ego integrity theory asserts that if one is able to remember their life as meaningful, then he or she will have enhanced peace with the prospect of death (Kasl-Godley & Gatz, 2000). Additionally, continuity theory emphasizes that individuals adapt to new changes by recalling their perceived past and creating continuity in psychological and social characteristics (Lin, Dai, & Hwang, 2003). When I facilitate a group working with women who are addicted to drugs or alcohol, I have used feminist theory, as well as solution-focused therapy (SFT), and cognitive behavioral therapy (CBT). CBT emphasizes changing thinking or behavior in order to change affect (Wright, Basco, & Thase, 2006). SFT, a precursor of CBT, focuses on patient empowerment through future-oriented, creative thought. Feminist theory in psychotherapy focuses on analyzing gender inequality and how mental issues can arise from societal oppression (Lerman & Porter, 1990). I have come to understand that these therapies and theories are powerful alone, but are most potent when used in combination, especially for patients with multiple presenting issues and unique cultural factors.

In my CM job, I see people every day who are ashamed of their illness or addiction. Unfortunately, mental illness and addiction still carry a large social stigma, and a patient often feels that he or she has brought the affliction upon herself or himself, and they internalize that they are not worthy of respect. The part I like most about my CM job is when a patient realizes that I am there to help him or her regain a perspective of *self-worth*. As a trained social worker, I don't see the illness first: I see the person. It is a gift (to me) every day when that realization becomes clear to the patient. I believe that is when true healing can begin, because I "mirror back" the respect they need to give themselves in order to grow. It is important to me to never lose that respect, or to become too hurried in my job and all its nuances, that I neglect to continually show respect and compassion to people who feel ashamed, abandoned, and often without hope.

This is not to say that we are successful with every patient. Many patients are admitted involuntarily, and they are often confused and angry. In these instances, the patient is often focused only on getting out and will "go through the motions" to get discharged from the hospital. However, for the patient who is motivated in making changes in her or his life, the hospital is a stabilizing, safe environment where the patient can begin meaningful work. A successful CM in the environment will be comfortable with meeting a wide range of people and will be open to taking on new challenges on a daily basis. While there is a routine to each day (i.e., team meetings, group facilitation, etc.), no day goes exactly as planned. A social work CM must be good at time management, in order to successfully work with the many unexpected challenges that come with the job.

If I were to help plan a MSW curriculum, assuming the BSW curriculum covered all foundation theories, I would focus more on practical issues that social workers need to know to complete jobs effectively. For example, I would include case examples on the basics of how to help patients apply for Medicare or Medicaid. In addictions classes, I would have the students complete a project on the various long-term residential addiction programs in their respective communities, as well as including half-way houses and transitional housing programs, and the *requirements* of each. By doing so, the new social work CM would leave the program with a fundamental understanding of the differences in these programs, and could enter their communities of care with increased practical knowledge about services and with professional confidence. Such social workers would be more effective with patients earlier in their careers and would be more attractive to employers that are looking for staff who have practical "work-ready" skills.

Concluding Remarks

An in-patient social work CM needs to have a variety of skills in order to succeed. He or she needs to be able to investigate and communicate with community resources, and provide empathetic and helpful client interactions. The successful worker needs to tolerate ambiguity and distressing situations, while actively looking for solutions and providing comfort to both clients and co-workers. An in-patient CM will be challenged in all spheres of social work and will have amazing opportunities to differentiate themselves from other allied health care workers through the use of systems theory. A competent CM should be as versed in financial and practical matters as emotional, relational, and spiritual concerns.

While the previous discussion paints a rosy picture of CMG, working with severely distraught psychiatric patients can be extremely complex, difficult, and stressful. Part of the job of an in-patient CM is to work through the inevitable disappointments and disrespectful clients in ways that preserves your integrity. While many clients and families view CMs as unnecessary and intrusive, in-patient CMs are vital to the continuing care of clients after hospitalization. The client lives in the community, not in the hospital, and so the client, knowingly or not, relies on the CM to establish stability in their normal environmental context. Without a CM, the client would be left with discontinuity of mental and social services and quickly relapse, making hospitalization nothing more than a temporary removal of risk of harm to self and others, with little prospects of long-term recovery.

Although in-patient social work CMs encounter unique challenges and barriers including a lack of community resources, clients who are challenging, and high workloads, they are also privileged to help clients make meaningful changes in their lives. Social work CMs are the only professionals in our in-patient setting that readily provide direct therapy and resources linkages for the client. They are also the only professionals (in this setting) that address family dynamics as part of a treatment plan, recognizing that long-term stability comes from a supportive social and environmental context. In this manner, in-patient social work CMs are uniquely positioned to help clients achieve sustainable wellness. While social work CMs may not be successful with every client, it is their willingness to continue showing up and advocating on behalf of their clients that makes it possible for many clients with little to no hope achieve greater happiness, stability, and productivity in their lives.

Case Example

John was admitted to our hospital, newly diagnosed with Alzheimer's disease. This gentleman truly felt that his life was over, and he had attempted suicide, which necessitated his admission to the in-patient hospital. When I first met with him, he was angry and dismissive of me. However, he agreed to talk to me in order for me to conduct the necessary biopsychosocial assessment with him. He was grieving over his diagnosis of Alzheimer's disease and said to me, "My life is over." At this time, John was very angry and was crying. I ignored the time constraints dictated by my schedule, and listened to him and validated his current grief, as well as his past successes. John participated in my process group later that day, and became a leader in the group by helping other patients process their recent experiences that led them to being admitted to the hospital.

After the group was over, I asked to speak with him and I told him what I had witnessed him doing. He said he did not realize he was being a "leader," but then recognized that he was, in fact, helping other people. I then gave John resources for contacting local Alzheimer's groups near him, and I asked him if he thought he would be willing to take his leadership skills to the organization and help others there when he was discharged from the hospital. John took this information and told me he would "think about it." The next morning, when I walked onto the unit, I saw John talking with a new patient. When John saw me, he smiled at me and winked. There was nothing in particular that I did, other than to assist this man in understanding that his life was not "over," at this moment—and that he still has much to offer. The best I can do in a fast-paced work environment is meet all patients with genuineness and respect, and sometimes plant a seed that the hospital is not the "end-of-the-road" for them, but instead a chance for a new beginning.

REFERENCES

Eden, J., Maslow, K., Le, M., & Blazer, D. (2012). The mental health and substance use workforce for older adults: In whose hands? Institute of Medicines: National Academies Press. Retrieved from http://www.pasrrassist.org/sites/default/files/PASRR_webinar_August2012_Mays.pdf

Erikson, E. H. (1959). Identity and the life cycle: Selected papers. *Psychological Issues*, 1–171.

Kasl-Godley, J., & Gatz, M. (2000). Psychosocial interventions for individuals with dementia: An integration of theory, therapy and clinical understanding of dementia. *Clinical Psychology Review*, 20(6), 755–782.

Lerman, H. E., & Porter, N. E. (1990). *Feminist ethics in psychotherapy*. New York, NY: Springer.

Lin, Y. C., Dai, Y. T., & Hwang, S. L. (2003.) The effect of reminiscence on the elderly population: A systematic review. *Public Health Nursing*, 20(4), 297–306.

Szasz, T. (2007). *Coercion as cure: A critical history of psychiatry*. New Brunswick, NJ: Transaction Publishers.

Wright, J. H., Basco, M. R., & Thase, M. E. (2006). *Learning cognitive-behavior therapy: An illustrated guide*. Arlington, VA: American Psychiatric Publishing.

ANCILLARIES

Internet Resources for Additional Reading

Anthony, W. (1996). *Managed care case management for people with serious mental illness*. Retrieved from http://cpr.bu.edu/wp-content/uploads/2011/11/anthony1996b.pdf

Case Management Association of America. (2015). Home page. Retrieved from cmsa.org.

Commission for Case Management Certification. (2015). Home page. Retrieved from ccmcertification.org.

National Association of Social Workers. (2007). *Indicators for the achievement of the NASW standards for cultural competence in social work practice*. Retrieved from www.socialworkers.org/practice/standards/NASWCulturalStandardsIndicators2006.pdf

National Association for Social Workers. (2013). *NASW Standards for social work case management*. Retrieved from https://www.socialworkers.org/practice/naswstandards/CaseManagementStandards2013.pdf

Scott, J. E., & Dixon, L. B. (1997). Community-based treatment for severe mental illness: What are the benefits and costs? *Medscape Psychiatry & Mental Health eJournal*, 2(5).

Hard Copy References for Additional Reading

Eack, S. M., Anderson, C. M., & Greeno, C. G. (2012). *Mental health case management: A practical guide*. Thousand Oaks, CA: Sage.

Longhofer, J. L., Kubek, P. M., & Floersch, J. (2013). *On being and having a case manager: A relational approach to recovery in mental health*. New York, NY: Columbia University Press.

Manoleas, P. (1996). *The cross-cultural practice of clinical case management in mental health*. London, UK: Taylor and Francis.

Rapp, C. A., & Goscha, R. J. (2006). *The strengths model: Case management with people with psychiatric disabilities*. New York, NY: Oxford University Press.

Rosenberg, G., Weissman, A., & Wong, D. F. K. (2014). *Clinical case management for people with mental illness: A biopsychosocial vulnerability-stress model*. London, UK: Routledge.

❖ JOB DESCRIPTION

In-Patient Psychiatric Case Manager Job Description

- Conduct psychosocial assessments to document patient history and identify preliminary issues for treatment focus by interviewing the patient and his or her family members

- Participate in the development and implementation of treatment plans, ensuring that concise, realistic care plans are maintained and carried out

- Provide individual, group, and family solutions-focused interventions using appropriate therapeutic techniques and models; facilitate process-oriented and didactic groups

- Document treatment and case management provided to patient in medical record legibly and in a timely manner

- Develop and coordinate an individualized discharge plan for the patient by utilizing information obtained from the patient, treatment team, and medical record to determine discharge planning needs; identify available appropriate family or community resources such as group homes, half-way houses, or treatment providers

- Attend and participate in regular interdisciplinary treatment team meetings to provide Social Services perspective to total case management of the patient; provide communication regarding patient's case, resources, and progress toward treatment plan and discharge planning goals; make treatment recommendations and actively coordinate each case with all members of the treatment team

- Report incidents or suspected incidences of sexual/physical abuse, neglect, or exploitation of a minor, elder, or disabled person to appropriate state or community protective agencies; represent the facility in legal proceedings as required by law

- Actively address safety issues as part of discharge planning process

- Assess patient's stage and extent of chemical use when appropriate

- Communicate with referral sources and other appropriate parties regarding patient's progress

- Provide thorough communication to Social Services staff regarding status of assigned tasks; provide clinical updates regarding patients to facilitate effective continuity of care

- Participate in department and other program or clinical and administrative meetings; support maintenance and development of clinical program services

- Adhere to all safety policies and safe work practices

- Adhere to all hospital policies and procedures

- Perform other duties as assigned

Educational Requirements

- Individual must hold a master's degree in social work, counseling, or related field

- Candidate must be licensed or license-eligible in Georgia

11

La Frontera: Coordinación de los Servicios de Trabajo Social para los Menores sin Acompañante en Arizona*

Rebecca A. Matthew and Anna Marie Smith

Introduction

The position of Children's Specialist/Case Manager (CM) at the Florence Immigrant and Refugee Rights Project (FIRRP) is a case management CMG and program development position working with unaccompanied minors in Phoenix, Arizona. Founded in 1989, FIRRP is a non-profit organization that provides free legal and social services for detained unaccompanied immigrant youth and adults in Arizona. The Children's Specialist/Social Worker (the second author, Anna Marie Smith) supports clients

---

*La Frontera: Social Work Case Management With Unaccompanied Minors in Arizona.

by coordinating various social service needs related to their legal cases, particularly crisis prevention and intervention. In this role, the CM is expected to have 35 cases with varying degrees of needs, continually develop resources and best practices for clients, and serve as a resource to attorneys and staff to ensure clients' legal and basic needs are met.

The Clientele

Unaccompanied minors are individuals legally under the age of 18 who have crossed the United States border without parent(s) or legal guardian(s). Upon apprehension, they are taken into the custody of the Office of Refugee Resettlement (ORR), then are detained in youth-only shelters, and afforded legal access to medical care and educational opportunities. Within Arizona, the shelters in which they are detained are operated by non-profit organizations that are sub-contracted through ORR. Of primary importance while being detained is the identification of familial or organizational sponsors to whom these children can be eventually released. At the point of release, these youth often face significant barriers accessing social services given their lack of legal guardians and tenuous immigration status. By virtue of their legal status, they are for example, disqualified from receiving medical insurance and have no access to the Supplemental Nutrition Assistance Program (SNAP) or other social benefits. It is for these very reasons that organizations like FIRRP are critically important to ensuring access to legal counsel and representation during immigration proceedings.

Once a case is accepted by FIRRP, initial efforts focus on determining whether the child has any legal relief to stay in the United States with permission, which may include securing legal immigration status for these minors through four main visas: Special Immigrant Juvenile Status, Asylum, U non-immigrant visa for victims of qualifying crimes, or non-immigrant visa for victims of trafficking. In this process, FIRRP attorneys are charged with representing these minors in their cases, but often and quickly call upon the social work CM to attend directly to their social and emotional needs. The CM will, for example, facilitate school enrollment, procure stable housing, and arrange for counseling and psychological evaluations to support legal claims.

Socio-demographic profile of clients. The demographic profile of the 110 youth receiving services from FIRRP in 2014 mirrors national trends. The U.S. ORR (2015) indicated that the majority of children detained in 2014 were male (66%), 14 years old or older (73%), and migrated from El Salvador, Guatemala, and Honduras (95%). Although FIRRP clients have been reported as young as 3 years old, the average is between 14 and 19, with several remaining active cases until the age of 20 as they await final court decisions regarding their immigration status (ORR, 2015). Also of note is the rising numbers of female clients, with an 11% increase from fiscal year 2012 to 2014 (ORR, 2015).

There are various reasons why these children leave their home countries. According to a study by the United Nations High Commission for Refugees (2014), which interviewed 404 children from El Salvador, Guatemala, Honduras, and Mexico, the five most common reasons cited were: "violence in society, abuse in the home, deprivation and social exclusion, family re-unification or better opportunity, and other" (p. 23). While each of these countries has distinct cultures and unique experiences, 48% of all children interviewed expressed how they experienced violence due to organized crimes such as drug cartels, gangs, and state-sponsored groups (United Nations High Commission for Refugees, 2014, p. 6). The individual and collective impact of these forces results in thousands of children fleeing to the United States each year.

With respect to country of origin, children migrating from non-contiguous countries, are automatically transferred to the custody of the ORR; however, youth from Mexico (2% in 2014) must demonstrate reasonable fear resulting from, for example, experiences as victims of trafficking to avoid swift deportation (ORR, 2015). Language barriers present significant challenges to ensuring adequate council and attainment of social services, given that 97% of the children in the custody of ORR come from Spanish-speaking countries (ORR, 2015), with the vast majority of them speaking Spanish and, at times, indigenous languages (e.g., Mam, K'itche', Ixil) only.

Based on personal experiences prior to, during, and following migration to the United States, the vast majority of these minors have experienced one or multiple traumatic events, which include rape, domestic violence and abuse, trafficking, abandonment, and extreme poverty. Given their prominent trauma history, these clients present common behaviors (for survivors of trauma) such as aggression, sleep disturbances, substance abuse, learning disabilities, attention difficulties, low self-esteem, unhealthy attachments, and increased medical problems (Social Work Policy Institute, 2010).

One, if not *the*, most immediately pressing and continual needs of these clients is access to safe and stable housing. Many do not qualify for housing programs given their immigration status, language abilities, or inability to work. In Phoenix, we currently have four organizational programs that do accept these youth; however, significant unmet needs remain. Housing is fundamental to creating stable lives for these youth.

There is also a legal issue for those detained by ORR who are not re-unified by their 18th birthday; youth unable to secure a viable individual or organizational sponsor prior to their 18th birthday will be taken into the custody of Immigration and Customs Enforcement (ICE). ICE then processes these individuals and may release them on their own recognizance if they have a release plan. If such a plan is not in place, however, they are immediately transferred to an adult detention facility where they have fewer legal rights and less access to services. Therefore, finding housing for these "age-outs" is crucial to avoiding subsequent adult detention and guaranteeing access to social and legal services.

Also a significant need is mental health counseling and support services. As mentioned previously, many FIRRP clients have suffered multiple, sustained traumas throughout their lives. As such, the need for culturally and linguistically appropriate, as well as financially accessible counseling, is of critical importance to the social and emotional well-being of these clients, as well as instrumental to effectively document-ing their asylum claims.

A final area critical to the support of these clients is CMG. For example, FIRRP cli-ents often need assistance enrolling in school, completing the necessary paperwork to obtain a social security card, determining eligibility and enrolling in state-sponsored health insurance, and finding free or reduced-cost available health care providers. Successful attainment of these services is critical to the long-term social, physical, and emotional well-being of such a vulnerable population.

Typical client. Ivan, a 16-year-old male recently migrated from a small town in Guatemala, was newly released to a brother in the Phoenix, AZ area. He reported that his father abandoned the family at a young age, and his mother died shortly there-after. Ivan had completed the sixth grade and resided with various family members in Guatemala during which time he experienced physical and emotional abuse from multiple family members. To support the family and himself, he began working around the age of 12 in agriculture; however, due to limited economic opportunities, lack of parental care, and the pervasive presence of violent gangs in his hometown, Ivan migrated to the United States. In so doing, he hoped to escape the threat of forced gang life, unite with his family members, and obtain gainful employment. FIRRP is currently assisting with filing for his Special Immigrant and Juvenile Status, as well as school enrollment, assessing safety issues in his brother's home, and accessing health care for free or at a reduced cost. A typical case like Ivan's can last between 4 to 12 weeks.

Atypical client. Jesus, a 17-year-old male from a middle-class Mexican family, has been working in the United States for 6 months and was recently detained by the Border Patrol. He has no family in the United States and does not have supportive relationships with those he has met through work. He reports his stepfather was a leader of one of the drug cartels in Mexico and was severely abusive toward him. To escape, he fled to the United States. At the time of his entrance into the United States, he did not know how to apply or avail himself of asylum status. Now with FIRRP as his counsel, he has applied for asylum and is awaiting his interview. In addition to supporting his asylum case, which is exceptionally time sensitive, given he will turn 18 in 3 weeks, FIRRP is trying to coordinate a counselor to document the abuse and its emotional/psychologi-cal effects, obtain a medical assessment to document the physical scars, and procure safe and stable housing so that he will not be transferred to an adult detention facility on his 18th birthday. An atypical case like Jesus's can last between 10 to 20 weeks.

Practice Roles and Responsibilities

The social worker CM position at FIRRP is both micro and macro. The CM is expected to perform referral and direct CMG services, as well as engage in program development and advocacy efforts. An appreciation for the ways in which these two spheres of practice are mutually supportive is critical to supporting clients. For example, being aware of resources that accept our clients, the legal processes concerning referral mechanisms, and specific documentation guidelines concerning

Carlson, B. E., Cacciatore, J., & Klimek, B. (2012). A risk and resilience perspective on unaccompanied refugee minors. *Social Work, 57*(3), 259–269.

Center for Public Policy Priorities (2008). A child alone and without paper: A report on the return and repatriation of unaccompanied undocumented children in the United States. Austin, TX. Retrieved from http://forabettertexas.org/images/A_Child_Alone_and_Without_Papers.pdf

Chang-Muy, F., & Congress, E. P. (2009). *Social work with immigrants and refugees: Legal issues, clinical skills and advocacy.* New York, NY: Springer.

Chomsky, A. (2014). *Undocumented: How immigration became illegal.* Boston, MA: Beacon Press.

Cole, P. L. (2012). You want me to do what? Ethical practice within interdisciplinary collaborations. *Journal of Social Work Values & Ethics, 9*(1), 26–39.

Fix, M. (2009). *Immigrants and welfare: The impact of welfare reform on America's newcomers.* New York, NY: Russell Sage Foundation.

Kandel, W. A., Bruno, A., Meyer, P. J., Seelke, C. R., Taft-Morales, M., & Wasem, R. E. (2014). Unaccompanied alien children: Potential factors contributing to recent immigration. *Congressional Research Service: Issue Brief,* 1–21.

Martinez-Brawley, E. E., & Zorita, P. (2011). Immigration and social work: Contrasting practice and education. *Social Work Education, 30*(1), 17–28.

National Association of Social Workers. (2008). *Immigration policy toolkit.* Retrieved from https://www.socialworkers.org/diversity/ImmigrationToolkit.pdf

Organista, K. C. (2009). New practice model for Latinos in need of social work services. *Social Work, 54*(4), 297–305.

Perreira, K. M., & Smith, L. (2007). A cultural-ecological model of migration and development: Focusing on Latino immigrant youth. *Prevention Researcher, 14*(4), 6–9.

Sotomayor-Peterson, M., & Montiel-Carbajal, M. (2014). Psychological and family well-being of unaccompanied Mexican child migrants sent back from the U.S. border region of Sonora-Arizona. *Hispanic Journal of Behavioral Sciences, 36*(2), 111–123.

❖ JOB DESCRIPTION

The Florence Project Children's Program educates, empowers, and provides legal assistance to unaccompanied immigrant children in removal proceedings in Phoenix and Tucson, Arizona. Many of the children served are held in shelters, group homes, or long-term foster care overseen by the Office of Refugee Resettlement (ORR) while awaiting deportation hearings. Our office works as a team to provide unaccompanied children "know your rights" presentations at shelters, individual intakes, pre-court counseling sessions, and representation in front of the immigration court, family court, and U.S. Citizenship and Immigration Services. We also provide services to children released from ORR custody, reunified with sponsors or family members in Arizona.

The Position: Caseworker for Children's Program

The Caseworker/Social Worker will work on a legal team comprised of five to seven people, serving immigrant children who have been released from ORR/Federal care to Arizona. The Caseworker will maintain a caseload of approximately 30–40 cases. The position includes extensive client contact with children, including indigenous children and children who have suffered abuse, abandonment, neglect, or other emotional and physical trauma. The position also includes substantial administrative work including file management, data entry, and referral services, as well as supporting the attorneys representing released children. The position is not a counseling position, but rather a CM position that links children with services in the greater Phoenix area, and works collaboratively with legal staff.

The Case Worker's major responsibilities include but are not limited to:

- Connect clients to non-legal services including housing, medical, mental health, vocational, and educational services. Meet regularly with legal staff to discuss client referrals.

- Under supervision and in collaboration with other social services team members, develop and update a manual of social services available to our clients in Arizona. Identify new resources and services in the community.

- In collaboration with legal staff, create case plans for clients, addressing most pressing social needs.

- Act as a liaison between clients and staff attorneys, including assisting clients schedule meetings with attorneys and other legal case-related appointments, understand the legal processes, and gather factual information from clients for legal cases, as needed.

- Accompany clients to USCIS or ICE appointments as needed, and assist clients in attending medical and social services appointments as it relates to the legal case.

- Communicate with client's CMs at school or other community agencies, as needed.

- Respond to clients in crisis and refer clients to appropriate agencies.

- Help clients prepare and understand forms and paperwork.

- Teach clients how to use public information resources (i.e., library) and transportation systems.

- Communicate effectively in person and by telephone with clients.

- Maintain clear and concise case file documentation to reflect the needs of the individual client.

- Be an effective, supportive team player—work with legal teams, and with other

Florence Project social services team members to coordinate and share knowledge among our three offices and different programs.

- Adhere to organization's policies particularly those related to confidentiality and client privacy.

- Participate in "Know-Your-Rights" trainings and intakes with detained children as needed, for coverage purposes.

- Participate in all program meetings and staff development activities.

- Participate in organizational fundraising and communications efforts as needed.

Requirements for the Position

Background in social work is strongly preferred, including BSW or MSW degree or studies. If the successful candidate has social work education, the position title will be social worker (instead of caseworker). The ideal candidate will have prior supervised experience with social services CM. Fluency in Spanish is required. Prior experience working with teenagers and traumatized individuals is a plus.

We are seeking applicants who have a demonstrated commitment to immigrant rights, social justice, or human rights issues with excellent interpersonal skills who enjoy working in a collaborative, client-centered law office environment. Must have excellent organizational skills with regard to administration and logistics, and use time effectively and efficiently. Must be flexible and able to handle multiple tasks at once. Must be a self-starter and able to work independently, as well as part of a team. Must be culturally competent. Must have reliable transportation.

12

Children's Wish Foundation International in Atlanta, Georgia

Melinda Williams Moore and Elizabeth Darby

The Clientele

As a case manager (CM) Wish Coordinator, I (the second author) serve families who have a child (or sometimes children) with a life-threatening illness at Children's Wish Foundation International (CWFI) located in Atlanta, Georgia. CWFI is an organization that was started in 1985 after its founder lost her daughter to pediatric cancer. Since then, it has been working with children and families who are facing the fear and challenges of receiving a daunting medical diagnosis by providing them a brief escape from hospitals and doctors' visits in the form of a wish. We also send out shipments of toys and supplies to pediatric hospitals all over the country to put smiles on the faces of children who are stuck in the hospital for extended periods of time.

CWFI has one central office in the Southeastern United States, but we serve clients all over the country and the world. Most of the families we serve live outside of the state of Georgia; most of my families are from Florida and South Carolina. Our families have varying levels of income, where some involve a single mother who is living off of Medicare, while other families can economically afford to go on a trip at any time, but choose not to take advantage of that option. I work with mainly Caucasian, African American, and Hispanic families. A typical family I work with is an African

American family with a single mother and two to three children. The atypical family is a wealthy white family with one to two kids.

All of these families are dealing with the fear that their child or sibling might not live much longer, which also tends to make them a little preoccupied and sometimes hard to contact. The children we serve must to be under the age of 18 and must have a life-threatening condition. The most common illness we see is cancer, with the most common type being acute lymphoblastic leukemia. We also work with many children who have cystic fibrosis, which affects a child's lungs and their ability to be very active. For example, one of my wish clients who was diagnosed with cystic fibrosis was unable to go on a scuba diving excursion on his cruise because he was unable to breath well with the scuba mask. Typically, it takes about 4 months for the whole Wish process to unfold, from receiving the initial referral, to contacting the doctors involved, to finally planning and executing the wish. However, sometimes it can take up to a year to plan a wish, if a child is not well enough to take her or his trip, or if we are waiting for an outside party to help us with the wish, such as a celebrity meet and greet, or a specific sporting event.

Practice Roles and Responsibilities

As a CM Wish Coordinator, my main roles are to communicate with all families, social workers or child life specialists, doctors, and travel agents to plan the wish for a child. This may involve planning a trip to Disney World, the Galapagos Islands, or for some, a simple shopping spree. Before a wish can be approved, I have to talk to social workers or child life specialists to see if the child meets our wish qualifications for eligibility. The two main reasons a child would not qualify is if the condition is not life-threatening or if the child has received a wish from another organization. Once the social worker or child life specialist confirms the child meets those qualifiers, I send them medical forms to have the doctor complete, just to double check that the doctor agrees with the other providers. If there is not a social worker or child life specialist on the client case, it can be very hard to get in touch with the doctor. Sometimes, it will take months for a doctor to get the two forms back to us, because they are so busy. When that happens, I have to be extra diligent about calling the doctor's office at least once a week to ask them to complete the form. I often have to be pushy with the doctors because the children we are working with do not have the time to wait.

Approval. After we hear back from the doctor, the child's application is passed on to our Wish Review Board for final decision. The majority of the time, the Board will approve the wish if it has made it to their last step in the process, but sometimes they raise red flags about certain wishes that might not be possible. We have a budget in place for each type of wish, to make sure we have enough funds for every child who qualifies. If the Board does raise a concern about a wish being too expensive, we try to come up with a more cost-effective way of making the requested wish happen, or we move on to the child's second wish. This is why our children provide us with three different wishes that would make them happy in the application stage of the process. An example of a wish that was too expensive was a trip to Bora Bora at a private resort with a stylized photo shoot thrown into the mix. Because this wish would have taken away from other funds that could make another child's wish a reality, we moved on to the girl's second wish for a trip to London, England.

Planning. Once a wish has been approved, I begin the process of planning for it. I start by finding out from the families when they would like the wish to take place. We like to let families choose their own time frame, because we want to make sure the child will be healthy enough to enjoy the wish with as few complications as possible. Sometimes, a family may want to plan their trip for the next month, and I may have to deny their request, because we are unable to plan effectively in that little amount of time. Although, the one exception I will always make is for a child who may be in hospice care and does not have much time to wait for a wish. Other times, the family may want to wait a year to plan their wish, because of school or because the child is recovering from surgery or chemotherapy at the time their wish is approved.

Once I have a time frame from the family about when they would like their wish to take place, I contact all parties necessary to help plan the wish. For example, if the child wants to take a trip somewhere, I contact our travel agent to book flights and hotels. If the child wants a game room or another tangible gift, I reach out to the retailers where we will be purchasing these items and then to volunteers in the family's area to see if they can help deliver the wish. In cases where there are not volunteers in the area, we will send party supplies and order a cake or other dessert for the child to celebrate being approved for their wish.

Social work skills used. Without question, the most important skill I use is *empathy*. Many parents know that their child may not qualify for a wish, but they will often call our office anyway, just to talk to someone about what they are going through. It is important to extend genuine empathy to show the parent that I understand what she or he is going through, and that I understand her or his fears and frustrations (Gerdes & Segal, 2011; Pinderhughes, 1979). I also use empathy with my co-workers. Because we are working with very fragile children and families, it is common to hear about the death of a past wish child, or of one who has become too ill to use their wish. During these times, I exhibit empathy to my co-workers to indicate that I understand what they are going through and can relate to the loss and pain they are feeling (Gwyther et al., 2005).

I also use *active listening* constantly to determine if a child qualifies for a wish, if the child's wish is actually being conveyed or if it's the parent's wish, and to plan the wish best suited to the child's individual needs (Huerta-Wong & Schoech, 2010). For example, I receive calls weekly from parents and providers who want to refer a child for a wish. They will tell me a long, detailed story of everything the child has had to endure, what the family has been through, and what type of supports the family has received. In the middle of the story they might say something about a child receiving a wish from another organization, but then they will gloss over it and not share many details. If I am not actively listening to the conversation and I send the child an application, I will have to deny them a wish later, once I note that they have received a wish already. I could have saved the child and family the disappointment of being denied and the work of filling out the application, if I had only been paying more attention.

I also have to set *boundaries* with all of my families, as I do not allow them to contact me after work hours, unless it is an emergency, and I do not accept any "friend requests" on any social media sites. Indeed, there is a fine line between practicing empathy and becoming unable to work because you are so involved in a client's life, and I think I walk that line well (Newell & MacNeil, 2010).

Challenges and Barriers

One of the main (and rather unpleasant) challenges of doing my CMG job is having to reject a child's wish. This happens when a child has had a previous wish, or if the child's illness is not truly life-threatening. It is indeed difficult to deliver this bad news, but it is necessary for us to be able to make sure that every child has an opportunity to receive a first wish. It is really hard to say no to families who are experiencing especially difficult personal circumstances, such as a relapses, loss of jobs, etc., because I feel that they are all just as deserving. Another challenge is trying to discern whether or not a wish is actually from the child or the parent. Sometimes it is obvious, such as a 5-year-old wishing for her or his college to be paid for, but other times it is much harder (i.e., does the child want to go to NYC instead of Disneyland because that's what she wants, or what mom wants?). A third challenge is trying to figure out how to work an expensive wish into a budget. As mentioned earlier, we have a detailed budget for each type of wish, from international travel wishes, to more tangible gifts, to shopping sprees. Usually, the children we work with do not have a hard time coming up with three different wishes that they would be happy to receive. There was one instance however, when a young man wanted to go to the Galapagos Islands to learn more about Darwinism, and nothing else. His heart was completely set on going to those particular islands. I had to determine if we could make the wish happen with the help of extra fundraising, or if we would have to ask the child to re-think of another wish. Fortunately, with a travel agent's help, we were able to send the child and his family to the Galapagos Islands—without taking away from another child's wish. A final CMG challenge involves working with doctors and other people involved in the child's wish. For instance, we could be waiting months for one doctor to sign a medical waiver because he or she is so busy. Also, if a child has a special wish to meet a celebrity or sports star, it takes months and sometimes years, before we ever hear anything (we offer the child to change her or his wish every 3 months, if we don't hear back). It is very frustrating to know that an ill child is waiting for her or his wish to be fulfilled, but not being able to do anything about it because you are waiting for someone else to do their professional part.

Role Development Potential

Unfortunately, there is not much room for career growth at my organization. The next step would be to be in charge of all of the CMG Wish Coordinators as a Program Manager, but the management has made it clear that I would not move into this position for many years. Since starting at the job, I have been given the added responsibility of managing volunteers who come to help us, but that is as far as my professional growth will go. However, this added experience has enriched my skillset as a CM and social worker and will help me be better prepared for a wider variety of positions in the social work realm.

I believe the School of Social Work at the University of Georgia (UGA) definitely prepared me for this position. I learned how to manage multiple cases at one time in my internship, and I would be unable to do my job now without that experience. During my BSW education, I also learned how to practice empathy, active listening, and use open-ended questions in the countless practice interviews we had to record for our upper-level classes. These skills have been meaningful for me to perform the CM Wish Coordinator job effectively.

If I were to plan a BSW curriculum, it would be important to emphasize more course content about both self-care and balancing one's work with life. I believe that social workers cannot help their clients to their fullest potential unless they are first taking care of their own needs. For example, I would have a hard time helping a client if I could not detach myself from their situation, re-frame, and think logically. Another concept I would teach BSW students is about the importance of having good time management. As CMs, it is expected that we will have many cases to juggle at once. Thus, we cannot afford to become bogged down by one case at the risk of neglecting others. It is important for us to learn how to prioritize what needs to be completed, and accomplish tasks in that order. Finally, I think it is also important to really focus on the fact that you can never know what is going on in a person's life completely. As such, it is important to not jump to conclusions or judge a client based on what you believe about her or him. As social workers, we cannot help any client reach her or his full potential if we are de-limiting what they can do in our own minds.

I bring empathy and active listening to the table daily at my job. Since none of my co-workers are social workers, I can see how they are lacking in these skills when I listen to them. Instead of listening to a client share her or his story, they are often quick to cut them off and get to the point. They also sometimes miss key parts of a child's situation, such as the need for a wheelchair, while they are focused on getting the logistics of the wish planned and over with. I believe the driving reason behind our professional differences is the idea that I want to help the families by giving them some sort of escape, something to look forward to, while my co-workers just want to check the box and make our numbers look better. Instead of investing in our families, they seem more interested in moving them along to get to the next person. While there is some validity to wanting to reach as many people as possible, I believe it is also important to show our families that we care about them individually and want to be invested in their stories. As social workers, we are taught that every person is impor-tant and should be given the opportunity to make their voice be heard and valued. This is especially true when it comes to our wish children. For instance, I had one child who just wanted to see the river running through San Antonio because she had never seen water in a city before. Instead of choosing to go to California because that's what her sister wanted, or getting a new gaming system like her younger brother wanted her to choose, I was able to discern that the child's true wish to go to San Antonio was the third wish on the list. Thankfully, we were able to bypass the first two wishes and make the trip to the Riverwalk in San Antonio a reality for that little girl, despite her family members wanting other things.

Concluding Remarks

It is very important for CMs to learn how to prioritize tasks and follow through on what you plan to accomplish. It is easy to become attached to specific clients and pour all of your heart and soul into one case, but then you are neglecting and potentially harming other clients. Each client deserves our full attention to the level that they need it, and we must make sure we give them such attention, so that they can reach their full potential. It is also important to talk to someone, whether a co-worker or counselor, if you are feeling overwhelmed. We are only human, and we can't handle helping others with their problems, if we are neglecting ourselves. Of course, client confidentiality is still of the utmost importance, but we must practice self-care. If you need to stop watching *Law and Order: SVU* because it reminds you too much of a case you are working on, then I recommend you stop watching the show. We must better learn how to help ourselves, so we can help others.

It is also important to recognize when you need help on any case. If you need advice on how to best help a client, ask for a coworker's or supervisor's opinion. It is better to ask for advice than to offer something that will do nothing to help the client. For instance, instead of telling a family to apply for a second wish with an organization that I know for a fact does not fulfill second wishes, I had to ask where else we could send families who did not meet our qualifications for a second wish. Further, if you need to say no to a client because they are asking for something inappropriate or for something you cannot give, it is better to ask for advice on how to appropriately turn a family away without burning bridges or making the family believe they are not worthy or eligible for assistance. Finally, all CMs need to practice the very help-seeking behaviors we expect of all our clients.

Case Example

I once had a 17-year-old male wish to go on a Disney Cruise to celebrate his 18th birthday. The young man was living in a low-income foster home because his biological mother was unable to care for him and his twin brother after he was diagnosed with leukemia. He had been bouncing from home to home, because he had no relatives who were capable of taking care of him and his twin. I practiced empathy toward the client to better understand what he was feeling about being in a foster home and being diagnosed with this horrible illness. He was very open about talking about the journey that he had been on regarding his diagnosis, his mother's inability to provide for him and his brother, and about being placed in multiple foster homes before settling down in his current placement. I believe showing him empathy and an openness to learning his story led the child to be so vulnerable with me, someone he had never met face to face. I also focused on empowering the client by giving him as much control as I could, over his own wish choices. He was able to decide when he wanted to go on his cruise, which cruise ship he would be boarding, and the special excursions he would get to do with his twin and foster family. When I let the family know that the client could decide all of these details, he was very excited to feel like he was in control of something. When so many things in his life are currently out of his control, it was a positive experience for him to be able to make seemingly small decisions on his own, and to know that he was capable of making them.

Besides working with the client, I also had to work with multiple different service providers, including the CM, child life specialist, and foster parents to make sure the young man had all the documentation needed to take the trip. This involved getting him a passport, having the state sign off on the trip, and making sure the doctor thought he was well enough to go. The foster family was unable to pay for the child or the rest of their family to purchase passports, so I had to request for our organization to fund that cost. We also provided the family with extra money to cover the cost of extra food and gas that they might not have been able to afford on their own. Further, I had to provide the DFCS CM a detailed outline of the flight itinerary, what the family would be doing each day, as well as contact information and addresses for where they would be staying each night. I also had to practice good time management and make sure his trip was planned with plenty of time for the CM and family to be able to go over everything that would happen on the trip.

When the week of the trip finally arrived, I made sure that I was available at all times during the day, in case the family needed to call. Each CM Wish Coordinator has to be on call while one of her or his families is on a trip in case an emergency arises, or they have some kinds of questions. When we do not hear from a family during their wish trip, we consider it a success because that means we planned their trip well enough that they did not have any problems. Fortunately, I did not hear from the young man or his family at all during his cruise. The family called me a couple of days after they got home to share with me what a wonderful time they had on their trip. The young man was able to fully enjoy his special excursions of swimming with stingrays and exploring Atlantis, and his foster parents were thrilled to be able to be there as he and his twin celebrated their 18th birthdays together. They were very thankful to be given the opportunity to take the young man on a trip that he so greatly needed and deserved. Despite the extra work that came along with coordinating this client's wish, I would not have traded it for anything.

❖

REFERENCES

Gerdes, K., & Segal, E. (2011). Importance of empathy for social work practice: Integrating new science. *Social Work, 56*(2), 141–148.

Gwyther, L. P., Altilio, T., Blacker, S., Christ, G., Csikai, E., Hooyman, N., . . . Howe, J. (2005). Social work competencies in palliative and end-of-life care. *Journal of Social Work in End-of-Life & Palliative Care, 1*(1), 87–120.

Huerta-Wong, J., & Schoech, R. (2010). Experiential learning and learning environments: The case of active listening skills. *Journal of Social Work Educations, 46* (1), 85–101.

Newell, J., & MacNeil, G. (2010, July). Professional burnout, vicarious trauma, secondary traumatic stress, and compassion fatigue. *Best Practices in Mental Health, 2,* 57–68.

Pinderhughes, E. (1979). Teaching empathy in cross-cultural social work. *Social Work, 24*(4), 312–316.

ANCILLARIES

1. The Center for Building a Culture of Empathy. Retrieved from http://cultureofempathy .com/references/Experts/Karen-Gerdes.htm

2. Hospice and Palliative Nurses Association. *Clinical practice guidelines for palliative care (Social workers, nurses, doctors, health care professionals).* Retrieved from https://www.hpna.org/ multimedia/NCP_Clinical_Practice_Guidelines_3rd_Edition.pdf

3. The National Association of Social Workers. Professional impairment and self-care. Retrieved from http://www.naswnc.org/?358

4. TED Talks. Ernesto Sirolli: Want to help someone? Shut up and listen! Retrieved from http://www.bestmswprograms.com/top-10-ted-talks-for-social-workers/

Indiana teenager whose courageous struggle with HIV/AIDS, and against AIDS-related discrimination helped educate the nation. (Fulton County, 2011)

Clients receiving Ryan White subsidies for medical care also obtain medications through the AIDS Drugs Assistance Program (ADAP), which is a "state administered program that provides HIV/AIDS medications to low-income individuals living with HIV disease who have little or no coverage from private or third party insurance" (Georgia Department of Public Health, n.d.).

Race is also important to consider in our caseloads due to reasons of continued racial disparities in HIV/AIDS infections and lack of access to care (Hallfors, Iritani, Miller, & Bauer, 2007). Approximately 87% of our clients are African Americans, 11% Latinos, and 3% white. About 57% are homeless living on the streets, residing in transitional housing, and/or staying at local homeless shelters. Finally, due to the co-occurring disorders of mental health and substance abuse among our clients assigned to this floor, many of them have problems maintaining their medical appointments or adhering to their HIV medication regimen. For example, it is more likely for someone with a mental health condition to forget their appointments or misplace medication. Someone with an addiction problem is also more likely to stop taking medication or to have unstable housing. Housing issues then lead clients to prioritize looking for a place to stay in the short-term rather than focusing on their health.

In sum, most of our clients receive Medicaid and SSI benefits, struggle to maintain any stable housing, see the psychiatric nurse for mental health services, and constantly seek assistance for food, clothing, and/or substance abuse treatment. Some of our clients are not compliant with their psychotropic and antipsychotic medications and are hence unstable. It is also not uncommon to serve clients who are actively psychotic and/or suicidal. On the other hand, an atypical client is someone who is maintaining long-term stable housing, while being adherent to medical and mental health services. This atypical client could have been in medical CMG services in the past, and completed her or his goals, and is maintaining progress. Moreover, this type of client knows many of the resources in the community and has a strong relationship with the providers in our multidisciplinary team.

Practice Roles and Responsibilities

The primary goal of medical CMG at ASO is to ensure that all clients are a) appropriately linked to necessary services; b) accessing medical care for their HIV/AIDS diagnosis on a regular basis; and c) being adherent to their medication. Therefore, the main role of CMs is to support the biopsychosocial needs of the clients and remove barriers that prevent/challenge them from getting medical care, support accessing and maintaining their care, and from obtaining or taking their medication as prescribed. When a client seeks medical CMG services, he or she needs to provide the ASO with all eligibility documents, namely proof of income and residency, state picture identification, and proof of HIV status through a letter from the medical provider or a copy of test results. Then, a CM completes a comprehensive screening with the client to determine if medical CMG is the appropriate service for that client at that time.

This screening gathers pertinent information regarding the person's mental health, substance use, housing, access to food and personal hygiene items, legal needs, and sexual health behavior. Here, questions are scored and tabulated to determine if the client could benefit from medical CMG or if he or she needs to be referred to a lower level of care, such as self-management, for minor support. If the client has needs in multiple areas, then he or she is given an appointment to complete an intake process that includes confidentiality forms, gathering of additional personal information, orientation of rights and responsibilities, and an Individualized Service Plan (ISP).

The client and the assigned CM cooperatively develop the ISP, which minimally covers the following areas: medical health (including vision and dental), medication adherence, health insurance, income, housing, food, mental health, substance abuse, social support, family and child care, transportation, furniture and clothing, legal, and sexual health harm reduction. Together, the client and CM identify the client's needs, strengths, and goals and determine the "best plan" to address her or his needs. Subsequently, the CM refers the client to the appropriate services and empowers the client to take full responsibility and ownership of the tasks outlined and agreed upon in the ISP.

The CM then maintains regular contact with the client on a monthly basis through face-to-face meetings or phone calls to work on identified goals, evaluate ongoing progress, troubleshoot issues that may be impeding achievement of previously established goals, and establish new goals, as necessary. Special focus is given to medication adherence and keeping up with medical appointments with all primary care providers. If a client is having difficulty with their maintaining adherence and/or keeping up with medical appointments, the CM evaluates what psychosocial areas present as barriers to care. The CM then provides appropriate referrals and reminds the client of the importance of adherence to medication and medical care. Some examples of barriers identified in these encounters are often inability to find transportation for medical appointments, lack of food to take medications that are directed to be taken with meals, and being incarcerated at the time of their medical appointments at the clinic. The ISP is revised and signed every 4 months for Medicaid recipients and every 6 months for Medicare or Ryan White beneficiaries.

When working on assisting clients to achieve their goals, we contend there are three main responsibilities for CMs. These responsibilities are advocacy, education, and referrals. Moreover, in order to perform these responsibilities, there are several social work skills that the CM uses to provide effective services to clients at the ASO. First, based on knowledge of existing evidence-based practices gained by attending continuing education trainings, the CM utilizes the SBIRT Model, which stands for taking the steps of *Screening*, *Brief Intervention*, and *Referral to Treatment*. According to the Substance Abuse and Mental Health Services Administration (SAMHSA), the SBIRT Model is

> an evidence-based practice used to identify, reduce, and prevent problematic use, abuse, and dependence on alcohol and illicit drugs. The SBIRT model was cited by an Institute of Medicine recommendation that called for community-based screening for health risk behaviors, including substance use. (SAMHSA-HRSA Center for Integrated Health Solutions, n.d.-b)

More specifically, the SBIRT Model could be utilized by social workers practicing as case managers by considering the intersection of their responsibilities and other tools and techniques within the following SBIRT steps:

1. Screening: Engage in practice informed by cultural humility, especially because most of the clients come from diverse racial/ethnic backgrounds and are affected by internalized, perceived, and societal stigma about HIV/AIDS. Considering culture and themes such as stigma provides the basis for more comprehensive and accurate screening. Furthermore, interviewing and clinical skills aid the CM in building rapport with their clients, formulating diagnostics impressions, and conducting biopsychosocial assessments that guide their planned interventions. The ASAM (American Society of Addiction Medicine) criteria are used to assess a client's level of substance use acuteness and the level of care/treatment adequate to the symptoms. For example, the ASAM criteria guide the CM's referral process to the appropriate (and available) community resources, such as out-patient or in-patient treatment.

2. Brief Intervention: When conducting a screening, the CM performs crisis intervention utilizing Motivational Interviewing (MI). It is important to understand that the SBIRT steps are not mutually exclusive from each other, and that in many occasions the CM screens for needs while engaging in brief intervention. For example, clients are sometimes discharged from housing services onto the streets due to client's non-compliance with rules. These situations create a need for assisting clients with re-evaluating their goals and attaining a more stable mental health situation. In this, the CM screens for important information regarding housing needs while performing crisis intervention skills with a client that has now become homeless.

   SAMHSA describes MI as "a clinical approach that helps people with mental health and substance use disorders and other chronic conditions such as diabetes, cardiovascular conditions, and asthma make positive behavioral changes to support better health. The approach upholds four principles—expressing empathy and avoiding arguing, developing discrepancy, rolling with resistance, and supporting self-efficacy" (SAMHSA-HRSA Center for Integrated Health Solutions, n.d.-a). MI aids the CM with assessing the client's position in the sequential and identified stages of change (pre-contemplation, contemplation, preparation, action, maintenance). Assessing these stages of change and the client's motivation guide the CMG process of referral to treatment.

   Finally, it is CMs' responsibility to educate clients not only about requirements needed to obtain community services, but also about the consequences of their decisions. For instance, many of our clients face problems with the law due to substance use and mental illness, and it is a CMs' responsibility to educate them about the limitations of certain housing programs availability due to their criminal records. CMs should also educate the clients regarding expectations of attaining services, waiting lists/periods, processes to be followed, documentation that needs to be gathered, and limitations of the CMs' power and/or influence over other agencies' protocols.

3. Referral to Treatment: In order to provide effective referrals, there is also a need for having knowledge of community resources and state and federal programs that could assist or impact clients. Some of the known programs and resources that impact the work of the CMs include: Ryan White policies and procedures; Medicaid and Medicare benefits; social security eligibility; programs that assist with paying utilities, rent, and

mortgage; agencies assisting in obtaining birth certificates and picture identifications; and how to obtain medical services at various facilities. Furthermore, it is important for CMs to constantly verify and research changes on such local, state, and/or federal programs, amendments to policies, funding changes, and other changes on eligibility and availability of services, knowing the community is integral to doing effective CMG with all clients we see.

The responsibility for making referrals is constant and requires regularly following up with the agencies receiving our referrals. Some referrals are not only for basic needs, but are also for services. These include payee services that assist individuals in managing their money as a requisite by entities like social security, legal aid, and assistance for obtaining school supplies and gifts for the holidays. Advocacy skills are necessary when a client encounters barriers related to the bureaucracies of systems or when there is miscommunication between the client, providers, and organizations. For example, a client who has difficulty understanding English and is re-scheduled due to the interpreter not being available, may need help advocating for herself to be seen on the day of the appointment by using the phone translation services.

CMs' main challenges when working with our clients are directly correlated to the clients' functional levels and the acuteness of co-occurring disorders. For example, it is challenging to work on concrete goals with a client who is psychotic and homeless, and will not remember an action plan, instructions for a referral, or a follow-up appointment. Furthermore, other barriers come into play when a client with active addiction is motivated by her or his desire to constantly acquire substances and cravings. These clients often tend to not show up for follow-up appointments and therefore are more responsive to motivating incentives such as food vouchers or assistance with public transportation.

Other challenges present when working with interdisciplinary teams. Expectations between the client, medical provider, and CM could differ significantly regarding realistic outcomes or resources available. For example, it is not unusual to have a request from a medical provider to a CM to locate resources for a client on the same day. These requests could include emergency housing or lodging, access to food, or referrals to substance use treatment. The challenge with accessing some of these services comes from the requirements established by community agencies. For example, some agencies provide financial assistance for emergency lodging if a client has a medical form completed, stating that they are medically fragile and must have an intake completed by their staff before 2PM. Another example is the constant unavailability of beds at substance use in-patient facilities and the preparation required for someone to be admitted, such as the client needing a 30-day supply of all of their medication. This discrepancy on expectations is sometimes due to the limited time frame that a medical provider has to see the client and the multiple and complicated medical conditions needed to be addressed in one abbreviated visit.

Finally, skills related to organization and attention to details when completing forms, tracking due dates of various documents, and keeping up-to-date documentation are important for all CMs. Special attention to documentation is in part due to the need to comply with funding provided by State and federal grants. Moreover, documentation is essential for liability purposes when working with individuals who report suicidal or homicidal ideation or abuse and neglect. CMs at the ASO are required to enter an encounter with a client within 48 hours.

Role Development Potential

The ASO provides the opportunity to participate in their Leadership Program where CMG skills and tools are taught. Moreover, employees are also encouraged to participate in continuing education trainings and are supported with flexible scheduling in order to attend such trainings. The ASO has multiple "lunch-and-learns" every year from pharmaceutical companies, experts in the field, knowledgeable staff with the ASO, and governmental agencies. The topics include, but are not limited to, mental health, new agencies in the community, changes in requirements for various programs, new HIV medications, and best CMG practices.

BSW and MSW social work curricula prepared the CM (Luis Alvarez-Hernandez) to perform many CM roles and responsibilities. Generalist social work interventions and community practice models from the BSW program has been integral in practice as a CM, as well as the clinical micro skill practice learned from the MSW social work education. For example, courses related to cultural humility and interviewing prepare social work students on how to better engage and work more effectively with clients from diverse backgrounds, as well as building rapport and obtaining necessary information from clients. MSW assessment and psychopathology courses provide students with opportunities to learn assessments and clinical skills of formulating diagnostic impressions. Moreover, field practicum from both BSW and MSW programs provided the CM with the knowledge and experience of crisis intervention skills. The basis of these experiences provided the CM with the basis to learn and practice MI later on in his professional practice. However, the CM could have benefited from more specialized elective courses like social work in medical settings, mental health, and addictions.

It would also be beneficial to offer medical CMG/medical social work MSW courses more consistently in social work academic schedules. Social work focuses on a person-in-environment perspective and systems theory and it would be helpful to offer courses that teach a medical or biological oriented model to students. Although we tend to talk (in our social work education) about ""biopsychosocial assessments," the focus is on the psychosocial areas and interventions and the "bio" part of the assessment (model) was often ignored. Conceptualizing a client from a biological or more medical perspective amplifies our understanding of an individual's health needs and limitations. For instance, knowing the most common neurocognitive diseases could be a valuable part of such a course.

Social work students bring a uniquely social work perspective informed by the person-in-environment and the strengths perspective, which is a great fit for the position of medical CM. As a CM for clients with HIV/AIDS and many other co-occurring problems, it is easy to focus solely on crises. However, adept social workers are trained to look beyond the immediate "crisis" and explore the multi-layered factors that lead the individual to have an acute need for food, housing, and social support. Many times our clients have many assets or strengths that could assist them on improving their situations on their own. Therefore, CMs are constantly required to have conversations with their clients about how they have addressed a specific issue in the past, what worked and didn't work, what social support they have, and what community resources they know or have used in the past.

Concluding Remarks

It is important to remember that we aspire to be agents of change in the life of our clients—however, we should remember two things. First, our clients are able to change their situations on their own, and thus come to us seeking support and guidance. Sometimes, we tend to forget to go past the deficit model and focus on the use of the strengths perspective. Our client's many strengths include a knowledge of community resources, social supports, and knowledge of how the systems really operate. Second, as social workers, we should be aware of our altruistic tendency to "save" our clients. Our clients have managed without us in the past and were able to come to us for assistance. Our presence in a client's life could last one session or several years. Moreover, at the end of that intervention, our clients will be able to go on with their lives and we may never know the real outcomes of their situations. We can only hope that we have fostered some sort of empowering change in them and that it will be enough to aid them to surpass other crises or difficult events arising in their lives. If not, we could only hope another social work colleague in another clinic, hospital, or agency will utilize her or his empathy, competency, and skills to assist this person.

Case Example

Marcos is a 65-year-old Latino male diagnosed with AIDS a few years ago. Marcos displayed an onset of dementia and was experiencing symptoms of forgetfulness and trouble in understanding and concentrating. Marcos has been homeless for more than a year. Marcos has been referred to me (the second author) by the medical staff due to problems with medication adherence, forgetting primary care appointments, homelessness, and language barriers.

After meeting with Marcos, I was able to gather most of his personal and medical history through self-report and many consults with various medical staff members and his previous social worker at the agency. The guiding framework for my interventions has been driven by a person-centered approach. I let him set the pace for working toward the goals in his ISP, while ensuring his medical and personal needs were met. I also utilized the strengths perspective by asking Marcos where he usually finds food and how he was able to secure temporary housing at a nearby shelter. My first impression of the client has changed as we addressed diverse situations and his strengths and resourcefulness were evident. For example, Marcos was able to find a community service opportunity on his own as part of his probation, which was due to having committed a minor offense. Marcos was also able to secure housing and have his basic needs met while being homeless for about a year. Moreover, I learned from him how he sees the world and what culture he identifies with. This knowledge aided me in utilizing systems theory to better understand how his previous experiences shaped his worldviews and how he typically interacts with the community and the system. I also utilized referrals and advocacy skills to help Marcos obtain adequate medical services and housing. Marcos and I were able to eventually stabilize his housing situation. He then became more adherent to medication and primary care appointments, and he is now compliant with hospital policy regarding his eligibility documents. Marcos and I are still working toward new goals on his Individualized Service Plan. Undoubtedly, I will continue utilizing his strengths by working collaboratively with him and the medical staff.

❖

REFERENCES

Fulton County. (2011). Ryan White Program. Retrieved from http://www.fultoncountyga.gov/ryan-white-home

Georgia Department of Public Health. (n.d.). The Georgia AIDS Assistance Program. Retrieved from http://dph.georgia.gov/adap-program

Hallfors, D. D., Iritani, D. B., Miller, W. C., & Bauer, D. J. (2007). Sexual and drug behavior patterns and HIV and STD racial disparities: The need for new directions. *American Journal of Public Health, 97*(1), 125–132. doi: 10.2105/AJPH.2005.075747

Substance Abuse and Mental Health Services Administration. (n.d.-a). Motivational interviewing. Retrieved from http://www.integration.samhsa.gov/clinical-practice/motivational-interviewing

Substance Abuse and Mental Health Services Administration. (n.d.-b). SBIRT: Screening, Brief Intervention, and Referral to Treatment. Retrieved from http://www.integration.samhsa.gov/clinical-practice/sbirt

What is a cd4 count and why is it important? (2015). Retrieved from https://www.aids.gov/hiv-aids-basics/just-diagnosed-with-hiv-aids/understand-your-test-results/cd4-count/

❖

ANCILLARIES

Internet References for Additional Reading

1. AIDS.gov. Retrieved from http://www.aids.gov/federal-resources/policies/care-continuum/

2. Centers for Disease Control and Prevention (CDC). Retrieved from http://www.cdc.gov/hiv/

3. Georgia Department of Community Health. Retrieved from https://dch.georgia.gov/medicaid

4. infoSIDA. Retrieved from http://infosida.nih.gov/

5. Substance Abuse and Mental Health Services Administration (SAMHSA). Retrieved from http://www.samhsa.gov/

Hard Copy References for Additional Reading

Mericle, A. A., Martin, C., Carise, D., & Love, M. (2012). Identifying need for mental health services in substance abuse clients. *Journal of Dual Diagnosis, 8*(3), 218–228. doi:10.1080/15504263.2012.696182

O'Neal, G. S. (2012). Self-assessment and dialogue as tools for appreciating diversity. *Journal of Social Work Education, 48*(1), 159–166.

Simoni, J. M., Huh, D., Wilson, I. B., Shen, J., Goggin, K., Reynolds, N. R., . . . Liu, H. (2012). Racial/ethnic disparities in ART adherence in the United States: Findings from the MACH14 Study. *J Acquir Immune Defic Syndr, 60*(5), 446–472.

Sun, A. (2012). Helping homeless individuals with co-occurring disorders: The four components. *Social Work, 57*(1), 23–37. doi:10.1093/sw/swr008

Turan, R., & Yargic, I. (2012). The relationship between substance abuse treatment completion, sociodemographics, substance use characteristics, and criminal history. *Substance Abuse, 33*(2), 92–98. doi:10.1080/08897077.2011.630948

❖ JOB DESCRIPTION

Job Title—Medical Case Manager

Job Summary

The Medical Case Manager (CM) works with members to remove barriers to HIV/AIDS medical care by facilitating a collaborative process that identifies members' needs, a plan to address those needs, and continuous follow-up to ensure that members obtain the necessary services that help them to maintain adherence to medical care. The CM also coordinates with other service providers through a comprehensive and active referral process to link HIV+ individuals into appropriate services and care.

Essential Duties and Responsibilities

- Provide direct service coordination and support to people living with HIV/AIDS.
- Provide CMG services to members on a walk-in, scheduled, and on-call basis.
- Manage a caseload of up to 75 members.
- Conduct initial comprehensive assessment and intake for eligible members.
- Collaboratively develop and implement Individualized Service Plan (ISP) for each member on caseload, including conducting ISP updates every 6 months for each member.
- Assess and evaluate member's initial needs through the EMA screening tool.
- Educate members about CMG and policies (Grievance, HIPPA, Member's Rights and Responsibilities) and other agency program policies to ensure member has clear expectations of services.
- Provide regular monthly (or more) contact with members to follow up on treatment plan goals and provide intervention as needed.
- Advocate and mediate on member's behalf to decrease or eliminate barriers to care.

- Educate members about the importance of participating in medical care and ensure that members have full access to primary medical care.
- Assess and Educate members about the importance of medication and medical adherence to improve member's clinical outcomes.
- Assess and educate members about harm reduction, prevention, and other HIV related sexually transmitted infections (STIs).
- Conduct home and hospital visits, accompanying members to appointments as needed.
- Assess, verify, and maintain records of a member's eligibility for CMG and various entitlement programs.
- Document all interactions with or on behalf of a member within 48 hours.
- Assess, collect, and maintain accurate member information and records in a confidential manner.
- Complete monthly reporting to ensure accurate programmatic reporting (based on position/site assigned).
- Provide active referrals and application assistance and support to members.
- Educate members about various community resources and programs to increase their knowledge of appropriate referrals.
- Collaborate with physicians, nurses, and other clinical staff in the development and execution of member's plan of care.
- Attend monthly interdisciplinary meetings with medical providers (based on-site).
- Maintain up-to-date resources of community services.
- Participate in and volunteer for intra- and interdepartmental activities/events across the agency.

(Continued)

(Continued)

- Communicate regularly with staff about changes, updates, and improvements in service delivery issues or other agency related issues that directly or indirectly impact staff and/or members.
- Attend agency, local, state, and national meetings, conferences, or workshops as needed or required.
- Adhere to policies and procedures for ASO and other off-site programs to ensure quality standards are met.
- Abide by NASW code of ethics, HIPPA, and Atlanta EMA CMG Standards to ensure a high level of professionalism is maintained.
- Address member's concerns utilizing the Customer Service Standards.
- Perform routine self-audits and maintain charts to ensure members information and eligibility documents are current.
- Meet with supervisor at least on a monthly basis to staff member cases, discuss chart audits/observation results, and to discuss performance and progress of stated goals.
- Attend all required internal and external (for off-sites) meetings.
- Participate in various trainings held internally and externally ensuring a continuous knowledge base of programs that benefit members.

Competencies

- Embraces and displays the agency's core values of compassion, leadership, equality, and empowerment
- Culturally competent and able to work effectively with diverse populations
- Possesses exceptional customer service and interpersonal skills with staff, colleagues, members, and community partners
- Able to be a team player who can work effectively independently and also within a team with co-workers, other community care providers, speakers, etc.
- Self-motivated, innovative, and creative

- Possesses excellent organizational and planning skills
- Able to prioritize scheduled and unscheduled tasks
- Has a basic knowledge about HIV/AIDS
- Able to maintain confidentiality of health and other information
- Able to multitask/manage/de-escalate multiple crises
- Possesses excellent problem solving skills
- Empathetic, caring, and patient
- Detail oriented
- Basic knowledge of harm reductionist principles and approach in providing services
- Able to effectively resolve conflict and cope with crisis situations
- Is goal and task oriented
- Has effective written and verbal communication skills
- Has excellent assessment and active listening skills
- Displays leadership ability/skills
- Able to motivate and inspire members
- Willing to improve on a continuous basis
- Able to be flexible, dependable, and resourceful
- Possesses a positive and caring attitude
- Open and responsive to coaching/feedback from others and other self-development and improvement opportunities
- Proficient in using Microsoft Windows and Microsoft Office Applications, including Excel and Word; Proficiency with Internet
- Proficient in the use and/or experience with client record database systems
- Ability to operate standard office equipment including computers, fax machines, copiers, printers, telephones
- Able to travel to meetings offsite, home/hospital visits, etc., as required for the job
- Able to pass criminal background review

the knowledge to evaluate the role that developmental disabilities play in the lives of so many children. As a professional, I now feel a calling to educate the wider social work community about signs, symptoms, and services related to ASD.

Working with this population has been quite a personal journey as well. The parents I get to know, and learn from on a daily basis, teach me what it means to love your child and to boldly face what you are given in life with courage, grace, and love. I know how draining and trying things can be for our clients. I also get to witness families celebrate victories—no matter how small—and find the strength within themselves to keep on going. I once had a mother tell me how much it bothered her when people said "I don't know how you do this," as if she had a choice. She just does it. They all "just do it," every single day.

As a parent of a young child myself, doing this work also compels me to wonder about the impact of parenting a child with autism. Many of the professionals I work with also have small children and think about this as well. When my daughter is talkative, social, engaged, and affectionate, I think about what it would be like if she wasn't. When I ask her what's wrong and she can tell me, I think about what it would be like if she couldn't vocalize anything. I try not to take any of this for granted. I find myself acutely aware of how it might impact someone if I were to boast about all the things my daughter can do as she grows and develops. So, I brag less and I appreciate more. I also know in my heart that if she wasn't developing the way she is "supposed to," it would still be ok, and I would love her just as much, and we would make it together. Every day. I might not know what it's like to have a child with autism, but I know that helping families who do this every day is a humbling, inspiring, and life-changing experience. I am filled with gratitude for how, every day, my clients help to make me a better professional and parent as well.

Case Example

Bobby first came to MAC when he was 6 years old. He and his mother lived in a rural area in South Georgia, almost a 5-hour drive to Atlanta. Bobby's father had had no contact with them for many years, and they were socially isolated due to Bobby's problem behavior. They couldn't attend church anymore, or participate in the local events and gatherings they had enjoyed before.

Bobby was non-verbal and used hand signs he and his mother had created to communicate his needs to others. Bobby had recently begun to display severe self-destructive behaviors. His mother hadn't been able to work for the last 6 months because she had to leave work so often to pick Bobby up from school due to his increasingly disruptive behaviors. He had begun to hit his head against walls and doors, and he repeatedly ran away from school. He would run away whenever he was outside, usually in the direction of water or a playground. At home, his mother couldn't take her eyes off of him. She was constantly trying to prevent him from hurting himself, and his head banging had caused him to have a lot of bruising and swelling on his head and face.

The family lacked insurance coverage for services for autistic children, and Bobby's mother was beginning to feel more and more desperate for help. She battled depression and a growing sense of hopelessness that things would ever get better. One day, when Bobby was acting out in the local grocery, a woman approached her and asked her if she'd heard of MAC, and she reached out to us feeling like it was her last resort.

As her care coordinator, I worked with her for months to help find the financial resources she needed to access our program. We looked at local lodging options and finally found an extended stay hotel, where she felt they could be comfortable. Given that it was outside of her budget, I helped her apply for grants and worked with Medicaid to get reimbursement for their lodging.

Bobby finally came to Atlanta and began to participate in our 12-week intensive day treatment program. His mom was alone here in Atlanta, didn't know anyone, and felt very isolated and overwhelmed. I met with her on an ongoing basis, providing emotional support and a listening ear. She also participated in a parent support group I had started, learning for the first time ever that she was not alone. She learned that there are other parents in her same situation with children who also showed such intense behaviors. She found it to be very healing to get peer support and eventually made friends she will keep for a lifetime.

As the team developed a treatment plan to help Bobby stop the head banging and running away, it became clear that it would be very difficult for her to maintain the level of specific treatment intervention strategies recommended at home. As we trained her on what she would need to do at home, she became overwhelmed thinking about how she was going to manage Bobby on her own.

I provided encouragement and emotional support, and together we developed strategies to help her utilize the limited supports that were available at home. We then located respite programs in her community where she could find someone to watch Bobby for a few hours a week, so she could get a break and take better care of herself. We explored different things she could do to take care of herself while Bobby was in school. She was always so preoccupied with how he was behaving in school, that she could never relax. We referred her to a therapist in her local community, as well as a parent support group and a school advocate familiar with children struggling with ASD. With this help, she learned how to advocate for Bobby at school, to make sure he was getting the services he was entitled to, instead of calling her to come pick him up when an intervention plan was already in place at the school to manage his behavior. The school personnel participated in a specialized training program at MAC as well, so they would be better equipped to support Bobby.

After discharge, Bobby and his mom returned home and participated in after-care services. Slowly we stopped hearing from them as Bobby's behavior improved. Bobby's mom had become active in her community again. She was able to find a rewarding job. She re-kindled old friendships and developed a supportive social network of her own and even got married!

Many months later, she called me to say that Bobby was banging his head again and had developed new behaviors that were disruptive and frightening. Given the demands on parents to maintain the treatment interventions recommended by MAC, sometimes they return to old familiar ways of parenting and need help bringing the home intervention strategies back to the levels required to successfully manage their child's behavior. She was able to come back to MAC for some intensive follow-up sessions to maintain the progress they had made. Sometimes she calls me when she needs support, and I often wonder how they are doing. I believe sees us as a kind of extended family that will always be there to provide guidance and a healing relationship connection that helps her through the hardest of times.

❖

REFERENCES

Dababnah, S., Parish, S. L., Brown, L. T., & Hooper, S. R. (2011). Early screening for autism spectrum disorders: A primer for social work practice. *Children and Youth Services Review, 33*(2), 265–273.

Hepworth, D. H., Rooney, R. H., Rooney, G. D., Strom-Gottfried, K., & Larsen, J. A. (2006). *Direct social work practice: Theory and skills* (7th ed.). Belmont, CA: Thomson Brooks/Cole.

Kohut, H. (1977). *The restoration of the self.* New York, NY: International Universities Press.

Mount, N., & Dillon, D. (2014). Parents' experiences of living with an adolescent diagnosed with an autism spectrum disorder. *Educational & Child Psychology, 31*(4), 72–81.

Rogers, C. (1951). *Client-centered therapy: Its current practice, implications and theory.* London, UK: Constable.

Skinner, J. (2014). Social work practice and personal self-care. In K. Corcoran & A. R. Roberts, *Social workers' desk reference* (3rd ed.; pp 130–143). New York, NY: Oxford University Press.

Winnicott, D. (1965). *Maturational processes and the facilitating environment: Studies in the theory of emotional development.* London, UK: Hogarth Press.

❖

ANCILLARIES

Autism. (2015). Retrieved October 12, 2015, from http://www.minddisorders.com/A-Br/Autism.html

Autism Ontario. (2015). Retrieved October 12, 2015, from http://www.autismontario.com/

Autism Speaks. (2015). Retrieved October 12, 2015, from https://www.autismspeaks.org

Autism Spectrum Counseling Center. (2015). Retrieved October 12, 2015, from http://autism-spectrumcenter.com/

Autism Spectrum Disorder. (2014, June 3). Retrieved November 8, 2015, from http://www.mayoclinic.org/diseases-conditions/autism-spectrum-disorder/basics/causes/con-20021148

Data & statistics. (2015, August 12). Retrieved October 12, 2015, from http://www.cdc.gov/ncbddd/autism/data.html

First Path Autism. (2015). Retrieved October 12, 2015, from http://www.firstpathautism.com/

A history of autism. (2015). Retrieved October 12, 2015, from http://www.webmd.com/brain/autism/history-of-autism

Marcus. (2015). Retrieved October 12, 2015, from http://www.marcus.org/

❖ JOB DESCRIPTION

Case Coordinator

1. Assists patients and their families in coping with illness, treatment, and hospitalization based on principles of growth and development

2. Assists families and health care team in making plans for discharge related to psychosocial needs

3. Assess, diagnose, plan, and implement care for the pediatrics patient working collaboratively with the community and health care professionals to develop an interdisciplinary approach to care

4. Responsible for maintaining relationships with community clinicians and pediatric psychiatric hospitals for referral and follow up

5. Responsible for creating and maintaining a resource database for referral and follow up care related to the psychiatric needs of the patient

6. Provides information and clarification regarding child protection, custody, and safety issues

7. Documents and maintains updated patient information pertaining to services provided

8. Assists with teaching and provides supervision of MSW students, or assumes special project and/or program planning assignments

Minimum Qualifications

- Master's degree in social work from an accredited graduate school required

- Previous work experience in a medical setting and/or work with children and families is preferred

- Previous work experience in a mental health/psychiatric setting with children and families preferred

- Minimum 4–5 years of post-graduate social work experience

- Must have excellent assessment and evaluation skills

- Must have excellent written and oral communication skills

- Licensed as a Clinical Social Worker (LCSW) either in the State of Georgia or in another state. Candidates holding an out-of-state clinical social work license must be eligible and obtain their Georgia LCSW within the first 90 days of employment

- Must be able to successfully pass the Basic Windows Skill Assessment at 80% or higher rating within 30 days of date of hire

15

Youth At-Risk of Socio-Economic Exclusion, Information and Communication Technology (ICT), and Case Management Practice in Hong Kong

Chitat Chan and Stanley C.Y. Ho

The Clientele

Youth at-risk of socio-economic exclusion are the clientele for this chapter. This umbrella term covers a range of closely related risk scenarios such as "non-engaged," "socially withdrawn," "working poor," "NEET" (*Not* in *Education, Employment, or Training*), "marginalized," and "hidden" (*Hikikomori*) (BGCA, Caritas, & HKFYG, 2015;

Centeno, Cullen, Kluzer, & Hache, 2012). There are also many unique issues associated with these risk scenarios, such as mental health and substance abuse (Ngai, Cheung, To, Liu, & Song, 2013). This umbrella term refers more to the common risk "factors," more so than the often diverse "scenarios" (Centeno et al., 2012; Haché et al., 2010). That is, these clients apparently present different and unique problems, but they are considered as having common underlying risk factors—weakening their various connections with socio-economic institutions, such as families, education, and employment. This unique cohort has drawn attention from governments across the globe, and there are increasingly more initiatives being offered for this group of young people, for example, pre-employment training and continuing education programs (Bynner & Parsons, 2002).

Nonetheless, all over the world, various economic structures and employment environments have changed rapidly. This results in any well-designed and large-scale programs or initiatives easily becoming quickly outdated. For example, the Hong Kong government has implemented various large initiatives to provide pre-employment training programs for young people, but many have continuously received public criticism, perceiving they have stigmatized young job seekers, are disconnected with reality, and that they cannot really help young people obtain jobs (Ngai & Ngai, 2007). To date, many of these programs have been combined and re-tooled to fit the changing local market trends, but service users and social workers generally still perceive that such government initiatives fail to catch up with the local market reality. Similarly, youth services in Hong Kong have themselves been re-structured and re-integrated several times in the last two decades, but practitioners and service users generally perceive that these community-based centralized services are constrained by their geography and office hours, and they cannot effectively address the needs of various hard-to-reach clients and unique populations (Cheung & CYRP, 2011; Lee, 2003).

Under these circumstances, some youth work practitioners contend that proper use of information and communication technology (ICT) may help better serve this cohort in our rapidly changing economies. There are some common reasons for this. First, practitioners gradually see that managing discrete quality information is much easier (or less risky) than investing in a large-scale service program. Second, compared to many other vulnerable client groups, it has been shown that young people at-risk of socio-economic exclusion are more willing to express themselves and seek help online (Clarke, Kuosmanen, & Barry, 2015). This is partly because, most of the time, they are living at home, and the Internet has provided them with a relatively safe environment allowing them to experience or experiment with various social relationships. Third, studies have revealed that they are likely to encounter more "risks" when online, and ICT-enhanced initiatives are deemed more suitable for engaging them (Cullen, Cullen, Hamilton, & Maes, 2011). Fourth, ICT can provide a range of online resources to construct their identities, such as nicknames, avatars, profiles, photos, videos, and codes (Subrahmanyam & Smahel, 2011). Finally, ICT can help connect them to various offline and/or online contexts to experiment with alternative identities, such as online job searches, and participating in interactive activities online/offline (Cullen, Cullen, & Hamilton, 2011).

There are increasingly more social services programs that have operated solely on online modes. For example, Youth Online (www.youth-online.com) has operated since 2000. "CryOut," a charity group that does not have an official website, has proactively outreached "hidden" (non-engaged) youth via multiplayer online game platforms since 2007 (CryOut, 2013). More recently, the Social Welfare Department (SWD) of the Hong Kong government also have started funding some pilot online youth work projects since 2011 (BGCA et al., 2015; SWD, 2011).

These ICT-oriented youth work units adopt a form of case management (CMG) practice that focuses more so on resource management than resource development. Practitioners in these units usually do not focus on developing a mega service center or a larger scale program, but they see themselves as a hub to liaise and coordinate tools and services that fit their clients. CMG practice presented herein is used in the Boys' & Girls' Clubs Association of Hong Kong (BGCA) with the Nite Cat Online Pilot Cyber Youth Outreaching Project (http://nitecat.bgca.org.hk/), which is a pilot project supported by the Hong Kong government targeting youth at-risk of socio-economic exclusion. This program served young Internet users aged under 24. Started in 2011, the project provided direct service from 3pm to 3am, 4 days a week.

Practice Roles and Responsibilities

The Nite Cat Online (NCO) hired an office venue in a commercial building, and the project was never designed for drop-ins. NCO had all full-time practitioners trained in social work or counseling. All cases were initially engaged online from different districts in Hong Kong. Their current CMG practice has two basic dimensions—enabling and facilitating (Moore, 1990). That is, CMG practitioners focus on both enabling individuals to better reach their potential and/or on facilitating more effective interaction with social systems. In addition, practitioners use ICT to enhance CMG in almost all activities (i.e., to engage, assess, intervene, and evaluate) at various levels (i.e., micro, meso, macro). These roles and responsibilities will be described.

Engage. NCO engages cases from different geographic districts in Hong Kong, via social media and the project's official website. We emphasize the notion that practitioners need to know the right place to engage the right type of client and to use the right ICT tool for the right task. This is comparable to practice wisdom in conventional outreach services regarding where to locate particular types of physical venues to engage particular types of clients—and meet the client "where they are at." For example, some NCO users might look for answers to particular problems, so they post their threads on a particular online forum, but not just any forum.

NCO clients become normally engaged via social media. Typical methods used here include searching, browsing, and using simple games and applications to engage potential clients. We have developed Facebook applications providing tools like personality tests and simple online games, so that practitioners can attract potential users. Second, clients can also be engaged via the project's official website. The "Nite Cat Club" Online Service Platform plays an important role for early identification and intervention for potential service users. The design of the website is simple, field-tested, and user-friendly, and it can be searched via search engines, Facebook, or forum. Moreover, the project uses a specially designed chat room, the Nite Cat VIP Room, to serve users' enquiries. This chat room has an instant messaging service, and user privacy is fully protected. There are more than 50,000 visitors who browsed the platform, and $N = 1,574$ were served via this chat room in the last 4 years.

Assess. The project assessed cases using select user-friendly online tools and/or some validated instruments. The message underpinning this role is that CMG practitioners need to know where to access these tools, how to use them, and which tools are used for what purposes. There are various validated online assessment tools which can be used for free. For example, many Hong Kong practitioners have used the Authentic Happiness website developed by the Positive Psychology Center at the University of Pennsylvania (www.authentichappiness.sas.upenn.edu/home). The website allows users to take a range of validated tests free of charge, including such as General Happiness Scale, CES-D Questionnaire, Fordyce Emotions Questionnaire, Brief Strengths Test, and the Work-Life Questionnaire.

There are also online tools funded by the local Hong Kong government. For example, to provide appropriate and personalized career orientation and employment support, practitioners can use Standard Career Assessment Tool (SCAT) provided by the government at www.yes.labour.gov.hk/ypyt/en/tby_assessment_tool.htm. This instrument helps practitioners understand the potential and abilities of trainees with career interests, personality, emotional intelligence, career maturity, and one's potential to start a new business. These assessment results help understand the local employment needs of trainees, allowing case managers (CMs) to formulate or modify training and career plans that suit the needs of trainees. In addition, practitioners may also use the Academic Programme Preference Inventory (APPI; http://student.hk/appraisal/appi/) that was funded by the Education and Manpower Bureau of Hong Kong, and the inventory was developed by the Open University of Hong Kong (OUHK) and the Hok Yau Club.

Intervene. NCO intervention focuses on enabling individuals to better reach their potential and on facilitating more effective interactions with various social systems. After practitioners engage participants online, they assess their needs and suggest a variety of online, and/or offline services, such as counseling, trainings, social activities, and job referrals. Practitioners are required to know these community resources, have connections with these resource providers, and provide consultations and/or recommend a suitable time for various communication modalities.

In order to enable individuals to better solve their own problems and/or reach their potential, practitioners may need to provide additional counseling services. Many hard-to-reach clienteles may benefit from such online counseling. In the NCO project, some online tools have been developed to facilitate this process. Sometimes users may not feel they are able to discuss sensitive issues via Facebook chat or WhatsApp, so practitioners may invite them to chat via the secured online platform called the "VIP Room," in which service users' privacy is protected. The system was originally an online customer service system named Actual Live. NCO CMG practitioners employed technical experts to modify and package it as an online reception and counseling tool. In addition, many existing peripheral online activities, such as sharing posts, tagging, putting on a "like" serve as significant strategic functions in the keeping in touch with our clients. These online communication forums enable CMs to earn the trust of their clients and subsequently develop more meaningful and ongoing conversations.

Conversely, it is equally important to facilitate more effective interactions with local social systems at various levels. In NCO, there are various collaborative initiatives which serve this purpose. For example, in "Nitecat Radio" (www.nitecatradio .org.hk), CMs, workers, volunteers, and youth clients may collaborate to produce their own online radio programs. There is a radio webcast one day a week, having several program sessions, focusing on different aspects of quality of life, value reflections, civic participation, etc. In "Checker Depot Hub" (http://nitecat.bgca .org.hk), youth can share their ideas and creative works of art, such as short stories, photography, songs, show clips, or other entity crafts and photos. There are also initiatives linking with local programs run by the government, such as on-the-job training and employment opportunities provided by the Youth Employment and Training Program (YETP; www.yes.labour.gov.hk). YETP is a platform for job searching with one-stop and diversified pre-employment and on-the-job training, for young school drop-outs aged 15 to 24 having educational attainment at sub-degree or below level.

Evaluate. Finally, different client cases have their own paces and evaluation criteria, and they are partly evaluated by using some user-friendly online tools and/or some validated instruments. We contend that practitioners need to know some basic evaluation designs, such as a pre-test/post-test design facilitated by online questionnaire systems, and how to conduct these processes (Holosko, 2006). For example, Google Forms (www.google.com/forms/about/) is a free application we use at NCO allowing practitioners to send a questionnaire to anyone with an e-mail address, embed it on a web page, or link the survey via URL. Our practitioners can also use Google Spreadsheets (www.google.com/sheets/about/), another free online tool, to analyze the survey results from Google Forms in real time using features that are similar to Microsoft Excel, and they can also export these results to other software such as SPSS. Questionnaires can support many different types of evaluation designs in social work evaluation studies (Thyer, Artelt, & Shek, 2003), and this type of free online tool can efficiently and economically enable the evaluation.

In addition, some online platforms can help advance evaluation studies by enabling practitioners to recruit participants to control groups. For example, social work researchers suggested that Amazon's MTurk (www.mturk.com/mturk), an online crowdsourcing platform, can be used to develop comparison groups in experimental designs, and therefore increase the likelihood of generalizing evaluation findings and offset the ethical issue about using clients to serve in control groups in health and human service settings (Chan & Holosko, 2015).

Role Development Potential

Educationally speaking, we can make further progress in ICT-enhanced CMG practice only if we can have significant changes to overall social work training and pedagogy that supports both CM and ICT. Hence, we offer the following suggestions.

First, social work educational programs may need to better integrate CMG into the social work curricula overall. In Hong Kong, agency-based trainings tend to focus on operational details, and social work programs at universities tend to focus more on intervention theories and/or therapies. That is, by and large, the conceptual framework of CMG does not really occupy a place in our current local social work curricula. Our experience in CMG illustrates the equal importance both of conceptual models and more practical and ICT knowledge about relevant resources and opportunities related to various clienteles. Studies have long pointed out that CMG systems in general should address different levels of social work practice, and various levels of personnel can be integrated into more effective service structures (Moore, 1990; O'Connor, 1988). Positing CMG into new forms of "theory and practice" modules may help highlight any linkages between the conceptual and practical components in CMG.

Second, all social work curricula may need to involve more frontline CMG practitioners to share their knowledge about community resources and opportunities for better serving unique clienteles. One of the challenges of learning CMG is that it is not a set of principles that can be learned in micro-skill labs only, but it is carried out within the context of a community and macro-organizational structure (Moore, 1990). Current university faculty members may not have such firsthand knowledge. This can be done by inviting CMG frontline workers to be guest speakers, assisting CMG frontline workers to publish their cases, and assist CMG frontline workers to evaluate and report on their practices.

Third, social work curricula and training programs may need to teach more technology-oriented skillsets related to outreaching, referrals, assessments, interventions, networking, and/or marketing. We have observed (in our ICT outreach) that individual CM workers tended to render services and utilize technologies based on their own knowledge and preferences rather than a comprehensive assessment of the available technologies. Our own traditional "social welfare-based" institutional constraints might have limited our engagement methods, assessment, and interventions, as well as evaluation. For example, we mainly assessed the needs of our service users using a remedial mindset, and we prefer using social services rather than business solutions, and we may not involve enough stakeholders from different sectors to participate in our interventions and evaluations. This implies a need for CMG practitioners to establish a stronger cross-sector and interdisciplinary collaboration, requiring extensive partnerships with other stakeholders, business firms, and vocational training bodies.

Fourth, social work curricula and training institutes may need to eventually develop repositories to archive and showcase ICTs related to CMG. We have observed that many CMs do not really have any idea about the range of possible ICTs they can use. Their current technology use is more of an adopted convention rather than a rational choice. Eventually CMG practitioners tend to stay at a micro level, while interventions at meso and macro levels are not commonly implemented or supported by ICT. Extant literature is concerned more with ICT use in CMG "administration system" (Coursen, 2006; Coursen & Ferns, 2004; Weaver, Moses, Furman, & Lindsey, 2003) than "direct practice." There is room to further develop ICT applications at meso-level and macro-level interventions. For example, "crowdsourcing" is about presenting an idea to a crowd of donors and then pooling funds to actualize that idea (Callaghan, 2014). Some advocates have suggested using crowdsourcing/crowd funding to solicit humanitarian responses for help or assistances (Chan & Holosko, 2015). Some crowdsourcing platforms such as Kickstarter (www.kickstarter.com) or IndieGoGo (www.indiegogo.com) are particularly designed to help pool funds from people to create new products or projects. There are even NGOs that operate solely on a crowd-funding model. For example, Benevolent (www.benevolent.net) in Chicago supports people to face their life challenges. Such ICT repositories can help students and practitioners broaden their options and consider further technology adaptation and/or development.

Fifth, social work curricula should consider allocating more educational research grants to develop instruments to assess and develop ICT literacy among social work students and practitioners. As ICTs have become more diversified and prolific, social workers may be required to differentiate, evaluate, and harness social media more effectively. Social workers may need a conceptual road map supporting them to assess the performance of social media tools regarding the practice tasks they need to do. Currently, such an ICT literacy framework is neither addressed by current accreditation bodies nor the textbooks (Berzin, Singer, & Chan, 2015), and therefore, there is much room for further research and development.

Concluding Remarks

Many training programs for youth at-risk of socio-economic exclusion are bundled with specific program content and staffing protocols. Many training packages have standardized operational procedures, which orient CMs and/or social workers to function more as operators rather than practitioners making professional judgments. However, the economic structures and employment environments we work in keep changing, making any well-structured large-scale training programs difficult to catch up with the local market. Similarly, technologies also change quickly, and some popular online platforms used just a few years ago by NCO are no longer popular right now. The tension between more rigid program content and the fast changing environment raise questions about overall service efficiency, as well as issues about de-professionalization of some of workers.

The ICT-oriented CMG practice presented here is focused more on practitioner-level skillsets than agency-based operation protocols. Instead of relying on an all-inclusive service program or a powerful technical platform, our social work CMs hold a community conceptual road map supporting them to identify, adapt, and develop technologies/resources relevant to their ICT practice processes

❖ Table 15.1 **Case Management (CMG) Practice and Information and Communication Technology (ICT)**

Practice Processes	Practitioners' Skillsets	Examples of Related ICT Tools
1. Engage	Know the right place to engage the right type of client, and use the right tool for the right task.	Develop Facebook gadget to facilitate engagement: https://developers.facebook.com/
2. Assess	Know where to access these tools, how to use them, and which tools are for what purposes.	Validated tests and analysis provided by the University of Pennsylvania: www.authentichappiness.sas.upenn.edu/home
3. Intervene	Know these resources, have connections with these resource providers, and provide consultations and/or recommends at suitable time in various communication modalities.	Youth Employment and Training Program HK government: www.yes.labour.gov.hk/
4. Evaluate	Know some basic evaluation designs, such as a pre-test/post-test design facilitated by online questionnaire systems, and how to conduct these processes.	Google Forms and Spreadsheets: www.google.com/forms/about/

(see Table 15.1). This may assist CMG practitioners choose the right ICT tool for the right task and expand further resources and possibilities. Yet, this kind of ICT-oriented CMG practice is in infancy, and further research, discussion, and consolidation would be required.

Case Example

These two individual cases were selected here as they have some common characteristics that help explain the uniqueness of ICT-oriented CMG. First, the achievements of these clients were the results of quality information/connection rather than a quality pre-employment training program. Second, these clients were initially engaged online, rather than via physical job referral centers. Third, ICT was used in supporting them to further experiment their interests and identities.

Tommy met NCO 3 years ago. He loved to play a mobile game named "Tower of Saviors." When he found an activity offered by Nitecat and Tower of Saviors, he was attracted by the prize "magic stone." He joined the activity and met our worker. He was told that he can join many other programs like outdoor activities, volunteer services, art workshops, and disc jockey (DJ) training. This reminded him of his dream of being a DJ. He shared this idea with the NCO CMG practitioner. The CM assessed that he was not deemed to be in any high-risk category. After the CMG practitioner found out that he was interested in DJ work, he further invited him to hold webcast programs, and recommended him to an official training program run by the RTHK—the official radio channel supported by the Hong Kong government. Having this positive experience helped Tommy find his career path. Today, he is employed as a part-time DJ in a famous online broadcast channel in Hong Kong.

Bobby was an introverted and emotional high school student. The CMG practitioner discovered his blog at NCO and noted that he had some emotional problems and potential self-harming behaviors. The CM approached Bobby and successfully engaged him to receive direct counseling services. After an initial assessment, he was referred to the local Integrated Community Centre for Mental Wellness. He possessed a passion, talent, and interest in visual arts, therefore the CM further invited him to join the Checker Depot Hub and relevant programs. Bobby mentioned that counseling might not be a suitable service (for him), and he found out that he could be more relaxed and peaceful when he worked with creative artworks in a supportive environment. He then actively uploaded his numerous creative endeavors to the Checker Depot Hub, which immediately gained much appreciation from visitors. Afterward, the CM further invited him to participate in coordinating local art exhibitions, which he did. After a time, he showed some very noticeable positive personal changes. Currently, Bobby is an art tutor in a rehab service center in Hong Kong.

❖

REFERENCES

Berzin, S. C., Singer, J., & Chan, C. (2015). Practice innovation through technology in the digital age: A grand challenge for social work (Grand Challenges for Social Work Initiative Working Paper No. 12). Cleveland, OH: American Academy of Social Work and Social Welfare.

BGCA, Caritas, & HKFYG. (2015). A joint proposal for cyber youth outreach—a project on ICT-enhanced initiatives for youth at risk of social exclusion (internal document). Hong Kong: Author.

Bynner, J., & Parsons, S. (2002). Social exclusion and the transition from school to work: The case of young people not in education, employment, or training (NEET). *Journal of Vocational Behavior, 60,* 289–309.

Callaghan, C. W. (2014). Crowdfunding to generate crowdsourced R&D: The alternative paradigm of societal problem solving offered by second generation innovation and R&D. *International Business & Economics Research Journal (IBER), 13,* 1499–1514.

Centeno, C., Cullen, J., Kluzer, S., & Hache, A. (2012). *Information and communication technologies (ICTs) for disadvantaged youth: Opportunities and challenges (policy report).* Retrieved from http://is.jrc.ec.europa.eu/pages/EAP/eInclusion/youth.html

Chan, C., & Holosko, M. J. (2015). An overview of the use of Mechanical Turk in behavioral sciences: Implications for social work. *Research on Social Work Practice.* doi:10.1177/1049731515594024

Cheung, K. C., & CYRP. (2011). *An evaluation report of Integrated Children and Youth Services Centers (ICYSCs)* [In Chinese]. Retrieved from http://www.cheungkwokche.hk/sites/default/files/20101120_ICYSC_ReportSummar.pdf

Clarke, A. M., Kuosmanen, T., & Barry, M. M. (2015). A systematic review of online youth mental health promotion and prevention interventions. *Journal of Youth and Adolescence, 44,* 90–113.

Coursen, D. (2006). An ecosystems approach to human service database design. *Journal of Technology in Human Services, 24,* 1–18.

Coursen, D., & Ferns, B. (2004). Modeling participant flows in human service programs. *Journal of Technology in Human Services, 22,* 55–71.

CryOut. (2013). *CryOut–Youth service practice guideline* [In Chinese]. Hong Kong: CryOut.

Cullen, J., Cullen, C., & Hamilton, E. (2011). *Mapping and assessing the impact of ICT-based initiatives for the socio-economic inclusion of youth at risk of exclusion: Impact assessment of ICT-based initiatives.* London, UK: The Tavistock Institute.

Cullen, J., Cullen, C., Hamilton, E., & Maes, V. (2011). Conceptual Overview on youth at risk and ICT. In A. Teoksessa Haché, E. Sanz, & C. Centeno, *Mapping and assessing the impact of ICT-based initiatives for the socio-economic inclusion of young people at risk of exclusion.* London, UK: The Tavistock Institute.

Haché, A., Dekelver, J., Montandon, L., Playfoot, J., Aagaard, M., & Elmer, S. S. (2010). *Research and policy brief on ICT for the inclusion of youth at risk: Using ICT to reengage and foster socio-economic inclusion of youth at risk of social exclusion, marginalized young people and intermediaries working with them.* Retrieved from http://ipts.jrc.ec.europa.eu/publications/pub.cfm?id=3799

Holosko, M. (2006). *Primer for critiquing social research.* Belmont, CA: Brooks Cole.

Lee, F. W. L. (2003). Integrated team model for children and youth services: Yes or no? *Hong Kong Journal of Social Work, 37,* 125–137.

Moore, S. T. (1990). A social work practice model of case management: The case management grid. *Social Work, 35,* 444.

Ngai, S. S. Y., Cheung, C. K., To, S. M., Liu, Y., & Song, H. Y. (2013). Parent–child relationships, friendship networks, and developmental outcomes of economically disadvantaged youth in Hong Kong. *Children and Youth Services Review, 35,* 91–101.

Ngai, S. S. Y., & Ngai, N. P. (2007). Empowerment or disempowerment? A review of youth training schemes for non-engaged young people in Hong Kong. *Adolescence, 42,* 137–149.

O'Connor, G. (1988). Case management: System and practice. *Social Casework, 69*(2), 97–106.

Social Welfare Department (SWD). (2011). Invitation to operate pilot cyber youth outreaching projects service specifications. Hong Kong: Author.

Subrahmanyam, K., & Smahel, D. (2011). *Digital youth—the role of media in development.* New York/London: Springer.

Thyer, B. A., Artelt, T. A., & Shek, D. T. L. (2003). Using single-system research designs to evaluate practice—Potential applications for social work in Chinese contexts. *International Social Work, 46,* 163.

Weaver, D., Moses, T., Furman, W., & Lindsey, D. (2003). The effects of computerization on public child welfare practice. *Journal of Social Service Research, 29,* 67–80.

ANCILLARIES

Internet References for Additional Reading

1. The Digital Media and Learning Research Hub run by the University of California Humanities Research Institute. Retrieved from http://dmlhub.net/

2. Online Youth Outreach in the UK. Retrieved from http://www.onlineyouthoutreach.co.uk/

3. Social work and technology—A Google Plus community operated by social work academics across the globe. Retrieved from https://plus.google.com/u/0/communities/115588985317830085141

4. Studies about ICT and Youth At-Risk of Social Exclusion funded by the European Commission. Retrieved from http://is.jrc.ec.europa.eu/pages/EAP/eInclusion/youth.html

5. Youth Employment and Training Programme in Hong Kong. Retrieved from http://www.yes.labour.gov.hk/

Hard Copy References for Additional Reading

Cullen, J., Cullen, C., & Hamilton, E. (2011). *Mapping and assessing the impact of ICT-based initiatives for the socio-economic inclusion of youth at risk of exclusion: Impact assessment of ICT-based initiatives*. London, UK: The Tavistock Institute.

Davies, T., & Cranston, P. (2008). *Youth work and social networking: Final research report*. Leicester, United Kingdom: National Youth Agency. Retrieved online from http://blog.practicalpartici-pation.co.uk/wp-content/uploads/2009/08/fullYouth-Work-and-Social-Networking-Final-Report.pdf

Hill, A., & Shaw, I. G. R. (2011). *Social work & ICT*. Thousand Oaks, CA: Sage.

Szekely, L., & Nagy, A. (2011). Online youth work and eYouth—A guide to the world of the digital natives. *Children and Youth Services Review, 33*, 2186–2197.

Watling, S., & Rogers, J. (2012). *Social work in a digital society*. London, UK: Sage.

❖ JOB DESCRIPTION

The Boys' and Girls' Clubs Association of Hong Kong

Job Title	Social Worker (Case Management)
Division/Department	"Nite Cat Online" Pilot Cyber Youth Outreaching Project
Reports to	Team Leader of the Project

☒ Full Time ☐ Part Time

JOB SUMMARY: Identify youth at-risk of socio-economic exclusion via the Internet, and create and manage service plans for them.

KNOWLEDGE, SKILL, AND ABILITY REQUIREMENTS

- Bachelor degree or higher degree in social work, counseling, or related field
- Experience in casework and/or case management will be an asset, but not a necessary requirement
- Good knowledge and skills in information and communication technology (ICT)
- Good written and verbal communication skills
- Available to work flexibly during 3 p.m. and 3 a.m., 6 days a week

DUTIES AND RESPONSIBILITIES

1. Outreach potential clients via social media platforms.
2. Engage clients via the chat rooms and other interactive features on the project website.
3. Provide brief counseling via the project's official website and/or social media platforms.
4. Assess client needs, develop service plan, and make appropriate recommendations.
5. Plan and implement volunteer training activities.
6. Regularly update clients' contact information.
7. Regularly update online trends and available resources.
8. Plan and implement online and/or offline programs.
9. Help search, identify, and connect appropriate community resources to meet client needs.
10. Liaise with other NGOs and/or government departments to smoothen service provisions.
11. Help collect and provide data to evaluate the project.
12. Help draft project reports.
13. Attend external meetings on behalf of the project.
14. Assist publicity and promotion activities.
15. Perform other duties assigned by the team leader, the supervisor, and/or the head of the agency.

16

Case Management in Head Start Centers

Trasie A. Topple, Lynda Ritter, and LaToya R. Swanson

The Clientele

In the summer of 1965, Head Start (HS) was launched as an American initiative of President Lyndon B. Johnson's legislation coined as "The War on Poverty." The goal was, and remains, to break the cycle of poverty by preparing pre-school children for success in elementary education, giving these children a "head start" in school and in life (Ramey & Ramey, 2010). Fifty years later, HS is one of the longest-running federal programs targeted to compensate for systemic inequalities due to social and economic conditions. In 1995, HS was expanded to include children ages birth to age 2 through Early Head Start (EHS) grants. HS/EHS services are accomplished through a culturally responsive, comprehensive approach to early childhood education for children and families. These services minimally comprise education and child development, health, nutrition, mental health, family services, and partnerships and referrals with community agencies. Nationwide, the HS and EHS programs serve over 1 million low-income families with young children per year (U.S. Department of Health and Human Services, 2015).

In 1991, the YWCA in St. Louis, Missouri, received their first grant to partner with the HS program to provide services for 776 children and families in St. Louis County. Since that time, the YWCA has expanded services to include St. Louis City and County with 2,795 Head Start children and 200 Early Head Start infants, toddlers, and 2-year olds. The mission of the YWCA St. Louis HS/EHS programs is to equip children with the building blocks for lifetime success. Their partnership provides services to children and families through 10 early childhood sites, 11 childcare partner sites, and various services for pregnant women throughout St. Louis City and County. Within the 10 early childhood sites, the YWCA provides direct services through 54 HS classrooms and 11 EHS classrooms. These include full-day and part-day services, with some transportation provided for families who need it.

YWCA St. Louis HS programs strive for quality in classrooms by maintaining a ratio of 1 teacher to no more than 10 children with a maximum of 20 children in one room. The EHS classrooms are smaller in size to provide more one-on-one attention, with 1 teacher to no more than 4 infants and toddlers, or 2 teachers with a maximum of 8 children in one room. Curriculum used in both programs is evidence based and aligns with the Missouri Early Learning Standards. These classrooms provide comprehensive developmental and health screenings for all children. In addition, individualized educational services assess children's educational progress 3 times per year and meet with families to discuss the child's developmental progress 4 times per year. The majority of pregnant women services are provided through home visits.

YWCA St. Louis HS/EHS has specific requirements for eligibility determination, recruitment, selection, enrollment, and attendance of children in the program. To qualify for the services, children and families must be age and income eligible (equal or below the Federal Poverty Line); additionally, 10% of the total number of enrollment opportunities must be made eligible to children with disabilities. Homeless families and children in foster care automatically qualify as long as they meet the age requirements. A community assessment is conducted every 3 years to ensure that the services provided are meeting the community's actual needs.

Enrolled families vary drastically, but all have varying degrees of stress, crises, and trauma in their lives. Particular challenges arise with single or teen parent families. Other family stressors include caregivers with little education, homelessness, or in-transitional housing situations. Unemployment and underemployment continue to be a burden for many HS/EHS families, and increased financial stress often occurs due to limited resources for basic necessities and paying bills. The majority of families receive some form of public assistance such as Supplemental Nutrition Assistance Program (SNAP), Medicaid, Supplemental Social Income (SSI), Temporary Assistance for Needy Families (TANF), childcare subsidies, or other financial assistance programs. Transportation can also become a barrier to accessing program services particularly in areas where public transportation is limited. Some parents receiving services may also have disabilities or mental health challenges, and many of our families often need immediate help with basic resources such as diapers, food, housing, transportation, phone, and utilities. Children in the surrounding St. Louis City and County area normally come from diverse cultures and backgrounds with over 15 different languages represented in YWCA HS/EHS enrolled families. Thus, communication can become a challenge, so program staff has access to interpreters and translators from the community when needed.

Referrals to the program come through families who have attended in the past or through community agencies. YWCA HS/EHS also conducts door-to-door recruitments and hosts a program recruitment day once a year, where all staff in the program go out in the community to outreach and meet families that might be eligible. Recruitment for HS/EHS is a continuous process throughout the year since many of our families are transient.

Family Advocates (FAs) provide a wide range of CMG services to families. FAs must have a bachelor's degree from a 4-year accredited university. FAs at the YWCA HS/EHS have degrees in social work, sociology, and child life. The FA begins by meeting with families to assess their strengths and needs, as well as any immediate crises that need to be addressed. They provide referrals and follow-up with external community agencies. Then, the FA begins to work with families to set goals for the family and children, if the family so desires. These goals may include potty training, parent coaching for a GED, employment support, or car or home ownership assistance. The FA shares information with parents about the importance of maintaining their child's medical, dental, nutrition, and mental health status. The YWCA Head Start center employs one FA who oversees the cases of approximately 120 students.

Practice Roles and Responsibilities

Since HS emphasizes the roles of parents as their child's first and most important teacher, the FAs target the family system within their social environment to improve school readiness for every child enrolled. The guiding framework for service provision is rooted in systems knowledge and strengths-based practices. Practice roles and responsibilities of FAs involve linking multiple, dynamic layers of the client's social system from individual work with the child at the micro-level, family support at the exo-level, community connections at the meso-level, advocacy work at the macro-level, and knowledge of a family system's historical and developmental context at the chrono-level (Bronfenbrenner & Morris, 2006). System linkage responsibilities for FAs can be broadly categorized into four main roles: 1) case coordinator, 2) broker, 3) advocate, and 4) team member. FAs focus their work in collaboration with family members and other HS staff to meet individually tailored goals for each student enrolled in the center.

Case coordinator. Once a child is enrolled at a HS center, family engagement becomes of primary concern for all HS staff. Family engagement consists of two components: Family Partnerships Agreements (FPAs) and Education. The education staff conducts classroom assessments and collaborates with families about the educational concerns of the center, while the FAs collaborate with families through the Family Partnership Agreement (FPA), a contract between the family and FA for accomplishing goals either for the family or the child to support optimal development. The majority of practice responsibilities falls under the area of case coordination and is realized primarily by conducting ongoing needs assessments.

At enrollment, a Family Outreach Worker (FOW) invites families to participate in the FPA and conducts an initial needs assessment. This agreement begins by giving consent for a collaboration with a FA to set goals for themselves or their child and to connect them with referral sources as needed. The FOW assesses at enrollment any crisis need that may be present, such as housing, food, safety, etc. If such needs exist, the FA typically meets with the family at enrollment, or as soon as available to connect them with resources or referrals. Otherwise, the FA has 90 days to complete a follow-up needs assessment for additional referrals for community resources. Some families have no need for referrals or decline to participate in an ongoing Family Partnership at enrollment. In this case, the FA is required to follow-up with families who have denied participation within 90 days, to re-visit their participation in the FPA. The St. Louis YWCA HS/EHS center employs one FA, and she manages approximately 120 families' needs assessments, and approximately 60% of those families are actively working toward accomplishing set goals.

A guiding philosophy of case management in early childhood education is Maslow's (1943) hierarchy of needs. It is important that a family reach a certain degree of stability with basic resources (like housing, food, clothing) and safety, in order for their child to maximize learning in the classroom (Noltemeyer, Bush, Patton, & Bergen, 2012). Referrals can either be an internal referral, such as to a child development specialist or child mental health support, or an external referral to the community, as is the case with community food banks, clothing, or financial support. Families perceived to be in crises necessitate immediate referrals to meet their needs, such as instability in housing or financial matters, food insecurity, and safety concerns.

FA's case coordination centers on meaningful goal setting in collaboration with the family. Most families have the desire to see their children succeed in school and FAs work alongside families to help them accomplish their stated goals. Goal setting is typically a 5-step process: 1) identify the family's strengths, 2) assess needs, 3) discuss supporting strategies, 4) build a partnership for follow-up, and 5) make a referral if needed. During goal setting and implementation, FAs explore many areas of the family system with their clients and develop concrete and agreed upon strategies to improve family functioning and well-being. For instance, areas include family connections to peers and community, such as extended family members, spiritual support, and/or knowledge of community resources. During conversations and occasional home visits, FAs assess the family capacities and interests in supporting their child's education through having books accessible in the home, reading to their children, participating in cultural traditions, and supporting appropriate developmental expectations of their child. FAs support positive parent–child relationships by assessing and implementing strategies around caregiver stress levels, family transitions, and parenting skills to maintain structure and routine in the home environment. Family well-being factors, such as employment, transportation, financial security, and housing, are taken into consideration. FAs may also assist families in maintaining regular health care appointments with local primary care providers and dentists. Other areas of concern that compromise the overall development of the child and stability of the family system, such as custody issues, interpersonal violence, substance use, and caregiver mental health concerns, are assessed and appropriate referrals for support are made if deemed necessary.

The ability to identify client strengths while exploring and clarifying thoroughly a family's needs and goals are crucial in successful case coordination. FAs employ active listening skills to fully understand families' concerns and to build upon existing strengths. FAs empower families through the identifications of both family and child strengths. Families' strengths are then utilized in setting collaborative goals to help families and children thrive at home, in school, and the community. When families are able to successfully complete goals, either for themselves or their young children, parental efficacy is increased and children benefit from a more engaged, effective caregiver. Simple goals, such as book sharing, can enhance the parent–child relationship, and set the foundation for emergent literacy. However, effective case coordination and goal setting depends primarily on the social worker's ability to form trusting and safe relationships with the family. FAs perceive that every encounter with the family, either in the center, at the home, or in the community, are opportunities to build continued rapport and strengthen ties within the family system and across systems to increase successful outcomes for all HS children. FAs employ communication skills such as active listening, empathy, reflection, paraphrasing, and summarizing in order to establish and maintain strong relationships with families throughout their time at the HS center.

Day-to-day tasks of a FA are dynamic and may include interacting with an average of five families per day, placing phone calls to either families or community agencies, conducting face-to-face meetings, and attending community meetings. Documentation skills are essential to facilitate communication and monitor cases. HS utilizes an electronic database, and FAs are required to enter all communication, needs assessments, referrals, and special staff meeting notes into the system in a timely manner.

Coordinating cases of families who live in poverty and often in crisis can be very demanding and challenging. Overwhelmed families have multiple needs, which the HS center and the community cannot always help meet. To be in a helping role but unable to locate the resources needed can lead to frustration for the FA. At these times, FAs work with the family to think creatively about their situations and to identify any informal network supports, such as extended family, friends, or faith-based communities. Other barriers include the cumulative adverse effect of the physical and emotional demand that families experience parenting young children while living in poverty (Shonkoff & Garner, 2012). Often, families are depleted of emotional resources to engage in effective ways to accomplish goals for themselves or their children and are barely getting by. Knowledge of the impact of poverty on family systems helps social workers identify where appropriate intervention may effect change. At times, our families deny services or participation in the FPA. Social work values of client self-determination guide social workers' engagement with families (National Association of Social Workers [NASW], 2008).

Broker. Although families do receive internal referrals to services involving the classroom setting, such as behavioral support, FAs often serve as a broker to connect families with services in the community that are important to the promotion of school readiness. To perform the role of broker, it is essential that all FAs have a thorough knowledge of community resources available to young children and their families as well as the cultural context of the communities in which families reside. FAs participate in monthly community visits to foster relationships with local organizations that can serve as resources to HS families, and to learn about their eligibility requirements or special programs. FAs have established relationships with key people in organizations that can assist the family in a crisis, such as local food and clothing banks, government organizations, mental health services, and foundations. FAs also monitor referrals and follow-up with clients within 30 days for all non-crisis referrals to see if the need was actually met or to develop new strategies to meet the identified need. FAs are responsive immediately during crisis and may even assist clients physically in obtaining resources. For example, if a client has a toddler and a newborn infant, the FA may collect essential items, such as food and diapers, to deliver to the home in cases of shortage. Clients and FAs experience barriers in communities that are resource-strapped and unable to meet the need of clients, particularly in rural communities. In these instances, FAs help problem-solve with clients to access informal support networks, such as extended family members or faith-based communities that have the potential to serve as supports.

Advocate. FAs have many opportunities to advocate with and on behalf of their clients to obtain resources and services that would not be otherwise provided to them. As advocates, FAs work with families and teachers to identify and eliminate barriers to a child's classroom successes. This may mean helping to empower families to be their child's own advocate if the child needs additional evaluations to determine eligibility for special education, or additional supports in or outside of the classroom, such as speech therapy. Parental decision making is an important part of parent engagement in HS. For example, approximately 10% of children in our centers meet eligibility for special needs staffing. These children will have an Individualized Educational Plan (IEP) and special staff meetings to discuss their progress in school readiness areas of communication, gross motor, fine motor, adaptive, and social-emotional developmental domains, as well as any concerns around transitions, nutrition, health, and family needs. Special staff meetings consist of the family, the HS center manager, a child development specialist, the teacher, and the FA working collaboratively to address any concerns on a quarterly basis. An FA attends all IEP meetings and is there primarily to assist the parent in advocating for the needs of her child and ensure that all parties are receiving sufficient information about the family's needs. As an advocate, FAs help to build a better foundation for parental involvement in their child's education, which is essential for school readiness. A recent study conducted with previous HS children's transition to elementary education suggested that greater parental involvement is positively correlated with higher literacy outcomes (Dove, Neuharth-Pritchett, Wright, & Wallinga, 2015).

Team Member. Because parent, family, and community engagement practices intersect into different service areas, it is essential that HS staff collaborate in interdisciplinary teams. Such teams commonly consist of a center manager, teachers, specialist, therapists, FAs, and support staff. As FAs, social workers function as an integral part of the center's team allowing for a more holistic approach to early childhood education. FAs contribute knowledge related to family dynamics and needs, as well as resources available in the community. They work to ensure that all staff have in-depth understanding of the strengths and needs of the family. While HS/EHS teachers contribute knowledge about the progress and development of the child in the classroom, the FAs provide crucial information regarding the child in a large system within her family and the community. In addition to their roles in a specific center, FAs from other HS/EHS schools around the surrounding St. Louis County gather once a month to share community resources and provide professional support to one another.

Role Development Potential

The dynamic and challenging nature of the FA position allows workers to continually develop their roles and learn from families how to better meet needs of vulnerable young children. Relationships with clients and community agencies take time to build, but with each culturally sensitive and strength-based response, the FA has an opportunity to build a network of continual support for families that dynamically crosses systems within the HS center and the community. Monthly visits to partnering community agencies further foster and nurture ties with HS centers, as well as develop skills in building collaborative partnerships with local resource agencies. Case coordination skills are continually practiced and improved as FAs learn to be culturally responsive to what referral and follow-up strategies work best for each individual family system. Communication skills, such as empathy, reflection, boundary setting, and conflict resolution, are consistently practiced and refined as relationships are being built and negotiated.

FAs must possess timely knowledge concerning typical developmental milestones for young children, strategies to improve problem behaviors, and parenting skills to improve parent–child relationships. FAs develop strategies to help parents create sensitive and predictable routines in the home environment. Ongoing continuing education through HS/EHS centers provides many opportunities to stay abreast of current child development information and gain knowledge about family mental health, the impact of trauma on families, child development and a variety of parenting practices, including unique ways to engage fathers.

Social workers employed as FAs bring with them many strengths to the position. Four-year accredited social work MSW and BSW programs teach the necessary and essential direct practice skills of case coordination, and practicum experiences give students opportunities to put into practice direct practice knowledge and skills as learners. Students learn client engagement, effective communication skills, change-oriented treatment strategies, successful goal-setting, and respectful termination (Hepworth, Rooney, Rooney, & Strom-Gottfried, 2013). Students are afforded many opportunities to develop professionally as they enhance professional skills of self-awareness and reflection about their own personal beliefs and cultural values, as biases may impede the provision of their services. Social work education emphasizes critical analysis of ethical concerns and dilemmas to develop a strong foundation in the Social Work Code of Ethics (NASW, 2008). Finally, social workers' knowledge of how systems at multiple levels may interact to influence and impact individuals is an invaluable resource for successful outcomes for young children. Most noteworthy is that all of these skills are delivered in strengths-based perspectives that allow FAs to identify client strengths and empower them to effect positive change. Students desiring to work with young children in direct practice would benefit from additional courses in early childhood development that could provide more in-depth knowledge of key theories, practice, and assessment tools used than is typically offered in social work's traditional Human Behavior in the Social Environment courses.

Concluding Remarks

Direct practice work in early childhood education requires a unique set of knowledge and skills that make social workers a very good fit for this position. Apart from the knowledge and skillset taught in BSW and MSW social work education, effective work with such clients requires reflexivity and the willingness of the worker to be open, aware, and sensitive to cultural differences. Social work CMG in early childhood education requires the practitioner to meet the client wherever they may be in the process of change, support them with social work professional skills, and work collaboratively toward accomplishing the client's goals. Relationship-based centered work requires time, patience, and emotional energy that can indeed be draining. Working with young children and families can touch us deeply on many levels personally and professionally, reminding us of our own childhood dreams and disappointments, or of our current family situations. Social workers need a support system built into their practice fields, just as they are building support systems for their HS families, through quality and consistent supervision, peer support, and work-life balances that allows them to better stay effective in the field. Ultimately, the rewards outweigh the difficulties, as you see families rise above their circumstances and witness children set on a trajectory that gives them inherent self-worth and a love for learning that will last them a lifetime.

Case Example

I (LaToya R. Swanson) have had other social work experience with families prior to joining the YWCA HS/EHS program. However, this program, by its very eligibility requirements, provides unique challenges due to a variety of diverse needs and crises situations that many impoverished families face daily. My work sometimes requires home visits, but more often than not, I see families in my office at the HS center typically after drop off or pick-up hours. Many of my (client) families will come to me when they have a crisis situation. This is a story of one case that highlights the complexity of working with such parents and young children.

Ruth is a single mother raising her three children alone. At enrollment, we learned that she has two children in the public school system, a 15-year-old boy and a 12-year-old girl. Her youngest daughter, Alice, is 3 years old and is eligible for our HS program. Their primary language is English. The family lives in a public housing apartment that is pretty run down but in fair shape. She pays approximately $400/month in rent. Ruth has been unable to work for 3 years, but receives a monthly disability check. She has mental health challenges and sees a psychiatrist for anxiety. She takes medication and states that it helps calm her when she feels anxious.

The disability checks she receives amount to less than $11,000 per year, which qualifies her for our program at 46% below the Federal Family Income Poverty Guidelines for a family of four. She is receiving support from Women, Infants, and Children (WIC) and Supplemental Nutrition Assistance Program (SNAP). She also shared that Alice was removed from the home and placed in foster care for 6 months of this past year. Due to the many risk factors, Alice was placed high on our eligibility priority list and was guaranteed a slot into our HS program.

Alice is enrolled in the part-day afternoon program in a HS classroom, from 12:30–4:30 p.m. Alice is progressing well in the classroom, but Ruth expresses concerns about Alice's occasional stuttering. Alice also had some physical health concerns with a clogged tear duct and underwent surgery prior to enrollment. She is seeing well now and passed the vision screen at the HS center. Ruth declined to set Family Partnership goals at enrollment, but after a month in our program, she agreed to participate in the Family Partnership Agreement.

We began by conjointly identifying her strengths. Through asking open-ended questions, active listening, and reflection, we identified that Ruth desires for Alice to do well in school, an area where she has previously struggled. Alice's enrollment in the program is a positive strength. I reflected to Ruth, "You are bringing Alice to HS so that she will be prepared for school." Ruth is committed to bringing Alice; however, she struggles to pick her up on time after school. We discuss strategies to help Ruth be on time for pick-up, important to both the center and her daughter. We also identified that she had a consistent place for her child to live, and a grandfather who had a great relationship with the children and was willing to assist with childcare. Then we discussed goals that she may have for herself or her family. She mentioned that she would like to go back to work, at least part-time. We explored more about her interests. We set a goal to meet with Job Corp and to get more information on various job training programs. She also stated that she would like to help Alice not stutter anymore. So next we created a goal to meet with the Child Development Specialist to work with Ruth around strategies to help with Alice's stuttering in the home.

Recently, Ruth told Alice's teacher about a personal financial crisis situation. Since we work collaboratively in a team, Alice's teacher suggested that Ruth meet with me that day. Ruth shared with me that her electricity had been disconnected because she was unable to pay her bill. As I listened carefully, she shared that she had asked for help from Catholic Charities in the past, but did not want to ask them again. I empathized with her situation and reflected back that we all need assistance at times. I tried to reduce her feeling of shame and empower her to seek the needed resources to provide for her young family.

I referred her to the local Community Action Agency, who was able to assist her in paying her gas bill, but not her electric bill, since their policy is to assist only with electric bills in the summer, and gas bills in the winter. Together, we called and left messages at the United Way and St. Vincent Catholic Charities. I also took her next door to the St. George food pantry to replenish her food supply. When I asked if they would be all right until the electricity was turned back on, she stated that they will stay at the grandfather's house to keep warm. I will follow-up with her to see if the agencies we contacted were able to assist her in paying the electricity bill.

The time that Ruth and I have spent identifying strengths, creating goals and strategies together, and seeking resources during crisis is building a meaningful, trusting relationship between us, but most importantly, Ruth is being more empowered to participate in tangible ways to create a home environment by setting goals for herself and her family that will help her children succeed in school and life.

❖

REFERENCES

Bronfenbrenner, U., & Morris, P. (2006). The bioecological model of human development. In R. M. Lerner & W. Damon (Eds.), *Handbook of child psychology: Vol. 1, Theoretical models of human development* (6th ed., pp. 793–828). Hoboken, NJ: John Wiley.

Dove, M. K., Neuharth-Pritchett, S., Wright, D. W., & Wallinga, C. (2015). Parental involvement routines and former Head Start children's literacy outcomes. *Journal of Research in Childhood Education, 29*(2), 173–186.

Hepworth, D. H., Rooney, R. H., Rooney, G. D., & Strom-Gottfried, K. (2013). *Direct social work practice: Theory and skills* (9th ed.). Pacific Grove, CA: Brooks/Cole.

Maslow, A. H. (1943). A theory of human motivation. *Psychological Review, 50*(4), 370–396.

National Association of Social Workers (NASW). (2008). *Code of ethics*. Retrieved from https://www.socialworkers.org/pubs/code/code.asp

Noltemeyer, A., Bush, K., Patton, J., & Bergen, D. (2012). The relationship among deficiency needs and growth needs: An empirical investigation of Maslow's theory. *Children and Youth Services Review, 34*(9), 1862–1867.

Ramey, C., & Ramey, S. (2010). Head Start: Strategies to improve outcomes for children living in poverty. *Investing in Young Children: New Directions in Federal Preschool and Early Childhood Policy, 59*–68.

Shonkoff, J., & Garner, A. (2012). The lifelong effects of early childhood adversity and toxic stress. *Pediatrics, 129*(1), 1–15.

U.S. Department of Health and Human Services. (2015). Office of Head Start. Retrieved from http://www.acf.hhs.gov/programs/ohs/about/head-start

❖

ANCILLARIES

Internet References for Additional Reading

1. Administration of Children and Families, Office of Head Start. Retrieved from http://www.acf.hhs.gov/programs/ohs

2. The Early Childhood Learning and Knowledge Center. Retrieved from https://eclkc.ohs.acf.hhs.gov/hslc

3. Harvard Center on the Developing Child. Retrieved from http://developingchild.harvard.edu/

4. Head Start-YWCA St. Louis, MO. Retrieved from http://www.ywcastlouis.org

5. National Association for the Education of Young Children. Retrieved from http://www.naeyc.org/

6. National Head Start Association. Retrieved from https://www.nhsa.org/

7. Zero to Three. Retrieved from http://www.zerotothree.org/

Hard Copy References for Additional Reading

Copple, C., Bredekamp, S., Koralek, D., & Charner, K. (Eds.). (2013). *Developmentally appropriate practice: Focus on preschoolers.* Washington, DC: National Association for the Education of Young Children.

Dove, M. K., Neuharth-Pritchett, S., Wright, D. W., & Wallinga, C. (2015). Parental involvement routines and former Head Start children's literacy outcomes. *Journal of Research in Childhood Education, 29*(2), 173–186.

Early, T. J., & GlenMaye, L. F. (2000). Valuing families: Social work practice with families from a strengths perspective. *Social Work, 45*(2), 118–130.

Phillips, D. A., & Shonkoff, J. P. (Eds.). (2000). *From neurons to neighborhoods: The science of early childhood development.* Washington, DC: National Academies Press.

Swick, K. J., & Williams, R. D. (2006). An analysis of Bronfenbrenner's bio-ecological perspective for early childhood educators: Implications for working with families experiencing stress. *Early Childhood Education Journal, 33*(5), 371–378.

❖ JOB DESCRIPTION

Job Title: Family Advocate Supervisor's Title: Family Partnership Administrator Operating Unit: Children's Division: Head Start/ Early Head Start Program	Job Code: Currency Date: 5/4/2011 FLSA Status: Non Exempt

General Summary

Dimension	Description
Purpose	Ensure that the family of each enrolled child is afforded the opportunity to develop and implement an individualized plan of service based on their interest and needs. Operate as a liaison between the center and home setting in all functional areas while promoting family wellness and involvement through a case management process.
Formal Policy-Setting Responsibilities	Responsible for making recommendations that may or may not be acceptable at a higher level regarding the job's purpose, essential responsibilities, and operations.
Routine Decision-Making	Conduct timely follow-up on Family Assessments and Family Partnership Plan/Agreements, identify community resources, make timely referrals to families, monitor family files to ensure the accuracy and integrity of information and assist with application intake and data entry as needed.
Formal Supervisory Responsibility	N/A

Essential Responsibilities

Number	Description	% of Time	Impor-tance Rating
1	Ensure, through a case management system, that all families are provided an opportunity to participate in a Family Partnership Plan, complete a Family Assessment and provided timely resources and referrals as a result of identified needs and goals of parents and/or guardians during this process.	20%	5
2	Implement goals, policies, procedures, and activities designed to provide the full range of family support services in compliance with Head Start Performance Standards, including assisting with obtaining health and dental services, and other child/ family services identified, as part of ongoing case management. Implement a formal system of follow-up with families on referrals to community agencies, to assure the satisfactory provision of services.	20%	5

The most common maltreatment types resulting in children entering foster care are neglect and physical abuse resulting from parental/caregiver substance abuse, mental health, and/or domestic violence issues. Children are most frequently removed from the custody of a biological parent(s), particularly a birth or adopted mother only. While birth/adoptive mothers are typically the most common perpetrators, there has been a growing number of children entering foster care due to the abuse of an unmarried partner of a birth/adoptive mother. Additionally, there are often sibling groups of children (from two to seven or more) that enter foster care; and some groups enter as a result of a child fatality in the family. Children who enter foster care often present with significant behavioral, emotional, and mental health problems that parents alone could not handle and therefore, choose to relinquish custody of their children to either the foster care and/or juvenile justice systems. Older youth particularly present with issues related to running away, sexual exploitation and trafficking, teen pregnancy, low educational attainment (dropping out of school), gang affiliation, and criminal records. In fact, according to Georgia's 2013 statistics, children with reported disabilities (i.e., behavior, emotional disturbance, learning/intellectual, and physical) made up 22.6% of all child victims with "emotional disturbance" being the most common at 10.6% (U.S. Department of Health and Human Services, 2015).

Since most children enter foster care due to neglect, the most common permanency plan is for children to be returned back to the custody of their parent or caregiver (re-unification). In fact, 47% of foster children in Georgia exited care to be reunified with their parent or primary caretaker in 2013; and of these children 72.1% were reunified within 12 months of entering care (*Kids Count Data Center*, 2015). Approximately 20% exited foster care to live with another relative and 17% were adopted (*Kids Count Data Center*, 2015).

Practice Roles and Responsibilities

The primary responsibilities of a Social Services Case Manager (CM) working in FC include:

1. Assessing risk of harm at all times to ensure that children are safe and stable.

2. Engage children, parents or primary caregivers, and other relatives or supportive persons in developing a plan to re-unify and stabilize the family or achieve an alternative permanency option.

3. Managing cases to ensure that the needs of children are continuously being met and the case is progressing according to the plan to achieve permanency in the most appropriate and timely manner.

4. Communicate and collaborate with other agency personnel, juvenile court personnel, community providers, law enforcement, and other stakeholders.

Performing these primary responsibilities includes the following: visiting children, primary caregivers, and foster parents regularly; documenting visits thoroughly;

placing children in appropriate residential settings; ensuring children have regular visits with their family members; searching for permanent placement resources (i.e., other relatives, friends, etc.); ensuring routine and periodic medical, dental, and mental health appointments are made and kept; ensuring that children are attending school; preparing court documents; testifying in court hearings; attending case staffing, family team meetings, discharge meetings; keeping case files up-to-date; and numerous other related tasks necessary for case management (CMG).

Meeting these responsibilities successfully, however, requires a mixture of training to build the required skillset and competencies, and a natural proclivity to handle complex, fluid, and often stressful and heart-wrenching situations. As a CM in a child welfare system, particularly a state system, one may be trained, certified, and called upon to work in a number of CMG capacities. No matter which capacity or unit you work in, there are 14 key standards, per the *NASW Standards for Social Work Practice in Child Welfare* (2013) that guide performance, as well as agency policies you must adhere to in order to manage your caseload well (see Chapter 4). A child welfare CM must have an ability to empathize with others and be creative and resourceful, possess effective listening skills, have a strong sense of accountability, and be highly sensitive to all matters of privacy and confidentiality.

However, we believe (based on our collective case experiences) that the most important social work skill to employ when encountering and working with maltreated children and their families is being open and willing to learn from the family the true nature of the dynamics that led to their eventual involvement with the agency. Making quick assumptions and judgments about families that may be factually baseless are counterproductive—and often create more harm than good. What undergirds effective CMG is understanding that a general awareness of, and knowledge about, vulnerable and disenfranchised populations typically served by child welfare agencies does not automatically account for or supersede individual, family, or even community dynamics and needs. Such work can quickly become a battle when a CM loses her or his focus on gaining an understanding of the family, instead imposing judgements of what they believe a family's level of functioning and normalcy should be, to ensure their own safety, permanency, and well-being. For example, it really does no good for a college educated child welfare CM to automatically require every parent to attend parenting classes—overtly assuming that poor parenting skills are the reason that the agency is now involved with the family. However, a teenage mother who doesn't have a full understanding of child development may very well benefit from such parenting classes. But, parenting classes may not help an unemployed and depressed mother with her small children, who has just fled across the country in the middle of the night to escape an abusive partner, leaving a job and her social network behind, to survive. This mother may be better served receiving some level of direct counseling and tangible resources to help get her and her children stable.

Challenges. Proper supervision is also vital to effective CMG. Good supervision can make the difference between a CM being productive, effective, and fulfilled in her/his work, and one being so stressed that they inadvertently may put children at risk.

Although supervisors can also become overwhelmed with the enormous amounts of pressure on their shoulders, it is imperative that CMs always advocate for themselves, to ensure that they receive proper supervision (Munson, 2007; Simpson, Williams, & Brantley Segall, 2007). Given the endless array of situations and encounters a CM may face in the course of a day, which often present all kinds of ethical dilemmas and complex decision-making, it is very important that the CM-supervisor relationship is strong. Thus, good supervision, as well as peer-to-peer mentorship, can also help CMs achieve breakthroughs with clients that are difficult to engage.

Two of the most important and challenging standards to achieve and maintain as a child welfare CM are quality assessments and appropriate documentation. The child welfare environment is fast-paced, ever-changing, and always demanding (Holosko, 2006). While the national recommended caseload size for CMs is 12–15, oftentimes one may have up to 20 or more cases, which is double the number of children you are responsible for. When you are also charged with making quality visits for all children on your caseload, their caregivers (primary and foster parents), and ensuring parent–child and sibling visits take place for an excessive caseload, it is extremely challenging to always conduct the required assessments (formal and informal) to ensure safety and well-being. For example, there are two foster care agencies covering the largest metropolitan counties in Georgia that require CMs to visit with every child on their caseload twice a month in the first 8 weeks a child is in foster care, or when a child is placed in a new foster home. Although this mandate is required by a federal consent decree, it is based on best-practice evidence indicating that frequent visits positively correlate with decreased incidence of maltreatment-in-care and placement disruptions.

Frequent visits by actively engaged CMs are also associated with shorter stays in foster care for children. However, these visits must be of high quality, meaning CMs need to have time to interact with children and caregivers (separately and privately when possible) to assess what is really happening in the home. Otherwise, possible maltreatment and/or other issues may go undetected. Unfortunately, due to high retention rates, caseloads can be very high, and CMs find themselves making more low quality drop-by visits to meet the agency quantitative goals while sacrificing qualitative goals (Wodarski, Holosko, & Feit, 2015).

Working in such a high-pressure environment also makes it challenging to keep up with timely and necessary documentation and paperwork. Different from many other work environments, it is admirable to plan your day to get all visits, documentation, and paperwork completed and also submitted responsively. However, any given moment of that "well planned out day," can turn into utter chaos when a school calls to report that one of your kids has just been suspended for fighting, and you need to come pick them up because they can't reach the foster parent; and a few moments later, a foster parent calls to say they can't keep a child in their home and you need to find them another placement as soon as possible. A CM then finds themselves working late into the night trying to complete proper documentation, submitting paperwork, or preparing for a court hearing. Possessing excellent time management skills is very important to juggling the many tasks a CM handles daily. But, being flexible, and adaptable to change helps a CM move more smoothly with the ebb and flow of the work—without going out of her or his mind.

Role Development Potential

Despite the noted challenges that come with being a child welfare CM, there is no greater feeling than seeing the joy in children returning home to their primary care-givers and following up to learn that the family is sustaining and thriving or hearing of a foster child that aged out of the system graduating from college. Contrary to popular belief, there are many outcomes such as these that have kept my (Babette Stephens) feet planted in this work for many years. I am a "natural helper," which perhaps I came about honestly from the long line of social workers in my family. But my social work education and exposure to working in the child welfare system was through my practicum, which eventually solidified this setting for my calling. I have always viewed work in child welfare as an investment of my time and energies in the overall well-being of children, and hence the future well-being of our society.

Although the greatest teacher for me has been client real-life experiences, the practical classroom preparation I received is most reflected in conducting interviews, particularly engaging resistant and combative clients, conducting assessments, and documenting numerous encounters. Additionally, my BSW social work education instilled in me a level of consciousness and sensitivity to appreciate cultural differences, acknowledge awareness of my own biases and privileges, and sharpen my critical thinking skills, all of which are vital to effective CMG. The skills to organize my workload and manage my time effectively to meet critical requirements and deadlines were fortunately facilitated through good supervision, and "trial and error"—because short of participating in real-life CMG simulations, there is absolutely no way any class can prepare you for the totality of the encompassing work you will perform. However, the appropriateness of the practicum was the exposure to real work and, therefore, it is imperative that practicums are developed and supervised accordingly. To have a solid foundation entering child welfare CMG, it is critical that social work students receive the full benefits of quality practicum supervision. When this is not the case, students, with the support of their academic program directors, should learn to advocate for themselves, just as they would be expected to for a client, when they feel they aren't gaining such benefits.

While it has been my preference to stay on the frontline working directly with children and their families, versus moving upward to a management level, it would have been very helpful (to me) as a BSW student to have investigated the actual career trajectory paths for social workers within child welfare. Developing such a professional/career growth plan during my junior or senior year would have supported my earlier idealism with more practicality. All too often, I have worked with many CMs who are both despondent and stagnant, mainly for 2 reasons: 1) they did not have a plan for their career development, and 2) at no point did either the agency or their educational institution facilitate the creation of such a plan. Many social workers start their careers in a state child welfare system based on either idealism or the job stability and benefits. However, such idealism usually fades away and most end up staying with the state system for their future stability and health/pension benefits. In retrospect, it would have been helpful for me to know earlier on that professional development in the Georgia child welfare system was a linear, and rather limited, career trajectory path. Indeed, very few professional development trainings or workshops with CEU credits are offered. So, if a student wants to obtain a clinical license at some point in their career, there is little opportunity for supervision within child welfare, and there are no incentives to obtain a license. Furthermore, to advance or increase your salary, the next levels above CM are supervisor, administrator, director, etc. There are currently no other career tracks in our system that will allow someone who wants to remain on the frontline as a CM to be promoted within a CMG track. For example, it would be nice if I could have been promoted from an entry-level CM handling more basic cases to a senior CM handling more specialized or complex cases. Nevertheless—there is some good news on the horizon! According to the *Georgia Child Welfare Reform Council Final Report to the Governor* (Blank, 2015), our agency will work to develop career paths that will "allow for advancement within each position, such that caseworkers do not need to become supervisors in order to advance in their careers if they prefer being caseworkers" (p. 11).

Finally, all BSW and MSW students need to know how important it is to always have avenues for their own self-care (Skinner, 2015), but it is equally important to assess how aspects of their work may resurrect personal traumatic experiences, to better ensure the appropriateness of self-care methods (i.e., counseling, exercise, etc.). As child welfare research and practice now support trauma-informed practice, social work programs and child welfare agencies should also consider the extent of trauma and healing that students carry into the field or at least facilitate students assessing and addressing any unresolved trauma themselves (Wodarski et al., 2015). Furthermore, we (the authors) believe that a more proactive approach to assess or monitor for secondary traumatic stress or compassion fatigue among child welfare CMs is needed as well (ACS-NYU Children's Trauma Institute, 2012). These initiatives have great potential to strengthen the child welfare workforce and, in turn, improve outcomes for children and families (Wodarski et al., 2015).

Concluding Remarks

The reality of working in today's child welfare world consists of the constant navigation of multi-level barriers—micro, mezzo, macro—for effective CMG. However, the profession of social work, through its ecological and systems orientation, is uniquely grounded to facilitate improved holistic and sustainable outcomes for maltreated children and their families. This orientation allows a social work CM to assess the interconnectedness of the multiple systems clients are synced to, and the role each may play in bringing about a client's identified problem. For example, in child welfare the Comprehensive Child and Family Assessment (CCFA) tool is the by-product of a systems perspective that is used to develop the family case plan to ensure the safety, well-being, and permanency of children during and after foster care episodes.

Furthermore, foster care CMs trained in social work have the skills and capacity to humanize perpetrators of child maltreatment, just as they do their victims, which is especially critical if re-unification is the plan for permanency. In this work, CMs must remember that behaviors are often situational and maintaining a level of respect throughout the continuum of case progression can counteract and/or reduce tension and facilitate essential rapport and trust with clients.

In conclusion, we challenge future BSW and MSW students to remember what led you to our altruistic social work profession and particularly to your chosen specialty or setting. Realizing early on the impact you will certainly have on the lives of children and families humanizes the ultimate responsibility to care. Being genuine, attentive, resourceful, and humble will all increase your effectiveness with the various individuals, families, and in the communities you serve. Be a master in your field, but yet humble enough to appreciate that families will be the ultimate masters of their own success—with your guidance along the way.

Case Example

As child protective services CMs, we are often so-called first responders to varying allegations of child abuse and or neglect. One case type in particular that continues to test social work skills and techniques involves multiple risk concerns. New cases are typically received by e-mail and for those that require an immediate response, an additional phone call alerts the CM of the reported allegations. Each incoming report of child abuse and neglect is routed with a response time of immediate, 24-hours, or family support (5-day response). With all new cases, it is best practice to read client history and thoroughly review all screenings to prepare the CM with some indication of the family you are responding to. Although a case may require an immediate response, safety is important to the assessment process, therefore CMs should arm themselves with as much information about the family they are about to encounter.

In one particular situation, I (the second author) had to respond to a family with an extensive history with the department regarding parental drug abuse, domestic violence, and supervision concerns for a sibling group of three small children all under the age of 8. Being careful not to pre-judge this family based on their historical reports, I was aware of what could happen upon initial contact because of the past documented encounters of my colleagues with this particular family. I also typically do not involve law enforcement officials for initial visits to a home, as it often is intimidating to the family and raises emotional defenses in situations that could be handled more independently. However, I am always intensely aware of my surroundings when visiting homes, especially when responding to allegations of child maltreatment.

As I approached this home located on a large family plot of farm land consisting of three homes, I quickly noticed the residence I was responding to. Without surprise (to me) it was the mobile home with trash, standing water puddles, a loose pit-bull dog, and children's toys strewn in the yard. As I knocked on the door, it opened only to the 4 inch limits of a guard chain. The lock on the door was broken at the latch, and only the chain lock was securing the door. A young child, around 2 years old wearing only a t-shirt (and no diaper), appeared at the door as I announced my presence through the slight opening of the door. The toddler did not speak and was covered in what appeared to be hot Cheetos that had stained his hands and face. My attempts to get the toddler to get his mom were unsuccessful at first. At this point, I then had to call law enforcement for support. After about 10 minutes, a female with her hair and clothing in disarray appeared at the door. When she realized I was a DFCS CM, she immediately became defensive and began explaining things that had nothing to do with the reason for my visit. Observing only through the narrow crack of the door that the home was grossly unsanitary, the mother refused me entry into the home. As the mother picked the child up, I could see even more how unclean and unkempt the child was and how disheveled and disoriented she was.

My first priority was to gain entrance into the home, so that the safety of the children could be properly assessed. To do so, I had to share with the mother that I had to call the police, since she would not allow me entrance into the home to at least "rule out" any safety issues. This tactic worked and she let me in. It was immediately evident that there were serious safety concerns, inadequate supervision, and lack of parental capacity to provide much supervision. However, I was able to calm the mother down by first staying calm and not reacting to her resistance. As she began explaining the reasons for the conditions of the home, I employed my social work active listening skills and expressed that I understood she must be really overwhelmed right now and could use some help. I continued to speak to her in a non-judgmental tone and diplomatically asked her for ideas to best address her own situation, versus authoritatively telling her what was going to occur. This tactic "broke the ice" and we, together, were able to begin developing "a plan." While the police had been called to the home, once they arrived the mother was more cooperative and agreed to an immediate drug screen. We discussed if and how other relatives may be able to help her out, and she continued to provide additional valuable case information. The end result was that the children were placed in a safe environment with relatives, who could provide for their basic needs and whom the mother trusted, while she addressed her own mental health and substance abuse issues. The agency continued to work with the family toward a successful re-unification.

The outcome of this case exemplifies the value of family-centered practice in child welfare. Removing judgments and offering suggestions that are workable for all parties enhances both relationship- and capacity-building. Families are very fearful of change—even when their own norms are chaotic. However, using social work skills, such as empathy and collaboration from a strengths-based perspective (as we were educated about and trained), has proved to produce positive outcomes and has continued to be the basis for successful family growth.

❖

REFERENCES

ACS-NYU Children's Trauma Institute. (2012). *Addressing secondary traumatic stress among child welfare staff: A practice brief.* New York: NYU Langone Medical Center.

Blank, S. (2015). *Georgia Child Welfare Reform Council final report to the governor.* Retrieved October 12, 2015, from https://gov.georgia.gov/sites/gov.georgia.gov/files/related_files/document/Child%20Welfare%20Reform%20Council%20Report%20FINAL.pdf

Child Abuse Definitions, Georgia Code § 19-15-1 Stat. (2015).

Georgia Division of Family and Children Services. (2015). *Division of family and children services SFY 2014 fact sheet.* Retrieved from http://dhs.georgia.gov/

Holosko, M. J. (2006). Why don't social workers make better child welfare workers than non-social workers? *Research on Social Work Practice, 16*(4), 426–430.

Kids Count Data Center. (2015). Georgia Foster Care Indicators. Retrieved from http://datacenter.kidscount.org/data#GA/2/0

Munson, C. E. (2007). *Handbook of clinical social work supervison* (3rd ed.). Binghamton, NY: The Haworth Press.

National Association of Social Workers. (2013). *NASW standards for social work practice in child welfare.* Retrieved October 12, 2015, from https://www.socialworkers.org/practice/standards/childwelfarestandards2012.pdf

Simpson, G. A., Williams, J. C., & Brantley Segall, A. (2007). Social work education and clinical learning. *Clinical Social Work Journal, 35,* 3–14.

Skinner, J. (2015). Social work practice and personal self-care. In K. Concoram, & A. Roberts (Eds.). *Social workers' desk reference* (3rd ed.). New York, NY: Oxford University Press, 130–143.

Wodarski, J. S., Holosko, M. J., & Feit, M. D. (2015). *Evidence-informed assessment and practice in child welfare.* Switzerland: Springer International Publishing.

U.S. Department of Health and Human Services, Administration of Children and Families, Administration on Children, Youth and Families, Children's Bureau. (2015). Child maltreatment 2013. Author retrieved from http://www.acf.hhs.gov/programs/cb/research-data-technology/statistics-research/child-maltreatment

---❖---

ANCILLARIES

Internet References for Additional Reading

1. Case Management Toolkit: A User's Guide for Strengthening Case Management Services in Child Welfare. Retrieved from http://www.iss-usa.org/uploads/File/Case%20Management%20Toolkit.pdf

2. Child Welfare Information Gateway. Retrieved from https://www.childwelfare.gov/

3. Georgia Division of Family and Children Services. Retrieved from http://dfcs.dhs.georgia.gov/

4. NASW Standards for Social Work Practice in Child Welfare. Retrieved from https://www.socialworkers.org/practice/standards/childwelfarestandards2012.pdf

5. Real Cases: Integrating Child Welfare Practice Across the Social Work Curriculum. Retrieved from http://socialwork.adelphi.edu/realcases/

Hard Copy References for Additional Reading

Barker, J., & Hodes, D. T. (2004). *The child in mind: A child protection handbook.* London/New York: Routledge, 2004.

Cooksey-Campbell, K., Folaron, G., & Sullenberger, S. W. (2013). Supervision during child welfare system reform: Qualitative study of factors influencing case manager implementation of a new practice model. *Journal of Public Child Welfare, 7*(2), 123–141. doi:10.1080/15548732.2012.740441

Denby, R. W., & Curtis, C. M. (2013). *African American children and families in child welfare: Cultural adaptation of services.* New York, NY: Columbia University Press.

Gladstone, J., Dumbrill, G., Leslie, B., Koster, A., Young, M., & Ismaila, A. (2014). Understanding worker–parent engagement in child protection casework. *Children and Youth Services Review,* 4456–4464. doi:10.1016/j.childyouth.2014.06.002

Gray, K. A., Franklin, L. D., & Wolfer, T. A. (2013). *Decision cases for advanced social work practice: Confronting complexity.* New York, NY: Columbia University Press.

Hiles Howard, A. R., Call, C. D., McKenzie, L. B., Hurst, J. R., Cross, D. R., & Purvis, K. B. (2013). An examination of attachment representations among child welfare professionals. *Children and Youth Services Review, 351587*–351591. doi:10.1016/j.childyouth.2013.06.010

McLendon, T., McLendon, D., Dickerson, P. S., Lyons, J. K., & Tapp, K. (2012). Engaging families in the child welfare process utilizing the family-directed structural assessment tool. *Child Welfare, 91*(6), 43–58.

Salloum, A., Kondrat, D. C., Johnco, C., & Olson, K. R. (2015). The role of self-care on compassion satisfaction, burnout and secondary trauma among child welfare workers. *Children and Youth Services Review, 4954*–4961. doi:10.1016/j.childyouth.2014.12.023

Zell, M. C. (2006). Child welfare workers: Who they are and how they view the child welfare system. *Child Welfare, 85*(1), 83, 103.

❖ JOB DESCRIPTION

STATE OF GEORGIA

Division of Family and Children Services

Overview
The Georgia Department of Human Services (DHS), Division of Family and Children Services (DFCS) is seeking candidates for the position of **Social Services Case Manager**. This position will serve **Berrien County, Region 11 DFCS**. *The position requires the use of a car for travel and transportation of clients (children).*
DHS delivers a wide range of human services designed to promote self-sufficiency and well-being for all Georgians. The department is one of the largest agencies in state government with an annual budget of $1.8 billion and approximately 9,500 employees. DHS is comprised of three divisions and nine enterprise support functions.
DFCS is the division within DHS that investigates child abuse, identifies foster homes for abused and neglected children; helps low income and out-of-work families get back on their feet; assists with child-care costs for low income parents who are working or in job training programs; and provides a number of additional support services and innovative programs to provide aid to troubled families.
Summary of Responsibilities
This position reports to the Social Services Supervisor.
Under general supervision, the Social Services Case Manager:
1. Assesses the level of risk to children by conducting face-to-face interviews with the alleged child victims and their caretakers; collaborates with law enforcement when children are physically removed from caretakers when the child is found by the courts to be at risk in the home; testifies in court as to the level of risk to children placed in the agency's legal custody
2. Serves as the case manager for children in foster care; ensures that the children are placed in permanent stable families within as short a time frame as possible; visits foster homes; supervises visits between children and parents; testifies regarding the status of the agency and/or parent's progress toward the court approved placement
3. Is available for on-call scheduling
4. Engages in required state-wide travel
5. Performs other professional responsibilities as assigned
Core Competencies
1. Excellent oral, written, presentation, and interpersonal communication skills
2. Strong proficiency in the use of Microsoft Office Suite and/or standard software applications typically used in a corporate office environment
DHS provides services to ensure the health and welfare of all Georgians. In the event of an emergency, any employee may be required to assist in meeting the emergency responsibilities of the department.

STATE OF GEORGIA

Social Services Case Manager

Required Qualifications: Education, Experience, and Credentials
1. **Job Code 14204**: Master's degree in social work from a school of Social Work accredited by the Council on Social Work (www.cswe.org) based in an approved, accredited college or university
2. **Job Code 14205**: Bachelor's degree in social work from a School of Social Work accredited by the Council on Social Work (www.cswe.org) based in an approved, accredited college or university
3. **Job Code 14203**: Behavioral Science degree (any level) from an educational institution accredited by the Council for Higher Education Accreditation (www.chea.org) and/or the US Department of Education *and* one (1) year of social services work experience or a DFCS internship that involved a caseload *or* from an educational institution accredited by the Council for Higher Education (www.chea.org) *and/or* the US Department of Education *and* DFCS internship that included a caseload
4. **Job Code 14212:** Behavioral Science degree (any level) from an educational institution accredited by the Council for Higher Education Accreditation (www.chea.org) and/or the US Department of Education *or* from an educational institution accredited by the Council for Higher Education (www.chea.org) and/or the US Department of Education *or* Bachelor's degree from an approved, accredited college or university
Foreign Credentials: Required Evaluation Reports
Persons who attended colleges or universities outside the 50 states in the United States or the District of Columbia will not be offered employment until they submit a foreign credential report that includes English translations and information showing detailed, course-by-course evaluations and appropriate US degree equivalency. The foreign credential report must be an independent review prepared by an agency approved by the GA DHS. These agencies are private enterprises that charge a fee for their services and the expense is that of the selected candidate. To find an approved vendor, visit http://dhsjobs.dhs.ga.gov/Main/Default.aspx. Go to Related Links and click on Foreign Credential Evaluation Report.
Preferred Qualifications: Education, Experience, and Credentials
The ideal candidate will meet the required qualifications as well as the following:
1. Child Protective Services certification highly desirable
2. Case management experience in Child Protective Services, Child Welfare, or Foster Care
3. Case management experience that involves working with individuals, families, groups, organizations, and/or communication of the goal of behavioral changes
4. Law enforcement experience in areas related to DFCS (e.g., family/domestic violence, investigations, or interventions involving children or substance abuse)
5. Ability to provide transportation and evidence of a valid driver's license for required travel throughout the state

18

Case Management With Long-Term Care Applicants in Ontario, Canada

Deborah Ann Holosko and Derek Chechack

Introduction

Our agency located in Ontario, Canada, is responsible for determining eligibility and authorizing the delivery of in-home health care services for all patients with both short- and long-term health care needs. Here, "in-home" refers to a range of residences on a continuum of care including individual residences, permanent or transitional retirement/assisted living homes, supportive housing complexes, and Long-Term Care (LTC) homes (or "nursing homes," as is the name the public still uses). When care occurs in LTC, the facility has the established medical care, and in this case, eligibility is not for health care services, but for admission to the home itself.

This chapter focuses on clients seeking application into LTC and the department within our agency that manages these applications, waiting lists, and eventual placements. The first author (Deborah Holosko) has performed two related case management (CMG) jobs involved in the application and placement process. One is an assessment case manager (CM), who determines eligibility for LTC. The second is the authorizing CM, who maintains the waitlist and offers available placements into LTC. Because all LTC beds have public funds attached to them in our province, they must be filled in a procedurally fair and equitable manner, giving all patients equal access (*Ontario Ministry of Health and Long Term Care*, 2004). Both CMG positions mentioned above in this will be briefly addressed in this chapter, as they are both required for the client's movement into LTC.

Presently, our clients are no longer called "clients," but rather "patients." This change in phrasing occurred a few years ago. Our personal take on this is that the term patient reinforces that the primary focus on the individual is his or her medical needs for service eligibility. However, the primary mode of assessment completed with patients by CMs provides a biopsychosocial view of the patient, thus acknowledging the patient and their needs and situations in a more holistic way (Bruns & Disorbio, 2009; Engel, 1997). It is also currently mandated and expected that patients be full partners in all of their assessment, treatment decisions, and care planning (Heale, 2011; Health Quality Ontario, 2015; Mead & Bower, 2000; Scholl, Zill, Härter, & Dirmaier, 2014).

The Clientele

Patients seeking LTC must meet strict eligibility criteria set out by our province, as publicly funded dollars are provided for all LTC patients; each patient pays a co-pay, depending on their type of accommodations. (Approximately $1,800 for basic to $2,550 for private [https://www.ontario.ca/page/find-long-term-care-home]). Ironically, because of such funding, these beds may be cheaper than those found in retirement and assisted living homes offering similar levels of care. Admission to LTC is often viewed by the family and patient as "the less disruptive" solution, even if the patient is not actually eligible. These are the LTC department's short-term patients. When they are made ineligible for LTC, they become a "non-admit" for placement services; however, referrals and counseling on what next are still warranted. Being denied access when it is requested can provoke comments of shock and disbelief, as the alternative may have more personal financial costs that were not planned for. The arguments patients and families frequently voice is that the patient should be allowed to settle into before they decline further. Individuals see moving down continuum of care contradictory to the "age-in-place" philosophy promoted in the province (Holosko & Feit, 2004).

The legislated criteria for accessing a LTC bed include:

- Be age 18 or older
- Have a valid Ontario Health Insurance Program (OHIP) card
- Have care needs, including:
  ○ 24-hours nursing care and personal care
  ○ Frequent assistance with activities of daily living
  ○ On-site supervision or monitoring to ensure your safety or well-being
- Have care needs that cannot be safely met in the community through publicly funded community-based services and other care-giving support
- Have care needs that can be met in a long-term care home, https://www.ontario.ca/search/search-results?query=long%20term%20care%20home

It is not the medical diagnosis per se, but its impact on one's functionality that essentially determines LTC eligibility. Simply put, it is the patient's ability to manage the activities of his or her day-to-day living. In terms of LTC eligibility, a patient typically needs to include a level of personal care impairment impacting transferring and toileting; and/or needs for medical treatments that are complex and time consuming; and/or needs for supervision to remain safe, for example, as in the case of advancing cognitive problems. The types of medical problems with associated functional needs include, but are not limited to, cerebrovascular accidents (CVAs; i.e., a stroke with some paralysis), severe cardiac problems, primary or secondary dementia, amputations, chronic obstructive pulmonary disease (COPD), severe arthritis, and/or kidney failure. Many of these problems can co-exist together and are often coupled with other conditions such as diabetes, mental illness (as another primary illness or secondary to the illnesses), vision loss, hearing, speech, and/or swallowing impairments.

When facing these challenges, patients and caregivers typically lament and concur that "the golden years are not really golden," or "getting ill makes you old real fast." It can be difficult for them to see a good quality of life, or find a positive focus/goal in the midst of their decline. They often talk openly about such losses: what they can no longer do or the mounting costs and added responsibilities/burdens, etc. It is in the midst of such vocalized distress and perceived hopelessness that the patient, and/or caregivers, now must negotiate the health system for solutions, often with a sense of urgency because the patient's failing health means a solution is quickly needed. This consensual solution will demand that an informed choice be made. However, the rules, regulations, and options to be discussed can be complex, and the motivation to engage and plan is often very low.

More specifically, the following is what a patient, and/or caregiver, must rapidly process: 1) that the patient needs to live in a LTC; and 2) they must choose a LTC facility quickly. In this regard, patients/caregivers are encouraged to make an appointment to tour and understand their available options, while at the same time being told to do it rapidly. They are likely to discover their preferred LTC choice may not be available for some time, so another task becomes, How do they plan to manage the situation in the meantime? Or, will they be setting up care elsewhere or picking a less-preferred LTC home? Here the messages can seem mixed—as options can be presented and taken away at the same time. Choices may be deemed "forced," or perceived as "what other choice do I have?"

While professionals in the field understand health care changes and the progression of illnesses, much of the public does not; they have pre-conceived ideas of how medical care progresses and/or what a move to a nursing home really means. As a result, there is much discovery and education required during this decision time. Frequently expressed comments are, "I don't know what to do."; "I don't know where to look."; "I don't know what to choose."; "What would you do?"; "I can't keep track of all the information."; "What do I do next?"; and/or "Why can't he or she stay in hospital, he or she hasn't had a chance to get better?" Here, any inaction or lack of decision making on the part of the patient or caregiver can be quickly perceived as resistance and manipulation by the professional, about not wanting to make a choice. However, an alternate interpretation (which would alter the professional's approach to the patient/caregiver) can be ambivalence; as they are too overwhelmed and anxious to act (Rollnick, Miller, & Butler, 2008). Depending on the perspective held, patients and caregivers often report feeling different reactions from professionals in the process, and sometimes bitterness can occur when feeling pushed.

For some, the transition to LTC will be more seamless. In other words, despite what has been described above, there are patients who are quite successful in navigating the complex system. Whether innate or learned, there are patients and caregivers who possess good health management skills, including a better understanding of their own needs; good coping skills; problem-solving abilities; and advocacy skills to facilitate their seamless movement through the system. Often, they are also skilled in concisely articulating their experiences. These patients are actually invaluable to CMs, as they teach the so-called professionals (like us) about the impact of the local health system on their situations and changes within it. With their lived experiences, they are able through case vignettes and sharing to help professionals deepen their empathy and also understand the pitfalls of the existing care system. Thus, they serve as an important resource for many CMs in the care system, and an inspiration of hope that things can work when issues are seen as challenges, not problems with no solutions.

Roles and Responsibilities of the Case Managers

The overarching goal and mission of our agency is to "engage patients and assist them to move seamlessly through the health care system," which aligns us with the goal of transformative health care, in having patients actively involved and be more responsible for their own health care (Province of Ontario, 2005). While the formal application process is clearly laid out in provincial legislation, policies, and forms (a bureaucracy in its fullest sense), each individual's experience is unique to themselves and their personal situation. The implication is that there are numerous inevitable speed bumps to be negotiated. There is consensus that while the process may be standard, the patient is not. Most patients present as needing some types of modification to move through the rather daunting process. For instance, many patients often have sensory impairments that directly impact on their communication abilities. Their health issues can also be tenuous, so planning must be able to change as one's medical status improves or deteriorates. Patients also often have a situational crisis, such as a need for interim accommodations, a delirium or behaviors that make placement difficult, limited financial resources for planning, having been immigrants to Canada in the last 10 years, which limits government supports (this applies to both Canada and the United States), difficulties with family dynamics, which further delays planning, and/or no informal support systems to assist them. Here the CM may have to become more involved with advocacy until something is worked out.

As previously indicated, making an application and moving into a LTC facility in our agency will require two CMs with distinct roles to navigate the patient in this portion of the system. The first CM's role involves *assessing, collaborating, and determining eligibility;* and the second, occurring after eligibility, is about case *managing waitlists, collaborating on choices/options, and authorizing the placement* of a patient into a specific long-term care bed. While collaboration is noted in both roles, other overlapping tasks of the CM role include navigation, coordination, and/ or patient advocates.

In fact, CMs are also known by those formal titles: Navigator, Coordinator, or Advocate. Regardless of the title, all focus on assisting the patient/caregiver's evolution toward being a better manager of their own health care needs. The CM's tasks in this regard, regardless of their position in the health care system, are essentially the same: a) collaborate with the patient on their current situation and needs; b) assist in breaking down the decision making required into doable steps; c) ensure that the specific information levels are provided for informed decision making; and d) assist in keeping the patient movement at a manageable pace for the system at large. Also, since these decisions must be made often in the midst of a disability/medical complexity, there is also the task of determining who is the correct person to actually make decisions: the patient or their designated decision-maker.

Assessing CM roles and responsibilities. A patient typically initiates a LTC application from two different pathways: 1) with the assistance of a community CM, who is also managing home care and community service referrals supporting the patient in the community; or 2) through a hospital setting, when it has been determined that the patient's discharge back into the community is too risky. While both of these CMs assess and determine eligibility for LTC, the role described herein will be the second (in hospital) when going home is not a foreseeable option at the time of assessment.

The hospital assessing CM a) completes an assessment to determine if LTC eligibility is appropriate; b) determines if the patient is able to make decisions or if someone else must; c) has the "determined person" complete a request of application for LTC; d) requests a LTC medical be completed by a medical professional; and, if possible, e) collaborates and starts a waitlist of potential LTC homes and any interim plans that may be needed.

Collaboration starts with the initial assessment using a specific assessment tool known as the RAI-HC (see accac.com/innovation/Pages/assessment.aspx). While this tool is specific to the province, variations of Resident Assessment Inventories (RAIs) are used worldwide for varying purposes. On a micro level, it uses algorithms and embedded sub-scales to predict multi-levels of functioning/needs and scores to determine eligibility for actual service provision. On a macro level, it can provide statistical data for research and health planning (www.interrai.org)]. Despite its capability, the assessment is only as good as the skill of its user, as the instrument is just "the tool." While completion is a necessary task or "output," accurate information, patient collaboration, and appropriate planning is the necessary outcome for appropriate and personalized planning.

The real skill for this CM is how to prevent the tool from becoming too front and center in the conversations with the patient. It is a real challenge for CMs to keep a patient-directed conversation going, while completing a very detailed and long form. We believe that the key is to know the form well enough so it does not have to be completed in a linear fashion. Experience reminds us that when the discussion is patient led, there are richer data and insights into their needs/goals and the patient's abilities to reach them. This is viewed as the cornerstone of patient-centered approaches in social work (Institute for Patient and Family Centered Care, n.d.; National Association of Social Workers, 2013; Peterson, 2012). In this regard, the RAI-HC is to be braided around the patient's agenda of what needs to be said, with the CM knowing when to ask timely questions that the patient is not addressing, but must eventually be completed in the RAI tool.

The immediate challenge for the hospital assessing CM, when a patient is referred, is how to build an instant rapport, as the assessment and eligibility is to be completed as short as only one visit. A second appointment requires a rationale, as one visit is considered the professional norm. This can be managed by the CM demonstrating to the patient and their caregivers an understanding of where they are and by providing the context of how the health system is actually impacting them. Knowledge of current legislation/policy, health care partners, the community and LTC resources that foster their understanding help fill in the context of how everything works. The aim here is to provide such information in an open and transparent dialogue, drawing on an awareness of "where the patient is at, in his or her social environment."

Often there is a disconnect in the perceptions patients/caregivers have of the health system, in general. For example, many are still confused about the role of the hospital in their care. Some patients and their caregivers also often feel they are being discharged too soon and get stuck on insisting they stay in the hospital longer, rather than exploring options about moving on. Much of the public is still unaware that hospitals (in both Canada and the United States) are presently utilized to treat acute patients until they are stabilized; as ongoing treatments, convalescence and maintenance can and will safely be carried out in other environments including LTC. Clarifying this disconnect provides the assessing hospital CM an entry point into building the needed rapport. By validating the emotions of patients/caregivers, and clearly explaining the real situation at hand, the CM has the opportunity to be viewed as a transparent and thus trusted resource/guide. To be effective, the CM must display the basic skills of empathy and genuineness, as well as the demonstration of expert knowledge on legislation, process, and resources.

A second important and related message CMs use to build rapport is to clearly articulate to the patient/caregiver that the CM has no pre-conceived notions of the patient, and will have no opinions to share, until the patient/caregiver provides "their own story." This message again reinforces the CM's willingness to listen, hear, and value their viewpoint, setting the stage for the necessary collaborative process required for more effective and efficient patient movement (Attree, 2008; Leach, 2005).

Unfortunately, the true picture of transparency and collaboration does not always occur in the system at-large, as transitions are often clouded by false information and "passing the buck." "I was promised/told . . . if I agreed to accept/move . . ." is the start of some conversations about unrealized services (e.g., more therapy, activities, transportation); resources (e.g., supplies/equipment, better room); and plan (e.g., preferred placement). It is a sad indictment of the system, and the accompanying pressure professionals can feel, to move patients on when false promise/hope is promoted without thought about the next planning phase. Each part of the health system does not really feel accountable to the next, nor the patient, with whom they feel

❖ JOB DESCRIPTION

Placement Assessor

Position Duties

Reporting to the supervisor, the incumbent will

- Conduct patient assessments/eligibility within the hospital engaging the patient/family to meet the patient's needs using negotiating, problem-solving, and decision-making skills

- Provide information throughout the health care trajectory, review assessments, counsel patients in the area of community services and long-term placement

- Complete patient assessments for Long-Term Care Eligibility as required

- Develop collaborative working relationships with Hospital staff and enhance existing working relationships with a broad range of community agencies

- Collaborate with clinical leaders in the development of system-wide diagnosis-related pathway development

- Navigate patients to appropriate alternate sources of care and/or service

- Compile concise records according to Ministry of Health and Long-Term Care and internal policies and procedures

Qualifications

Knowledge and application of case management principles and practices acquired through membership in good standing, with the appropriate college, as a Registered Nurse, Occupational Therapist, Physiotherapist or Speech Language Pathologist, or Social Work, with a degree at the master's level preferred. All professions are to be in good standing with the professional colleges. Proven skills in the areas of case management, assessment, communication, interviewing, and problem solving. Minimum of 2–3 years of community care coordination and/or hospital care coordination experience is preferred. The ability to work independently in a highly organized manner is required. This position also requires proficiency in the use of a personal computer in a Windows environment, using Word and database software. Sound knowledge of health care system, relevant legislation, and community resources. The ability to travel. Fluency in French language preferred.

Serious Mental Illnesses and Dual Diagnoses Case Management

Edwin Ng and Polly Li

Introduction

In his message on World Mental Health Day (October 10, 2011), United Nations Secretary-General Ban Ki-moon (2011) stated,

> There is no health without mental health. Mental disorders are major contributors to illness and premature death, and are responsible for 13% of the global disease burden. With the global economic downturn and associated austerity measures, the risks for mental ill-health are rising around the globe.

Because mental well-being plays a significant role in the health of individuals, it is worthwhile to identify and review essential social services and interventions that address mental health disorders. One such service is case management; the collaborative process of assessing, planning, facilitating, coordinating, evaluating, and advocating for options and services to meet an individual's comprehensive mental health needs (Rapp, 1998). This chapter provides a first-person account of case management with individuals with serious mental illnesses and dual diagnoses.

The Clientele

Since 2004, the second author (Polly Li) has worked as a case manager in the Mental Health Intensive Case Management Program (MHICMP) at York Support Services Network (YSSN). MHICMP serves individuals who are at least 16 years of age and who, through no fault of their own or their families, have been diagnosed with a serious mental illness (SMI) and/or dual diagnosis (DD). Established in 1985, the YSSN is located in the Regional Municipality of York in Ontario, Canada. The York Region is a fast-growing global village, consisting of several different types of people of various ages, backgrounds, and languages (Statistics Canada, 2011). From 2006 to 2011, the region recorded a population increase of 15.7%, or about 140,000 residents. In 2011, it ranked seventh in Canada with a population of 1,032,524 residents and had the third highest percentage of immigrants in its population (45%), after Peel (50%) and Toronto (49%). Tellingly, 5% of the region's population are recent immigrants who arrived in Canada between 2006 and 2011. The top six visible minority groups in the region are Chinese (18%), South Asian (e.g., East Asian) (11%), West Asian (e.g., Iranian) (3%), Black (3%), Filipino (2%), and Southeast Asian (e.g., Vietnamese) (2%). Despite being known as an affluent region with a median family income of $97,374, low- and very low-income neighborhoods are scattered throughout Markham, Richmond Hill, and Vaughan, constituting 14% of the region.

Given York region's rapid growth in population, increasing cultural and racial diversity, and rising affluence and deepening poverty, the clients of MHICMP have evolved to reflect these changing population demographics. For example, the CM's typical caseload is diverse and includes clients who are male and female, aged 18–60, single and married, immigrants and non-immigrants, and who occupy different socioeconomic statuses. Most clients, however, live near poverty and are either underemployed or unemployed. If employed, clients often work within shelter settings. In recent years, a growing number of Mandarin speaking individuals from China have sought mental health case management (CMG) support. Within any given time period, the average number of assigned cases assigned ranges from 15 to 20. In terms of workload, the average amount of time required to successfully manage assigned cases and bring them to resolution varies from 2 to 5 years. It is also worthwhile to note that all CMG work takes place on an interdisciplinary team, which includes intake social workers, supervisors, case managers, administrative support staff, and a consulting psychiatrist.

The two most common presenting issues are individuals with SMI or DD. The former is defined by three criteria (Ruggeri, Leese, Thornicroft, Bisoffi, & Tansella, 2000). The first is *diagnosis*, or the identification of the nature and cause of SMI, which includes mental health disorders that produce psychotic symptoms. CMG clients present with severe impairments that adversely affect their feelings, moods, and overall affect (e.g., uncontrolled and disruptive emotions); thinking (e.g., presence of delusions, and/or hallucinations); family and friends (e.g., inability to maintain family and social support systems); role performance (e.g., unable to perform labor market, and/

and patient advocacy. The journal provides practical, hands-on information for day-to-day activities, as well as cutting-edge research.

5. CMSA Today. Retrieved from http://www.cmsatoday.com/

This quarterly publication delivers important news and information direct from the CMSA—the largest and oldest non-profit, multidisciplinary care management professional association in the United States. The magazine is the cornerstone of CMSA's member communications—incorporating print and digital publications, as well as e-newsletters and a complementary news website—all designed to deliver the latest news and information from CMSA and the care management industry.

Hard Copy References for Additional Reading

Burns, T., Catty, J., Dash, M., Roberts, C., Lockwood, A., & Marshall, M. (2007). Use of intensive case management to reduce time in hospital in people with severe mental illness: Systematic review and meta-regression. *BMJ, 335*(7615), 336.

Eack, S. M., Anderson, C. M., & Greeno, C. G. (2012). *Mental health case management: A practical guide.* Thousand Oaks, CA: Sage.

Forchuk, C., Ouwerkerk, A., Yamashita, M., & Martin, M. L. (2002). Mental health case management in Canada: Job description analyses. *Issues in Mental Health Nursing, 23*(5), 477–496.

Goering, P. N., Wasylenki, D. A., Lancee, W. J., Farkas, M., & Ballantyne, R. (1988). What difference does case management make? *Psychiatric Services, 39*(3), 272–276.

Hromco, J. G., Lyons, J. S., & Nikkel, R. E. (1995). Mental health case management: Characteristics, job function, and occupational stress. *Community Mental Health Journal, 31*(2), 111–125.

Mueser, K. T., Bond, G. R., Drake, R. E., & Resnick, S. G. (1998). Models of community care for severe mental illness: A review of research on case management. *Schizophrenia Bulletin, 24*(1), 37–74.

Nelson, G., Aubry, T., & Lafrance, A. (2007). A review of the literature on the effectiveness of housing and support, assertive community treatment, and intensive case management interventions for persons with mental illness who have been homeless. *American Journal of Orthopsychiatry, 77*(3), 350–361.

Onyett, S. (1998). *Case management in mental health.* London, UK: Nelson Thornes.

Rapp, C. A. (1998). *The strengths model: Case management with people suffering from severe and persistent mental illness.* New York, NY: Oxford University Press.

Rapp, C. A., & Goscha, R. J. (2004). The principles of effective case management of mental health services. *Psychiatric Rehabilitation Journal, 27*(4), 319.

Sackett, D. L., Richardson, W. S., Rosenberg, W., & Haynes, R. B. (1997). Critically appraising the evidence. *Evidence-based medicine: How to practice and teach EBM,* 118–128.

Stanard, R. P. (1999). The effect of training in a strengths model of case management on client outcomes in a community mental health center. *Community Mental Health Journal, 35*(2), 169–179.

Vanderplasschen, W., Rapp, R. C., Wolf, J. R., & Broekaert, E. (2014). The development and implementation of case management for substance use disorders in North America and Europe. *Psychiatric Services, 55*(8), 913–922.

Ziguras, S. J., & Stuart, G. W. (2000). A meta-analysis of the effectiveness of mental health case management over 20 years. *Psychiatric Services, 51*(11), 1410–1421.

❖ JOB TITLE: CASE MANAGER

Program: Mental Health

Summary

The Mental Health Case Manager is responsible for the provision of intensive case management and advocacy services to individuals 16 and over who are experiencing significant difficulties in daily functioning as a result of serious mental illness or dual diagnosis (mental health and developmental disability). The overall responsibility of the Mental Health Case Manager is to facilitate recovery and assist service users to improve their quality of life through a collaborative approach to service provision through community visits. The Mental Health Case Manager is responsible for direct service interventions, clinical support, and community development.

Responsibilities and Duties

1. **Service coordination:** To assist service users (and/or their families) to develop skills or to access resources needed to achieve goals.

Duties

- Assist service users and/or families in identifying their needs, strengths, abilities, and preferences from a biopsychosocial perspective, and to assist toward greater independence and service completion

- Engage service users in a collaborative ongoing process of identifying and monitoring a goal plan, progress, and achievement and clarifying goal-related tasks, roles, and responsibilities

- Assist service users and/or families to evaluate service effectiveness and to support the continuous quality improvement efforts of the agency, to address concerns, and resolve issues

- Provide information to the Supervisor regarding critical service issues and participate in the systematic advocacy efforts as requested

2. **Clinical Support:** To assist service users to improve their quality of life through a range of professional strategies.

Duties

- Assist service users to address identified needs including food, shelter, and clothing and develop strategies for healthy living

- Work collaboratively with service users to identify and develop a crisis management plan

- Provide information related to mental illness in a manner that is understandable to service users and others

- Provide and research information about services offered and other agencies through telephone consultation, written material, and other resource materials requested by the service users or others

- Assist service users in acquiring functional skills through direct teaching or through a group process

- Provide emotional support and encouragement through active listening, validation, and constructive feedback

- Utilize agency resources, formal and informal contacts to address the complex or critical situations concerning service users, in consultation with the Supervisor

- Provide Short-Term Support to service users as required

20

Juvenile Court Social Work Case Manager

Mark W. Flanagan, Margie J. Strauss, and Harold Briggs

The Clientele

The majority of clientele seen at our juvenile court are poor families on government assistance with unemployed heads of household. Approximately 80% of my (Mark W. Flanagan) clients are white, 19% Hispanic and 1% African American. Clients come to our attention primarily through schools, which file complaints with the local juvenile court. However, anyone can file a Juvenile Court Complaint: that is, law enforcement, Department of Family and Children Services (DFCS), neighbors, parents, or just concerned citizens. If the courts have not found any abuse, the client comes to our agency's attention. Usual problems include housing, transportation, school compliance, employment, and health care. Many also have significant barriers transporting themselves to crucial appointments with doctors, lawyers, and other community professionals. As noted, while abuse has not been assessed when they initially come to our attention, most cases end up having some kind of physical or emotional maltreatment.

Typical Clients

A 10-year-old child is not going to school and acts disruptive at school when he does attend. His parents are unable to control or make him go to school. The child is also left unsupervised for long periods of time, which exacerbates his overall ambivalence and negative behaviors. His parents are separated, and he mainly stays with his mother and grandmother. His mother is not working and is on government assistance and has no health insurance. Generally, there are also younger children in the home.

The best-case scenario here is when a case manager (CM) can arrange supportive services such as therapy, parent support, school interventions, youth mentoring, support groups or life coaching for parents. A CM aims to aid the youth and family by achieving services and ultimately self-determination. The goal of Juvenile Court services in this case is to divert the youth and family from becoming further involved with the court system.

Atypical Client

A 15-year-old boy is not going to school because he claims he is too tired from his other activities. The boy comes from a wealthy family, and his parents are not forcing him to go to school. He is also consuming pot, alcohol, or other drugs. The parents are largely absent and provide limited supervision.

In order to address this situation, a CM met with the family, and the parents first consented to a drug screen. The test was positive for marijuana. While his parents were astonished, his explanation for the positive test result was that he was at a party in a smoke filled room with others smoking pot, and he inhaled the smoke secondhand. Following his declaration of innocence, the CM explained that the likelihood of acquiring a positive drug screen resulting from passively inhaling pot smoke is highly unlikely, if not impossible. After their clarification, he admitted to smoking marijuana on a regular basis out of boredom and lack of supervision. The brief treatment approach used by the CM involved the following:

- The parents changed their schedules to ensure more supervision.
- The youth was referred to an out-patient drug treatment program.
- He was also placed on the drug self-report protocol, where he had to call a phone number at 7:00 am daily to determine if he needed to come in for further drug screening. If 'clean' for drugs during a 6-week period, the case would be re-evaluated by the CM for service delivery needs and eventual service termination.
- If the random 6-week drug screening resulted in a positive drug screen, then I would file a complaint with the court and the youth would appear before a judge. The judge would then decide on the disposition, which could be the implementation of a protective order and shift the case into dependency court. Dependency court could mandate an out of home placement, foster care, an ankle monitor, or supervision by the Department of Juvenile Justice (DJJ).

Practice Roles and Responsibilities

The main responsibilities of a Juvenile Court CM are as follows:

1. **Family Assessments**

   This includes meeting with the family and determining what they need through a lengthy interview and protocol. Then, the CM makes appropriate referrals. This could be as simple as referring them to a licensed therapist, or as dire as filing a complaint for an emergency hearing with the court. I (M.J.S.) have had parents come to this meeting under the influence of a substance and refuse a drug screen. This is where my experience comes to bear, and I have to evaluate if the child(ren) are safe, foremost. I have also had cases where the parents leave the assessment meeting. I would then make a referral to DFCS and perhaps ask for their welfare checks from local law enforcement.

2. **Liaising With Other Community Professionals**

The CM plans services mainly for cases involving abuse and neglect. In those instances, I would send a CM from DFCS to the home. DFCS CMs are only required to have a college degree. While some have master's or BSWs, most do not. We also send out a lot of CMs from "CASAs" (Court Appointed Special Advocates), who are lay Guardian *ad Litem.* These CMs do an extensive in-home evaluation and then report to the court or directly to me about what they find. These CMs have a college education, but are trained by the CASA program. If the case comes into court, then the judge may assign a CASA to it and they'll become the "field person." Here, they interview the child, the parents, grandparents, and extended family in the home. They may also be called upon to monitor any interstate travel of such clients.

3. **Case Evaluations**

As the CM with the court system, I am the point of entry for a given complaint about a given child or family. After the case is reviewed, I send clinical evaluators to client's homes. In order to determine what is most needed, I require an investigation conducted by the appropriate child serving organization in the community. For example, if a complaint comes from the school, chances are the school has already been at the home, because they have to make reasonable outreach efforts before it comes to us by law. However, they only go as far (physically) into the home as they are invited, which is usually the front door. If the school has a concern that there is abuse or neglect, then the school reports it to DFCS. If it is something like truancy, without suspicion of abuse, it would come into court, and I would assess what needs to be done. DJJ would then most likely make a home visit and conduct another assessment. I am actually not allowed to go out and do court assessments myself, because I then become 'a witness'. Here, my role is to *coordinate* the assessment of the client's overall safety.

4. **Care Management Coordination**

I coordinate the service system organizations participating in the life of the case in our "community of care." This involves coordinating different agencies involved in each client's case and then developing a treatment plan. It also involves follow through, or making sure that they do what they are supposed to do. For example, if a family comes in and they need mental services for therapy or assessments, I can order a psychologist to conduct such an assessment. If necessary, the court can often pay out of their budget. Sometimes, I have to coordinate with their insurance agency to arrange full or partial payment. Once the assessment comes back from the psychologists, I hand the case details to a Licensed Clinical Social Worker (LCSW) on our staff to review. The LCSW would then normally conduct a meeting with the parents and we would follow the recommendations of the assessment. Often, this involves contacting other community agencies to access services for mental health, health care, finances, or employment.

Main Social Work Skills Utilized

Establishing rapport. The first task of the Juvenile Court CM is to make families feel more comfortable—in efforts to have them talk openly and honestly to a stranger in a short amount of time. It is important to welcome new families with both open arms, and suspended judgments. I believe that this helps to build rapport very quickly. Generally, the first meeting is for an hour and a half. After that, I continue to maintain ongoing and open communication with the family as I coordinate care.

Problem-solving. It is no secret that complex problem-solving skills are crucial to effective case management (CMG). A CM must be flexible and willing to always look for multiple solutions. For example, I once had a parent with a transgender child who was having difficulties both socially and academically. We referred the mother to parental education classes in the community. However, the parenting she received was religious, which conflicted with her own way of life. She came back and told me, "These classes are not helping. They are telling me something is wrong with my child." I immediately helped her find other options, because I didn't feel this strategy was appropriate or helpful for this client.

Theoretical Framing for Interventions:

I rely on theories learned in my education to both better understand the lived experiences of my clients and to help me to contextually frame the interventions and treatment plans that I develop with my clients. Two theories I routinely use in this regard include: lifespan and attachment.

Lifespan Theory

CMs in this job need to appraise the age dynamics of everyone who is in the family. For example, we have clients who have several generations in the house: great grandparents, parents, children, and grandchildren. In such families, the central issue is how to help such clients progress, while acknowledging and honoring the age-related values of everyone in the home (Broderick & Blewitt, 2015).

Attachment Theory

I see a lot of co-dependency among my clients and their families. For instance, there was a case where a mother wouldn't let her daughter sleep in another room. Her husband had left her, so she was holding onto this child, physically as well as emotionally. However, the daughter wanted to sleep in her own, separate room. But, the mother wanted the daughter to sleep with her, not in a sexual way, but in an overly enmeshed way. The daughter also had to report to her mother for everything. The daughter was having problems, didn't want to go to school, and was getting bullied, and her mother would listen to her child and do whatever the child wanted.

A central principle in attachment theory conveys that a child needs to develop a trusting relationship with at least one primary caregiver, in order for him or her to successfully develop emotionally and socially (Goldberg, Muir, & Kerr, 2009). However, this mother was fostering an anxious attachment style by requiring her daughter to spend inappropriate amounts of time with her. When other professionals came to help with this case, the mother dealt better with her co-dependency, the child dealt better with her guilt, and we were able to more effectively help this child. This child needed to cope with her own deep-seated guilt from fear of hurting her mother by moving to a separate room. The daughter eventually did move out, and she is doing very well.

Main Challenges/Barriers

A lack of resources, especially mental health services. As an entry-level social worker, I am frustrated with the number of providers that don't take Medicaid, or who work with no health insurance. Indeed, there are few quality mental health residential facilities for children ages 9–16 (Mental Health America, 2016). Many of our clients don't have health insurance, therefore, there are very few providers that are free of charge.

Political climate, legislation, and funding. Politics and legislation have big impacts on Juvenile Court CMG. Presently, the state laws have taken much power away from judges, so they have to focus on putting these children with their parents. This has been challenging because what is needed is follow-up services, which costs money. Most of our clients have limited incomes or are on government assistance. There are very few professionals that will accept reduced payments and provide quality service for such clients.

Large caseloads. I am currently carrying 180 cases, which is actually a caseload for two CMs. Because of reduced funding for our court, and the increased number of cases the court is taking, I have had to take on more work. It has been a major personal and professional struggle, and we are actively working to resolve it. My job is to assess the needs of the family, which requires constant vigilance. I have to monitor the families and their progress, which sometimes is meager. However, I only have 120 days to meet, evaluate, and implement an intervention. If the family shows no sign of improvement, I have to promptly re-evaluate. There are times when the services offered are enough, and the child is doing better. In these instances, I would close such cases. There are other times when there is no progress, and I need to decide if court involvement is still necessary.

Role Development Potential

My job currently supports me in obtaining my MSW. It both supports me and gives me needed time off and flexibility with my schedule, although I have to still work 40 hours in each week. I hope to obtain my LMSW and LCSW eventually. These licenses will increase my salary and will change my job responsibilities. Presently, I am more involved much bureaucracy and paperwork. I spend about half of my time completing administrative tasks. My MSW and additional training will position me to primarily do more clinical work.

To date, my on-the-job social work education has helped me significantly. It has helped me mature and take judgments out of assessments and interactions. My clinical training has also helped me approach clients to develop rapport quicker, so I can make a more timely positive change. I believe it has also helped me mature into role of social worker more effectively.

If I were planning a BSW/MSW curriculum to educate students to work as social work CMs, I would recommend more course content on working with specialty populations. For example, I would like to see more classes focusing on transgender, hospice, young, and elderly populations. Within these courses, it would be helpful to practice interacting with diverse groups through teaching-learning interactive role-plays. I believe students learn effectively by enacting case situations rather than reading about them.

In addition, I think offering additional certifications for specialty skills would help new graduates better obtain employment. For example, I am forensically trained to interview outside by the police department. This is very marketable, outside of the university. Offering other shorter and specific trainings like suicide assessment, CPR, statistical training, and others could provide a more competitive advantage for BSW and MSW students.

Finally, I think the field placement is critical to our social work learning. I believe it would be advantageous to broaden our placement choices. The more hands-on experiences students have, the more prepared they are to practice social work. I feel currently there are limited choices for placement in many programs. For example, certain field placements only offer concentration internships and won't do foundation ones, and vice versa.

Case Example

A low-income Caucasian family presents with a husband, wife, a 10-year-old child, and a 5-year-old child. The younger child is not in school yet, and the older one is in school, but is having trouble. The school thinks that the dad may be sexually abusing the older son. The older child is asking questions about female anatomy, and the school thinks that the father is not handling it appropriately. The father also has symptoms of autism. In this case, after the father found porn on the child's computer, he decided he was going to get textbooks and go over the female anatomy with the child in an educational manner. The school decides that this is not appropriate behavior, so they make a report to DFCS.

When the case came to me, I began my CMG by conducting an interview with the father and older child. I see that the father is awkward socially, but determined that he did not have any malicious intentions in showing the son various textbook images of anatomy. He seemed very innocent to me, and it was what he thought was the best way to parent his child, and I did not see any abuse or inappropriate parenting. The mother didn't want to discuss female anatomy with the son, and the father felt it was his responsibility to fully educate his child about parts of woman's anatomy and what goes where, and what happens, and so forth. And the father talked about the porn and how it was inappropriate and illegal.

Again, DFCS felt this was inappropriate, and the family was recommended for ongoing services. Again, the family felt they were targeted, and for not doing anything wrong. So I went in and tried listening to the perspective from the school and DFCS. But my social work skills guided me to stop and listen, and try to better understand where this gentleman was actually coming from. I spent an hour and a half with him; afterward, I put in affordable services for an LCSW to come into the home and provide guidance on age-appropriate sex education. I then gave the recommendation to close this case. The case did not go to court, and the DFCS also closed the case. This case example illustrates the importance of discernment, suspension of judgment, and understanding complex biopsychosocial considerations: all skills and knowledge emphasized in our BSW and MSW social work training.

Concluding Remarks

Active listening has been the most valuable tool for me to understand what both clients and organizational entities want. Importantly, active listening has also helped me pay closer attention to what I (the worker) need. It is vital to be in touch with one's self while working with systems of vulnerable and challenged clients, because this work can be emotional and very draining. One needs to be aware of one's own needs and take care of one's self—it's something that I think should be mandatory for this job. Through such self-awareness and active listening, CMs become more effective for their clients.

Supervision is also critical. Support at the workplace or in a collegial group is very valuable for difficult and complex case situations. Workers should regularly seek help through supervision in order to reflect and process difficult cases. I have also had people work for me who get too emotionally wrapped up with their clients. Over time and with proper support, an effective CM is able to become less personally involved in cases. For me, the hardest part in learning this is how to let go of the client whom you want to help, but who doesn't seem to want to help himself or herself. That has been a lesson that I am still working on. Through my own supervision with LCSWs and Licensed Marriage and Family Therapists (LMFTs), I have begun to understand that many other clients both need and want our help. When you have really given it your all, and they are still not responding, you just have to let it go! If you find yourself doing more work than the people you are providing assistance and empowerment to, then you must be aware and change *your* behavior before seeking to change the client's actions. In this manner, you can grow into an effective CM who is healthy and happy, while providing the highest level of care to your clients. This is truly rewarding, but challenging work indeed!

❖

REFERENCES

Broderick, P. C., & Blewitt, P. (2015). *The life span: Human development for helping professionals* (4th ed.). New York, NY: Pearson.

Goldberg, S., Muir, R., & Kerr, J. (Eds.) (2009). *Attachment theory, social developmental, and clinical perspectives*. New York, NY: Routledge.

Mental Health America. (2016). *Mental health in America—Access to care data*. Retrieved from http://www.mentalhealthamerica.net/issues/mental-health-america-access-care-data

---

❖

ANCILLARIES

Internet References for Additional Reading

1. SCHOOLENGAGEMENT.ORG

   Colorado Foundation for Families and Children. (2007). *Truancy case management handbook: Advice from the field.* Retrieved from http://schoolengagement.org/wp-content/uploads/2014/03/TruancyCaseManagementHandbookAdvicefromtheField.pdf

2. DYRS.DC.GOV

   Department of Youth and Rehabilitation Services. (2010). *Case management manual version IV.* Retrieved from http://dyrs.dc.gov/sites/default/files/dc/sites/dyrs/publication/attachments/dyrs_case_management_manual.pdf

3. NSCS.ORG

   National Center for State Courts. (2014). Juvenile justice resource guide. Retrieved from http://www.ncsc.org/Topics/Children-Families-and-Elders/Juvenile-Justice-and-Delinquency/Resource-Guide.aspx

4. OJJDP.GOV

   Office of Juvenile Justice. (2016). Combating violence and delinquency: The national juvenile justice action plan. Retrieved from http://www.ojjdp.gov/action/sec1.htm

5. CHILDWELFARE.ORG

   Child Welfare Information Gateway. (2014). *Case planning for families involved with child welfare agencies.* Retrieved from https://www.childwelfare.gov/pubPDFs/caseplanning.pdf

Hard Copy References for Additional Reading

Cox, S. M., Allen, J. M., Hanser, R. D., & Conrad, J. J. (2013). *Juvenile justice: A guide to theory, policy, and practice* (8th ed.). Thousand Oaks, CA: Sage.

Murrihy, R. C., Kidman, A. D., & Ollendick, T. H. (Eds.). (2010). *Clinical handbook of assessing and treating conduct problems in youth.* New York, NY: Springer.

Potter, C. C., & Brittain, C. R. (Eds.). 2009. *Child welfare supervision: A practical guide for supervisors, managers, and administrators.* New York, NY: Oxford University Press.

Powell, S. K., & Hussein, T. A. (2008). *CMSA core curriculum for case management.* Philadelphia, PA: Case Management Society of America.

Rapp-Paglicci, L. A., Dulmus, C. N., Jongsma, A. E., & Wodarski, J. S. (2001). *The social work and human services treatment planner.* New York, NY: John Wiley & Sons.

❖ JOB DESCRIPTION: JUVENILE COURT CASE MANAGER

Provides supervision for a caseload of juvenile offenders released on conditions of Juvenile Court orders; supervises cases of first-time status or unruly juveniles placed on court probation; conducts initial review of all juvenile complaints filed and determines whether complaints may be processed as informal adjustments or forwarded to Department of Juvenile Justice; supervises juveniles placed on informal adjustment; monitors status of pretrial release cases throughout the court process.

Collects and investigates personal information regarding juveniles to determine residence, employment, and other data; conducts background checks for juvenile histories of prior offenses; schedules appointments for juveniles to report.

Performs drug/alcohol testing of juveniles; collects urine/saliva samples for drug/alcohol testing; administers drug/alcohol testing and interprets test results.

Performs a variety of services to facilitate rehabilitation of youth offenders; implements or oversees implementation of treatment/program plan for youth placed on probation of informal adjustment by the court; identifies sources of supportive services that may be needed; refers juveniles to appropriate supportive services; monitors and follows up on referrals to other agencies.

Attends court sessions involving conditionally released juveniles; attends bond/detention hearings of detained juveniles to assist in determining qualification for release supervision; testifies at court hearings as needed.

Compiles statistical data pertaining to caseloads, defendants, and related issues; performs research; makes applicable calculations; analyzes data and identifies trends; prepares and distributes reports.

21

Medical Case Management Social Work

Junior Lloyd Allen and Andy Allen

The Clientele

Our agency is a hospital in the Southern United States and the second author (Andy Allen) is a licensed master social worker (LMSW) who works on different floors and with different departments as assigned, offering case management services.

The clientele with which medical social work case managers (SWCMs) interact include patients who are admitted to hospitals for short-term issues, long-term issues, and/or end-of-life care. Examples of short-term issues, meaning 24 hours or less, may include broken arms, legs, and minor car accidents. Longer-term care may include hip replacement surgery, heart attacks, or major car accidents. While medical SWCMs work primarily with individuals in hospitals, in-patient agencies, and day facilities, they also work in conjunction with family members to address any potential and additional physical and mental health risks and/or concerns that could occur as a result of the patient's health and well-being. Finally, medical SWCMs may work with non-traditional clientele, which include the homeless and/or indigent.

Since the demographics (i.e., race, class, gender, sexual orientation, religious beliefs, etc.) of the clientele at our hospital includes patients and their family, it requires SWCMs to be culturally competent, and integrative, regarding a patient's specific needs. For example, we have to be open to alternative ideas when discussing care and treatment options, learning about a patient's living environment and/or how the patient may perceive medical treatments, that is, patients that practice holistic approaches to treating ailments, do not frequent hospitals or utilize traditional medications, or have trust issues with doctors. As such, it becomes the SWCM's responsibility to consider alternative perspectives and/or approaches that physicians may sometimes overlook. Additionally, SWCMs should recognize the contextual factors and learn the various cultural norms that are impacting the life of their client by examining the juxtaposed needs and wants of the patients and their social environment. One explanation for having such alternative outlooks is based on the perception that physicians are charged exclusively with treating illnesses as they examine, explore, and treat sicknesses using the traditional medical model regardless of who is affected (Leutz, 1999). However, once this knowledge is obtained, it is shared with the treatment team (physician, nurses, etc.), so that the patient's needs and wishes can be understood by all members involved in improving patient outcomes and providing optimal care (Wagner, 2000).

In thinking about a typical case, we present a patient who recently had her hip replaced; she slipped, fell, and broke her hip. She is a 78-year-old single female living alone, geographically far away from her family, and has limited mobility and social supports. As the medical SWCM on duty, you become informed that a medical patient with hip replacement will need post-operative care. After the surgery, the patient will need arrangements, at a minimum, tailor-made for her care, due to her lack of existing social support. However, the patient also has early onset Alzheimer's, and after surgery, when the anesthesia wears off, she is likely to be confused regarding who she is, where she is, or how she got there? This further complicates the post-operative care as she will be unable to make her own decisions because of her altered mental state. As the medical SWCM on duty, you have to find out who is her next of kin, are they willing to make decisions, or if the patient has a medical power of attorney (MPOA) in place to make decisions for her in the event she loses mental capacity. In this instance, the patient had a next of kin willing to make decisions and no MPOA documentation has been presented. The next of kin, her sister, stated that she wished to care for her at home once she has been discharged from her hip surgery, but since she works 8 A.M.–5 P.M., Monday through Friday, there will be no one at home with the patient during those hours of the day. As the medical SWCM assigned to this case, it was important to recognize the many unsafe issues associated with this discharge plan, as the patient will need immediate and continuous care that this family member, in this case, is really unable to provide. Acting as the patient's guardian *ad litem*, it becomes the medical SWCM's responsibility to work with the patient's sister and the complete treatment team in an effort to identify an interdisciplinary approach that meets the immediate and short-term needs of the patient post-discharge.

In a short time, the medical SWCM will need to identify the social supports that family members offer as well as identify the needed supports that will help the family members to mentally and physically decompress. The family members, and patient, may get pressure from the hospital, the insurance company, and other entities, to discharge the patient in a timely manner, as external and internal agents have their own guidelines and/or expectations of what should happen with specific parameters. While the medical providers and insurance companies are aware of the long-term psychological and/or mental health issues that a client may have, the focus may be based primarily on the medical model for treating illnesses and infections (Leutz, 1999). As such, the medical SWCM should not be afraid to confront a physician or insurance company regarding the needs of a patient, while being flexible with the physician who may not be aware of the specific socio-economic, cultural, environmental, or general wants/needs that the patient may not have shared with the physician.

The medical SWCM advocating for the long-term mental health needs of the patient must be able to respectfully disagree with a doctor, a hospital, and/or insurance company when advocating for what is deemed the most appropriate care for one's patient. At times, when advocating for the patient, the medical SWCM must firmly state, and require, that the treatment team create a plan that decreases the likelihood of the patient experiencing another slip and fall, and getting re-admitted to the hospital with additional injuries. However, the medical SWCM must be careful to not to be seen/labeled as the uncompromising team member who does not work well within a team setting. One has to be able to consult with team members such as nurses, therapist, dietitians, physicians, insurance companies, etc., who will be able to provide different perspectives regarding the team's view with respect to their own clinical areas of expertise.

However, one exception to discussing discharge planning options with patients, and families, in a pre-emptive manner could be hospice. It is never the medical SWCMs place to initiate conversations to either a patient or their family regarding hospice or end-of-life care, since it is not within our training or expertise to make such a decision (Leutz, 1999). To qualify for end-of-life or hospice care, a physician has to certify that a patient is within 6 months of dying and, therefore, must initiate that level of care (Health and Human Services, n.d.). You may however, feel comfortable discussing hospice care with a patient or his or her family members if, and only if, the patient or family specifically initiated or asked about hospice care.

While medical SWCMs may have diverse experiences within the hospital, there are also instances with atypical cases. An example of an atypical case was that of an Asian-Pacific patient's family who desperately wanted their father to return to his home country of China before he passed. However, to do so would require him being transported in an air ambulance. This is expensive and not generally covered by insurance; and in this case, the family could not afford it, as the cost of such services typically exceeded $100,000.

As part of a hospital medical SWCMG team, we had to re-assess the situation, taking into consideration terminal illness issues coupled with the probabilities of providing long-term care. While conducting in-depth interviews with the family, we learned about the importance of getting the patient back to his home. According to this patient's cultural norms, there is a belief that if he died in an unfamiliar area, then his spirit would be lost. The family vehemently did not want him to die in a hospital, or a foreign country, but rather in his hometown in China surrounded by familiar friends, family, and environment. These interviews and interactions with the family gave us the insightful a-ha moment about how to best identify the most financially solvent outcomes to this situation. It was within this moment, of death and dying locale, where our medical and social work background, education, and job descriptions are aligned.

The educational background allowed us to ask ourselves the following question: What can we do, in this moment, to get him fully discharged from this hospital with the most viable and appropriate treatment plan while working with the family to best serve the family's wishes, especially since they no longer meet criteria for admission or long-term care?

We also advocated to those closest to the patient in ways that other health care professionals might not be able to, in this instance family members. Taken collectively, we were charged with making the family comfortable and more understanding of the situation. For example, during our previous interviews with the aforementioned patient, we located a son who could assist with helping his father and that within the New Orleans area. We also found out that the patient had a large group of close family and friends who lived in close proximity. We were able to speak with other members of the patient's family about his health and well-being, found out about spiritual guidance through a spiritual leader within their faith, and helped the family be at ease with the idea that a transfer to the New Orleans area would be a more familiar place for his soul to find rest. It was important to get the patient in hospice care that was as close as possible to the New Orleans area, as well as close to the family. Eventually, we were able to agree that transferring him to an inpatient hospice facility in New Orleans would be a better alternative rather than having him die in a hospital.

Practice Role and Responsibilities

A SWCM, depending on employment location, may be identified using various professional titles. In some hospitals, they are assigned with a generalist social worker title, while at others, they are assigned a medical social worker or medical case manager title. However, each title is distinguishable based on the job description. For instance, social workers in our hospital spend a majority of their time conducting and completing clinical and biopsychosocial assessments that help to provide insights into a client's mental health. However, medical SWCMs are primarily solution focused regarding the specific barriers between psychosocial concerns that negatively impact a patient's medical recovery. Additional roles specific to medical case management titles are closely aligned with insurance payments, providers, and patient utilization review that ensures that the patient meets specific criteria for entrance into an acute care hospital. These medical SWCM positions happen within an array of settings that deal with patients, patient's rights, and insurance outside of hospital settings. Some of these include a family planning, access, care, and treatment (FPACT) program, a short-term acute care center at a hospital, or a long-term planning, access, care, and treatment (LPACT) facility for individuals that need multiple modalities and intense levels of care for extended periods of time.

Medical SWCMs and social workers can also work in various rehabilitation treatment facilities. However, some medical SWCMs outside of hospital settings may work in a physical rehabilitation hospital working with patients recovering from a traumatic brain or life threatening injury and has some physical incapacitation regarding their mobility and capability to be self-sustaining. Other medical SWCMs, outside of hospital settings, may also include nursing facilities, or work in so-called "swing beds"—a nursing home bed that can be transitioned from skilled nursing facility (SNF) status to nursing home status. Here, the actual bed/room does not change; but what changes is the level of care that the patient in that room receives. While there are a wide variety of external hospice care, the second author's (A. A.) experience is situated within the context of shorter-term acute care in a hospital setting that more so meets the needs of the general population. Finally, while the roles vary depending on the hospital where one is employed, the connecting responsibility and role factor between these positions is discharge planning. In other words, where will the patient go after he or she is discharged from our unit, hospital, or facility? For instance, if a patient enters our facility with a projected optimal outcome that includes both physical and mental health unison, the medical case manager has to decide what their discharge planning will resemble—home to recover or in a short-term health facility?

While the actual position title may differ depending on where a medical SWCM is hired, the duties can include, but are not limited to, a) discharge planning; b) utilization review; c) interdisciplinary collaborations that help determine the best outcome for discharge of a patient; d) patient advocate; e) supporting group leadership facilitator, which may include working with individuals who are diagnosed with cancer or those in remission and living in the community or any other life-threatening/alerting illness (i.e., stroke, spinal cord injury, etc.); f) identifying ways to provide support for out-patient family support groups; and g) providing resources for patient's and/or their families regarding external resources to help meet their appropriate mental and physical needs. These responsibilities are particularly important when advocating for the short- and long-term needs of patients.

Patient advocacy differs from the traditional textbook description learned in social work programs regarding how to best interact with and advocate for clients, especially when working with indigent and homeless populations. In many hospitals, SWCMs will routinely be consulted on the needs of homeless populations. There are instances when the SWCM is called in to help someone who is willing, and wanting, to help themselves. Also, there will be times when homeless individuals are content with their living arrangements. The medical SWCM working with this population has to think holistically and keep the central question within the forefront when addressing and implementing discharge planning: Is the patient mentally able to maintain himself, or is he at harm to himself? The SWCM must also be able to decide the patient's right to autonomy, and whether or not his or her decision to go back out in the streets is safe. While a SWCM should not judge a client's decision, they should be able to provide the patient with resources, contacts, opportunities for shelter, arrange transport to a shelter, or even arrange placement in a group home. All of these options should be presented to homeless patients, but at the end of the day, if a person who is homeless, having been provided access to resources, wishes to return to the street and is of sound mind to make that decision, it is not up to the health care professionals to judge.

One role that is often ignored in SWCMG is that of an emergency room social worker. Emergency room (ER) SWCM is different than acute care medical social work, as the ER SWCM is more trauma focused, and is heavily laden with mental health aspects that must be understood and considered. In the instance of a patient who either died in the ER, or in route to the ER, the SWCM is the person who assists the family with addressing the issues surrounding the death of their loved ones *only after* the physician has informed them about the death of the patient. However, sometimes the ER SWCM may accompany the physician when notifying, if and only if the physician wants the SWCM to be present to assist with immediate emotional support after hearing this news. Sometimes, again this varies per hospital and job location, but our ER SWCM helps the family with visiting the remains after the patient is presentable (e.g., cleaned up, or maybe closed up if the patient died during surgery) and addressing issues surrounding how to deal with the remains. Our ER SWCM may also help family and friends process any mental health issues that they may be experiencing at the time, as well as helping with the completion of necessary death and funeral paperwork and to mentally prepare for the funeral.

In addition to handling issues surrounding death, the ER SWCM may also assess issues/concerns regarding sexual abuse, child abuse, or elderly abuse among patients brought to the ER. The ER SWCM will assess the mental health and well-being of the patient, as well as communicate with various appropriate agencies (e.g., the department of human services, child protective services, and/or the police). Our ER SWCM must help patients navigate the overall process. In the event there was a domestic violence patient, the SWCM is charged with linking the patient to a domestic violence shelter and certifying that the patient receives reliable transportation to the shelter. As a SWCM, it is important to meet the patient "where they are at," or "where they were," in an effort to bring them to where they want to be. However, sometimes the patient does not want such resources; therefore, the ER SWCM must be supportive and provide the patient with timely information, and should they need services in the future, provide them with the information or access to those resources.

We contend that ER SWCMs need to have a strong stomach as they work primarily with more serious, gruesome, and at times emotionally macabre events. ER SWCMs are often the first professionals to be contacted when patients enter the ER, and at the time, patients may appear disheveled, delusional, and disoriented. During these times, it is the ER SWCM who becomes the "lead detective" working to identify the patient, as team doctors and nurses are steadfastly working to address their more immediate medical needs. As such, the ER SWCM is tasked with identifying who is the in-case-of-emergency (ICE) contact, and what state, and/or federal laws prohibits the SWCM from searching a patient's wallet, cell phone, and/or personal belongings. Further, in some states, searching a patient's private belongings without their consent is considered illegal. The ER SWCM needs to know the appropriate and legal course of action that must be taken to help identify a Jane Doe.

Role Development Potential

A degree in social work, specifically a MSW, provides the foundational insight and techniques required to complete a comprehensive biopsychosocial assessment, and helps to increase a SWCMs awareness of client issues. However, for the medical social worker or CM, there is not enough built into *most* social work curricula to holistically provide adequate information about the health care component of one's individual needs. While social workers are provided with a generalist approach to social work care regarding the person-in-environment approach, this paradigm often neglects the specific aspects that focus on health-related issues. For example, elective courses that introduced us to issues associated with death and dying, as well as working with grieving patients or family members, were taught in relative isolation from each other and were not integrated as they should be (Morse et al., 2006). These courses are important because they address ethical considerations that must be made regarding our clients that we often overlook, and are different from the usual clients that we frequently encounter in treatment centers. However, there is certainly room for improvement in the MSW curricula that must increase our multi-level thinking of ethics as not just issues to have with living individuals, but also, what to consider when thinking of individuals who are close to dying.

In the medical field, a lot of the learned experience cannot be studied within classes or found in textbooks, as experience happens through day-to-day job responsibilities and ongoing interactions with doctors, nurses, and other health care professionals. For example, the ICD code refers to a specific coronary artery bypass graft (CABG), but what does this particular medical illness and procedure mean, what are its particular outcomes, and how does this specifically affect the physical capabilities of the patient? Understanding and being able to readily provide answers to these specific medical questions are all "on-the-job learned skills" along with others, which helps the SWCM to navigate various SWCM and management positions. These may include the following: program director, assistant manager of a social worker or caseworker department, a director of social work or case management depending on the hospital, or allows the SWCM to work in other arenas of social work related to marketing, sales, and/or business management. Ultimately, while working, the SWCM obtains a smorgasbord of knowledge on medical terminology, illnesses, symptomology, and how to treat a patient, inclusive criteria for specific levels of care, background insights on insurance and insurance claim policies, and lastly, the requirements to fully meet the needs of a client. As a whole, these skills can help SWCM and social workers move upward or lateral, depending on the available positions, and are necessary to be taught in MSW curricula.

There are also additional ethical and cultural considerations that must be made when dealing with religious belief systems and ethnicities (Conner & Chase, 2015; Hallenbeck & Goldstein, 1999). As a medical SWCM, it is important to consider some of the typical approaches that we must address when dealing with issues surrounding death and dying (Kwak & Haley, 2005), coupled with unique cultural and ethical practices that are prevalent when working with Asians, English, Irish, Jamaicans, Jewish, Mexicans, Muslims, and others. One noticeable issue that arises here, and continues to arise, is the overt lack of awareness to external cultures that are not like ours (Hall, 2001; Hallenbeck & Goldstein, 1999; Kwak & Haley, 2005). Many times, social workers in the Western hemisphere assume that every death is the same and, therefore, we may ignore the different cultural values when an individual dies. Also, as Western SWCMs, we may ignore what is important for that patient during his or her final life stages. For some, death is seen as being left behind, while for others, death is leaving the body. This differentiation is important for SWCMs as they have to help clients find the easiest way to grasp the concept of death and dying.

To help here, a course that specifically addresses death, dying, and social work would be required for all MSW students interested in medical social work. Such a course may provide an ancillary introductory overview regarding key elements connected to the pervasive and daily pressures of working in hospitals, especially with vulnerable and/ or aged populations (Hegedus, Zana, & Szabó, 2008). In such a course, there are teachable and task-specific issues related to medical insurance policies, how to obtain medical compliance that holistically addresses clients' needs without prematurely releasing the client from the hospital, living wills and power of attorney issues, examination of cultural biases when working with specific populations, and navigating the multiple roles associated with medical SWCM. Also, with the many changes in insurance policies and advanced technologies, having a course that addresses current issues in health care, including medical changes and older persons, would be beneficial to enhancing one's learning environment. Lastly, such a course could also address Medicare/Medicaid changes and the various issues that a medical caseworker and CM need to know when asking insurance companies to provide the most adequate levels of care to their patients.

As indicated earlier, patient advocacy is ethically essential for client success (Toda, Sakamoto, Tagaya, Takahashi, & Davis, 2015). Regardless of the setting, advocacy is an important component for all social workers to know and be able to effectively execute. The SWCM should be able to identify the social and familial factors that the patient may be facing and have the wherewithal to address those issues more holistically. However, before advocating for the client, the SWCM must gather all available data and evidentiary backing that supports the *why*, and the *how*, or rationale for the required needs being requested for the patient. The SWCM should be able to effectively communicate with supervisors, medical providers, and insurance companies to justify the need for an increased level of care. This skill is especially important when requesting insurance companies to cover more specialized care that has been denied by others. For example, if an insurance company denies a claim for a patient because they assumed that the client needed one type of care, but working with the internal departments, there is evidence to support the additional need of inpatient care resources instead of outpatient care. The SWCMs should be able to advocate for their patient—arguing that sending them to an outpatient level of care may have negative effects on their recovery and well-being, which may result in poorer recovery outcomes—if that patient truly needs further inpatient care.

services, experience longer duration of untreated disorders, and use fewer health care services for mental disorders, particularly specialty mental health care. (p. 1097)

Many of our Asian and Latino American community members would be classified as limited English proficiency individuals.

Along with being primarily African American and Caucasian, most of our clients receive Supplemental Security Income (SSI), which is a federal income supplement program funded by general tax revenues (*not* social security taxes). It provides cash to meet basic needs such as food, clothing, and shelter for people who are elderly or disabled and have little or no income. Most of my clients receive SSI payments of exactly $733 a month, the minimum amount allotted. When a social worker (like me) sees $733, it tells me valuable information such as, not only is this client experiencing debilitating poverty, but also they have likely never, or very rarely, held a conventional job. This is definitely not much to live on, especially for someone with longstanding and complex mental health problems.

Most new clients I see have been battling mental health problems, on their own or through other agencies, since their teenage years or even younger. A good number suffer comorbidly from both severe depression and anxiety. Schizophrenia shows up frequently, as well as schizoaffective disorder. Also, many of our clients have experienced physical or sexual abuse in their life and are often diagnosed with PTSD. We do see some veterans, but not many because we only have one clinician panelled to see TriCare.

Substance use is definitely a problem with a significant number of our clients, and I have observed some differences in gender and age with this problem. Generally speaking, about 75% of my male clients are currently experiencing a moderate or severe addictions problem. Alcohol abuse is universally the problem. However, with younger clients, crack, marijuana, and the so-called designer drugs are often problems. For female clients, about 30% admit to having used illegal drugs or having had a drinking problem in the past, but most say they are now sober. We don't drug test them unless the court requires it, so often we take them at their word.

A recent abuse issue we've seen is prescription pill abuse, especially opiates. These clients (mostly female) actually receive prescriptions for these medicines, and they do not go out to the street to score drugs, so it is a rather unique problem for us to deal with. We think this will be higher on our radar in the future, as it seems that doctors are sending more people to pain clinics. We expect that this is going to be something new to contend with, that is, how it affects families and relationships and people's ability to parent effectively. Also, in terms of prescribed medications, many of my clients are on Seroquel, and without it, they tend to decompensate very quickly. Also, some have been in jail or prison for a long time, and do not really know how to re-integrate into society. Sadly, many do not have the basic skills to live independently. So addictions, mental health, and other issues including legal problems really put our clients in a very hard and rather detached [from mainstream society] place.

The literature reveals that the comorbidity of substance use and mental health issues for clients in community agencies is significant. For example, Chang et al. (2015) found that individuals with depression and substance abuse histories in such communities had higher clinical and psychosocial needs, regardless of the setting where they were screened. Most were also unemployed, over half lacked health insurance, and about one-fifth had witnessed violence in the past six months. Participants had moderate to high rates of psychiatric and medical comorbidities, including tobacco use, depression, anxiety, psychosis, or mania. (p. 289)

The intersection of mental health and substance abuse needs of individuals recently released from incarceration is also profound. Begun, Early, and Hodge (2016) found that, "Just prior to participants' release, AUDIT-ID, a well-known Alcohol Use Disorders Identification Test, scores reflecting the year prior to incarceration indicated that 82.5% of participants engaged in levels of alcohol and/or other substance use that placed them at-risk for a substance use disorder (Begun, Early, & Hodge, 2009). In fact, 64% of my clients were at very high risk last year (p. 213). I have certainly seen these statistics validated with our agency's larger client population.

Every client is different, but there are some similarities, certainly. As you get to know them, you often learn that their families and friends are very important to them, as is their faith. Living in the south, most of my clients are Christian and deeply religious. I think faith means "hope" for many, and hope is often the most important thing to them. Without hoping that things are going to get better, how can we ask them to keep coming to all these appointments and filling out all these necessary forms? Being able to understand how faith affects my clients is important, on a personal level and from a CMG perspective.

I am really not sure there is a "typical client." It is very broad, but I suppose that a most typical client is someone who's not working, receiving the minimum SSI, and has depression, anxiety, and substance abuse problems. Usually, they are over 40, and gender-wise, it is about half men and half women. The most atypical client I can think of was a client who was reclusive. He denied ever having a girlfriend (or boyfriend). His parents died, and he just didn't ever want to leave the house. A judge mandated that he obtain mental health treatment after he jumped on his brother, attacking him. He was rather unusual because he did not have any trouble with drugs or alcohol, he was always well groomed, and he kept his place neat. He just did not want to deal with anybody and said he was like this all his life. You can only imagine how difficult it would be to engage a client like this in a counseling setting!

Practice Roles and Responsibilities

I have many roles and responsibilities primarily including assessment, coordinating with therapists and other departments, recovery planning, care coordination, organizational planning, teaching basic life and living skills, and assisting clients in accessing community resources. In my opinion, advocacy is the primary and foundational role of any CMCW, in any setting, not just mental health. All CMs need to be legitimately concerned with social justice because most clients are underserved, and that means that the system can really disempower them by disillusioning them.

This was the time when I believe my CMCW skills were crucial to helping her recover. I was able to locate a support group for rape and sexual assault victims, and immediately referred Sarah, so she could have some sense of community and belonging. My agency also had a Dialectical Behavioral Therapy (DBT) group, which I also recommended, so she could develop the coping tools necessary to continue functioning despite frequent crying spells, feelings of hopelessness, and other symptoms of deep depression.

In the months after her uncle's acquittal she began abusing alcohol, but she has recently completed an inpatient substance abuse program. In our many one-on-one sessions, we focused on healthy daily activities and living, identifying warning signs of relapsing, and avoiding unhealthy people and environments. We also developed alternative strategies for coping with her negative emotions, especially surrounding loneliness.

One day, Sarah asked me very tentatively, "Do you think maybe I could get a puppy? I think maybe a puppy would be good for me." She had gone to an animal shelter and fell in love with an abandoned Black Labrador. I felt terrible. I wanted nothing more than to take her down to the shelter and get her that puppy. But instead, I worked with her to create a realistic budget including adoption fees, food, housing deposits, and the inevitable veterinary bills. She recognized that she could not afford a dog just yet. I felt so sad for her, but this is when creativity and persistence become crucial for CMCWs. I approached the shelter and advocated for my client. Within a month, she was volunteering 15 hours a week and receiving hands-on animal care skills, working beside the veterinary tech. Over time, the office manager took an interest in her and began training her as an office assistant. Sarah now works there part-time, takes at least a few community college hours each semester, and yes, has adopted a dog of her own.

For Sarah, as for Marcus, to be a successful CMCW, I had to be approachable, accessible, and an artful systems negotiator. What I mean by "approachable" is that you have to be able to experience that kind of deeper emotive empathy with your client, but not let it break you. You must be able to look across the table at your client, and not look down at them. I contend that no one should work in a helping profession unless they can care about each individual person uniquely, and actually see their humanity. I know the business side of this can be a big barrier, and there will be pressure for productivity, seeing as many clients as possible, but you cannot turn clients into numbers. They are not billable hours. They are, each one of them, a person. And I care for them. That's what I bring to the table.

❖

REFERENCES

Anakwenze, U., & Zuberi, D. (2013). Mental health and poverty in the inner city. *Health & Social Work, 38*(3), 147–157.

AUDIT. (n.d.). *Alcohol Use Disorder Indicator Test.* Retrieved from www.drugabuse.gov/sites/default/files/files/AUDIT.pdf

Bauer, A. M., Chen, C. N., & Alegría, M. (2010). English language proficiency and mental health service use among Latino and Asian Americans with mental disorders. *Medical Care, 48*(12), 1097–1104.

Begun, A., Early, T., & Hodge, A. (2016). Mental health and substance abuse service engagement by men and women during community reentry following incarceration. *Administration & Policy in Mental Health & Mental Health Services Research, 43*(2), 207–218.

Chang, E. T., Wells, K. B., Gilmore, J., Tang, L., Morgan, A. U., Sanders, S., & Chung, B. (2015). Comorbid depression and substance abuse among safety-net clients in Los Angeles: A community participatory study. *Psychiatric Services, 66*(3), 285–294.

Eack, S., & Newhill, C. (2012). Racial disparities in mental health outcomes after psychiatric hospital discharge among individuals with severe mental illness. *Social Work Research, 36*(1), 47–52.

Ex-offenders. (2011). Study shows ex-offenders have greatly reduced employment rates. *Prison Legal News.* Retrieved from https://www.prisonlegalnews.org/news/2011/dec/15/study-shows-ex-offenders-have-greatly-reduced-employment-rates/

SSI. (n.d.). Social Security Insurance. Retrieved from www.ssa.gov/ssi/

TRICARE. (n.d.). Retrieved from http://tricare.mil/welcome.aspx

ANCILLARIES

Internet References for Additional Reading

1. Department of Labor: Social Work. Retrieved from www.bls.gov/ooh/community-and-social-service/social-workers.htm

2. International Perspective-England. Retrieved from www.theguardian.com/careers/careers-blog/want-job-mental-health-social-work-step-by-step-guide

3. MSW Guide: Mental Health and Substance Abuse Social Work. Retrieved from www.mswguide.org/careers/mental-health-and-substance-abuse-social-work/

4. NASW and Mental Health. Retrieved from www.socialworkers.org/pressroom/features/issue/mental.asp

5. Psychiatric Social Work. Retrieved from www.socialworklicensure.org/types-of-social-workers/psychiatric-social-worker.html

6. Social Worker as a Guardian Ad Litem. Retrieved from http://www.citytowninfo.com/career-story/family-and-school-social-workers/social-worker-and-guardian-ad-litem-in-child-abuse-cases

7. Social Work and Homelessness. Retrieved from http://www.hhs.gov/programs/social-services/homelessness/index.html

❖ PSYCHOSOCIAL SERVICE PROVIDER JOB DESCRIPTION

Provides a wide range of paraprofessional social services to clients and their families. May provide supportive counseling to clients and their families and/or serve as a liaison to community agencies. Conducts client intakes, participates in treatment team planning, and assists in dealing with personal, mental health, and social problems. Performs case management duties.

Duties and Responsibilities

- Assists clients in identifying and accessing community resources, including but not limited to financial, legal, medical

- Meets with clients/clients' families to facilitate realization of case goals. Often in the form of home and school visits, and outings in the community; keeps documentation of face-to-face sessions and collaborative sessions with each client and/or provider

- Transports, or makes arrangements for transportation of, clients to appointments in a timely manner

- Contacts other health care professionals in the agency or community to obtain consumer background information as necessary

- Completes client intakes based on interviews with clients, their families, and any other support persons as necessary

- Develops and maintains a network of community contacts

- Collaborates with service providers to design and update treatment plans as necessary

- Participates in meetings pertaining to case management

- Provides social and psychological support to clients and their families through listening and discussing problems and progress as necessary

- Provides short-term case management and referral services to clients in emergency situations

- Complies with all regulations on client confidentiality

- Minimum Qualifications: High school diploma or GED *and* 2 years of experience in a social services related position *or* bachelor's degree in a social services related field or 1 year at the lower level or position equivalent.

Preferred Qualifications

- A bachelor's degree in social services or related field plus 2 years related work experience *and*

- Experience working with individuals who are currently homeless and individuals with a Severe and Persistent Mental Illness (SPMI) and/or Substance Abuse Diagnosis

❖ SENIOR RESOURCE CENTER, INC.

Senior Resource Center, an Equal Opportunity Employer, is seeking applications for the full-time position of Projects Coordinator.

Duties

1. In conjunction with other interested parties coordinates a community process assisting current Medicare and North Carolina Senior Resource Center enrollees' transition to the Medicare Prescription Drug Program benefits that became effective in early 2006.

2. Organizes public meetings and events throughout the county designed to explain the Medicare Prescription Drug Program process, the benefits, and their alternatives to residents 65 years of age that will be ongoing from September 2005 and continue into early summer 2006.

3. Maintains the various information and databases required for periodic mailing of timely relevant Prescription Drug information to individual members of the senior population as necessary.

4. Develops a volunteer corps to assist staff and the board implement the mission and programs for Senior Resource Center, Inc.

5. In collaboration with the County Volunteer Center and by other means coordinates volunteer recruitment, deployment, and recognition with Senior Resource Center, Inc.

6. Establishes and maintains an electronic database and helpline of resource in the community that are available to senior citizens.

7. Acts as a referral agent and case-manager in assisting senior citizens access existing services meeting their needs.

8. Develops issue specific publications informing senior citizens on resources that are available to assist them in living as independently as possible in the community.

9. Assists in the development and regular maintenance of a website for the Senior Resource Center with appropriate links.

10. Assists the President/CEO in strategic and program planning, program design and implementation, and other program development activities.

The appointee must be:

1. Highly organized and have ability to prioritize and manage multiple projects and be computer proficient

2. Possess excellent communication skills, both written and oral

3. A team-player and be capable of relating to a multifaceted and diverse colleague group

4. Knowledgeable of community resources and programs for senior citizens

5. Capable of meeting, communicating, and interacting with senior citizens from diverse backgrounds with respect, empathy, understanding, compassion, etc.

Education/Experience: A minimum of a bachelor's degree in human services, social work, or gerontology preferred with at least 3 year's successful case management experience in human services being desirable. A valid NC driver's license and access to a vehicle is required.

24

Social Work and Case Management: Homelessness Prevention

Lindsey Disney and Susan Bradford

The Clientele

In 2005, a task force united in Knoxville, Tennessee, to create a 10-year plan to end chronic homelessness. It included representatives from social service agencies, mental health centers, psychiatric facilities, law enforcement, homeless services, neighborhood associations, libraries, transportation organizations, and local, state, and federal government. Part of the plan included funding for new social work positions (Ploeg, Hayward, Woodward, & Johnston, 2008; Sadowski, Kee, VanderWeele, & Buchanan, 2009). A case manager (the second author, Susan Bradford) position was created to target homelessness prevention, because preventing homelessness, rather than re-housing after eviction, was thought to be more economical and more effective (Crane & Warnes, 2007). The Knoxville-Knox County Community Action Committee (CAC) funds the current CMG position, but the work setting is located within a subsidized high-rise facility for disabled and senior adults.

Love Towers houses 250 residents in two adjacent buildings. Building A is primarily seniors, and Building B is primarily persons with disabilities, although many residents are both seniors and disabled. Disabilities can be physical or mental, and the criterion is based on whether the resident receives social security insurance for their disability. Regardless of verified diagnoses, many of our residents struggle with mental health issues and/or substance abuse issues. Their average age is about 60 years old, and many experience the negative effects of aging, such as chronic health issues, increased social isolation, ageism, and feelings of a lack of meaning or purpose. In addition to issues related to aging, many also experience the frustrations of poverty. Most are single, which is partially attributed to a limited number of two-bedroom apartments in the buildings. There are some family combinations of a child and a parent, such as an adult child taking care of an elderly or disabled parent, and there are some couples, married or self-declared. There is a higher percentage of Caucasian residents and female residents in the complex.

The vast majority of residents are living below 125% of the federal poverty line. The average income is $732 per month. They are housed in Knoxville Community Development Corporation (KCDC) housing, which is part of the city's subsidized housing program, funded through the federal Housing and Urban Development (HUD) program. This means that residents pay one-third of their income, or about $240 a month, for their rent and utilities. There is very little money left over, despite the reduced rent. Food stamps are often not adequate enough to provide food for a month, and food insecurity is a chronic issue for our residents. Mobile Meals are delivered to those who are homebound Monday–Friday to assist with this issue, and Mobile Meals provides a hot lunch for all residents in the social hall 4 days a week. About 10 years ago, the residents' association advocated for themselves and organized for the Second Harvest Food Bank to hold a food drive every Friday at the apartment complex. We have a very active residents' association at Love Towers—and this is a real strength of our community (Yen, Michael, & Perdue, 2009). Given the criteria for eligibility, there is really no typical or atypical client per se. The demographics presented above generally characterize the vast majority of our clients.

Practice Roles and Responsibilities

The primary job of the CM at Love Towers is to prevent eviction. The CM does this in collaboration with the Love Towers Housing Manager. The typical protocol is that a housing manager makes a referral to the CM at the same time that he or she gives a resident an eviction notice. But that is not the usual way that we work. If the housing manager is even mildly concerned, he will say to me, "Let's do a home visit together." The housing manager writes all referrals, but I can also go to him and express client concerns—that is, "Ms. Smith is talking to herself and engaging in repetitive behaviors; I'm concerned about her." So in this way, through collaboration, we both target who is at risk for eviction, and do so as far in advance as possible. Once residents are added to my caseload, I begin proactive case management with them. I typically have 30–45 residents on my caseload. Working far in advance is particularly important to prevent eviction from occurring because once eviction occurs, the client is pretty much doomed. Re-housing someone who has been evicted from public housing is a daunting task. More abruptly, no landlord wants to take you. And, how could you house someone who makes only $732 a month? This is why our prevention model is crucial to our agency and clients.

If someone does receive an eviction notice, and the resident accepts CMG, then the CM serves as the resident's advocate in both the informal and formal hearings. If eviction is inevitable, then the CM works to develop a plan to re-house the resident prior to eviction. An eviction might be inevitable, for example, if a resident has broken a "one strike" public housing rule (i.e., any drug related activity or criminal activity), in which case there is no negotiation. At this point, the goal of the CM is to prevent eviction to the street, which involves finding alternative housing either in another apartment complex, or with family or a friend. Thus far, the program has had an extremely successful rate of no evictions to the street.

In addition to eviction prevention, the CM is also the in-house social worker for all 250 residents. In this role, the CM helps with a wide range of activities. Some residents only need 5 minutes of service time, and when they will drop into my office. I have an "open door policy," and I also try to be present when residents are gathered for group activities, such as during Second Harvest. During group activities, I often help keep the activities organized and engage and develop rapport with our residents. Other residents, however, require more intensive or long-term CMG around issues such as setting up hospice care or applying for social security benefits. The CM also assists with information and referrals for community services such as health insurance, establishing primary care, mental health treatment, and other needed community resources. Substance abuse and mental health issues are common, and connecting to the appropriate local agency or resource is very important. Currently, I have a good collaborative relationship with the local Alcoholics Anonymous and Celebrate Recovery programs to connect residents and organize transportation. I also have been looking for a non-faith-based substance abuse group in order to provide services for residents who prefer a secular option.

Administering and organizing support groups are also the responsibility of the CM. The "Chatty Café" group meets once a week for an hour, and the topics we discuss are varied. Sometimes outside speakers are invited, such as a recent speaker from a local attorney's office who provided education and counsel about living wills, power of attorneys, and other legal issues. Other times, the CM will present on topics such as "Healthy Boundaries," "Getting Through the Holidays," or "What Are My Strengths." This material is presented at a fifth-grade educational level, as many residents have low educational attainment and/or deficits in their interpersonal skills. As the CM, I have also collaborated with Peninsula, a local mental health provider, to conduct a peer support group twice a month. Having strong, supportive community collaboration is extremely important for the success of our program.

The greatest challenge for the CM is our residents' chronic poverty. Chronic poverty negatively affects one's mental health and human behavior in various ways, from food hoarding to poor hygiene. Residents with no income (usually from a history of chronic homelessness) are often the most challenging to serve. Love Towers has a minimum fee of $50 for rent. Where do residents who have no income, are disabled, and/or elderly get $50? Sometimes their relatives will pay it. Sometimes, they will sell their televisions. Sometimes they collect tin cans on the street; sometimes they panhandle downtown. Although they may scrounge together the $50 for their rent, there is usually no additional money available for toiletries, prescriptions, or for other necessities. The recent changes in our state public health system have particularly impacted this zero income population. For example, our local indigent health care provider, which is in conjunction with Tennessee's public health system, now charges a minimum of $3 per prescription, regardless of one's income. For residents who have no income but who need 10 prescriptions, this is a rather major issue and concern (Henwood, Katz, & Gilmer, 2015). Further, our health care provider is also no longer paying for transportation costs to doctors' appointments, which leaves many disabled and ailing seniors with no way to get to their appointments.

Role Development Potential

There is always potential for growth as a CM working in homelessness prevention with the elderly and disabled. Initially run as a pilot program, the CMG position at Love Towers has proved to be effective, and there is hope that other housing programs and communities will emulate the model. Serving as a CM here also provides opportunities for ongoing professional skill development. For instance, there are numerous trainings offered such as lunch and learns, workshops, and conferences, where evidence-based practice ideas are shared and discussed. As social work practitioners, bringing evidenced-based practices to our clients is essential. Attending trainings and other opportunities for evidence-based learning also helps to keep our abilities current and skills sharp.

In my MSW program, I focused on gerontology, which prepared me greatly to work in senior care. One area that I regret not gaining more knowledge in, and this was not a reflection of my program, but of my personal choices and where I directed my education, is the area of mental health. Many of our residents have significant mental health issues, including drug and alcohol abuse. An important component of any social work curriculum is a foundation in mental health and substance abuse issues. Additionally, a course in understanding poverty, the reasons for poverty, the cycles of poverty, and what it means to be in that particular class situation, would be a beneficial addition to any BSW and MSW social work curriculum. Unfortunately, there were no such courses offered in our MSW programs.

One area where social workers are recognized in the helping professions is ethics. CMs with a social work background possess an especially strong ethical base that is not always apparent in CMs from different helping disciplines. For example, one of our core social work ethics is to always protect the right of client self-determination. Thus, our clients have the right to make bad decisions just like everyone else, but these are their decisions foremost. Of course, the CM has her own hopes and dreams for every case of outcomes that he or she would like to see, and places that he or she would like to see the client move toward. But, that good might not be congruent with the client's own decisions. A CM needs to allow a client to direct their sessions, and the services engaged in, even if the CM does not agree with the decisions made. Further, a CM should not drop a client from his or her caseload under the pretext of the client being "non-compliant," if this occurs. Fortunately, ethics is a core part of our altruistic social work curricula, and social workers bring to the table a unique understanding of what it means to be ethical in social service positions. This is something that helps us greatly in our important work with all clients.

Concluding Remarks

Regardless of the employment setting in which we work, CMs have to be prepared to work with unique and diverse populations (Berkman, Gardner, Zodikoff, & Harootyan, 2005). Although my (Susan Bradford) educational focus was on gerontology, and I am currently working at a senior apartment complex, I have been continually surprised with the diversity of clients that I see. For example, clients may have serious mental health issues or serious substance abuse issues, which are their most significant presenting problems. Others may have a police record or a history of sex offenses. Some clients may have been low-income earners their entire lives, and others may find that, due to one reason or another, they are experiencing poverty for the first time in their lives (Petersen & Parsell, 2015; Sermons & Henry, 2010). Others are raising their grandchildren, and, ironically, their grandchildren may actually become our clients one day as well, even if a CM intends to work only with adults and not children. Within the senior population, seniors are very different according to generation. A senior who is 80 or 90 years old ("old-old") is quite different from a senior who is 50 or 60 years old ("young-old") (Holosko & Feit, 2004). The point is that some BSW/MSW students may have the idea "I'm never going to work with <u>BLANK</u> population." As a social worker, you cannot really say that. When you professionally serve your clients, you must learn to anticipate and respect diversity in all people and their lived experiences.

A final piece of advice for future social work CMs is not to underestimate the importance of being able to understand the client's world. In order to conduct effective CMG, a CM must be able to understand where a client is at, and what a client's life is like, in order to understand decisions that get made, and decisions that do not get made. Empathetically understanding the everyday life of an individual living in poverty is essential to becoming a successful CM, and it is the foundation of all services offered to our clients.

Case Examples

Mr. C was a 73-year-old man who had been a resident of Love Towers for 20 years. About 4 years ago, his wife passed away. His wife was our "social butterfly," while Mr. C was a quieter man. After she passed away, Mr. C began to self-isolate, and he went off of everyone's radar. He began having memory problems, and in his vulnerable state, a telephone salesman took advantage of him. He incurred multiple insurance policies, and a very expensive cable package, all being directly withdrawn from his bank account. Mr. C came onto my radar when he missed a rent payment. At that point, he had also bounced his bank account a couple of times, was behind on his rent, and terribly embarrassed. When I gently probed if he could tell me a little about what was going on, he responded, "Sugar, I don't even know." I then opened up a case file.

The first thing that I did was to connect Mr. C to a representative payee. I do budget counseling, but in his case I felt that he was no longer capable of managing his own finances. These are the kinds of judgments that a CM has to make quickly. Mr. C was actually relieved that there was someone who he could pay to manage his bills. However, assigning a representative payee is a rather serious and often emotional decision, and it may require documentation from doctors and multiple visits to social security offices. On our first visit to the local social security office, the worker could clearly see that Mr. C was confused, and the representative payee was set up. The payee and I then began working together to figure out how to curtail the extra expenses, and get Mr. C caught up on his bills. Meanwhile, Mr. C was 2 months past due on his rent, and eviction was pending.

I applied for a grant through my agency (CAC) to cover the 2 months, so that he could get caught up. The grant stipulated that there must be "an uncontrollable circumstance" and "a plan for sustainability." Mr. C was a good candidate because he had an uncontrolled circumstance (the deterioration of his memory) and a plan for sustainability (the representative payee). Of course, funding is not always there, and such funding is always limited. Because of this, CMs have to be good stewards of all grant monies. We have to consider whether the money is going to make a difference, and if it is going to help draw someone out of crisis. These can be difficult and complex decisions to make. In the case of Mr. C, the decision was clear and, fortunately, the funds were available. Currently, Mr. C is no longer in crisis with his housing, and he is caught up on his bills. However, I have continued to keep Mr. C on my caseload because of other issues that he needs help with. For instance, he is no longer able to drive and needs help with obtaining groceries. Isolation continues to be a real concern for his own mental health. He has physical health concerns as well, so I drove him to the hospital for diagnostic tests that he had put off for the past year. Recently, we discovered that he also has bed bugs. He is very neat and tidy, but he has over 20 years of personal possessions, many of which belonged to his deceased wife, and going through the necessary protocol to get rid of the bed bugs will dictate Mr. C disposing of many of his cherished possessions. So there are multi-layers of need for this client, and multiple roles for the CM. In short, this is the nature of this rewarding work that we were educated and trained to do.

❖

REFERENCES

Berkman, B., Gardner, D., Zodikoff, B., & Harootyan, L. (2005). Social work in health care with older adults: Future challenges. *Families in Society: The Journal of Contemporary Social Services*, 86(3), 329–337.

Crane, M., & Warnes, A. M. (2007). The outcomes of rehousing older homeless people: A longitudinal study. *Ageing and Society*, 27(06), 891–918.

25

Child Protective Services and Case Management

Jessica Parker and Tiffany Johnson

Introduction

In the United States, federal and state legislation prohibits child abuse and neglect (Primavera & Jackson, 2014). The *Federal Child Abuse Prevention and Treatment Act* (CAPTA), (42 U.S.C.A. §5106g) defines child abuse and neglect as "any recent act or failure on the part of a parent or caretaker, which results in death, serious physical or emotional harm, sexual abuse or exploitation, or an act or failure to act which presents an imminent risk of serious harm" (Primavera & Jackson, 2014). In practice, however, what actions classify as abuse or neglect are dependent upon the developmental age of the victim, the frequency and intensity of the behavior, the degree of intentionality, and extenuating circumstances (Primavera & Jackson, 2014). Thus, child protection case managers (CMs) are integral to the process of identifying child maltreatment on a case-by-case basis. At the state level, child welfare agencies such as Georgia's Division of Family and Children Services (DFCS) collaborate with law enforcement to investigate alleged reports of child maltreatment with the ultimate goal of protecting children from abuse and neglect, while attempting to preserve families.

The Division of Family and Children Services (DFCS) administers child and adult protective services, foster care and adoption services, and supportive services for low-income families. Within DFCS, Child Protective Services (CPS) is responsible for responding to reports of child abuse and neglect in the state of Georgia (DFCS, 2016). The focus of this chapter is the Liberty County DFCS, located within Georgia District 12, which serves Hinesville, Flemington, and Riceboro. Whereas Chapter 17 focuses on foster care within DFCS, this chapter complements that one and describes DFCS's Child Protective Services—the investigations branch of child welfare.

The Clientele

In 2015, Georgia's CPS responded to 109,570 alleged reports of child maltreatment involving 70,250 children. The bulk of these reports involved children ages 1 to 15, with less reports involving children under the age of 1 and above the age of 16. Children served by Georgia's CPS are primarily white (50.36%), black (43.40%), and Hispanic (7.95%). There are roughly as many boys (49.88%) as there are girls (49.80%) served by CPS.

In 2015, 928 reports were made to Liberty County's CPS, of which 130 cases were substantiated, involving 597 children. The ages of children served by Liberty County CPS are representative of Georgia's overall children's age distribution within DFCS. Compared to the entire state of Georgia, Liberty County serves about the same number of black (45.73%) and white children (43.72%), but disproportionately more multi-racial (9.55%) and Hispanic (9.21%) children. Additionally, and more locally, Liberty County CPS serves more girls (52.60%) than boys (47.40%) (DFCS, 2015).

Among the counts of reported abuse, girls experience sexual abuse more often than boys. According to national data, incidence rates of maltreatment are lower among younger children (ages 0 to 2). However, these cases may go unreported, as it is difficult to identify abuse before children enter school. Children enrolled in school have higher rates of physical abuse, but non-enrolled children have higher rates of sexual abuse. Additionally, recent national research has found that rates of maltreatment are higher for black children than for white or Hispanic children. Children with disabilities also have higher rates of emotional neglect coupled with serious injury or harm (Sedlak et al., 2010).

Perpetrators of child maltreatment are more often female (68%) than male, more commonly female in the case of a biological parent perpetrator, and male for a non-biological perpetrator (48%). The majority of children who experience maltreatment were abused or neglected by their biological parents, except in the case of sexual abuse, which is more often committed by someone other than a parent or a parent's partner. Although there is no archetype for caregivers who commit acts of child maltreatment, as child abuse and neglect occurs across all demographics, it is not uncommon for investigated caregivers to be experiencing hardship. Evidence suggests that children with unemployed parents have 2 to 3 times the rate of neglect as those with employed parents, and children in lower socioeconomic households experience maltreatment at 5 times the rate of other children (they were 3 times as likely to be abused and 7 times as likely to be neglected). Additionally, rates of abuse are higher for children from larger families (double the rates of households with two children [Sedlak et al., 2010]).

Children living with a single parent who has a cohabiting partner are more likely to experience abuse, 10 times the rate of abuse and 8 times the rate of neglect of children living with married biological parents (Sedlak et al., 2010). The ecological model comprehensively examines how child-mediated stressors (such as temperament of the child or physical/intellectual disability), parental pre-disposition (including parental history of abuse, or substance abuse), and situational stressors (for example, marital conflict, limited social supports, or financial stress) combine within the context of a family's cultural background likely to result in abusive situations (Primavera & Jackson, 2014). Thus, while there is no single explanation for what causes child maltreatment, the ecological model acknowledges the ways in which several factors interact to contribute to child abuse and neglect (Primavera & Jackson, 2014).

Types of Abuse. According to the 2012 *National Child Abuse and Neglect Data System* of the Department of Health and Human Services, the most prevalent form of abuse is child neglect (78%), followed by physical abuse (18%), sexual abuse (9%), and psychological or emotional abuse (8.5%). In Georgia, the primary reasons for opening an in-home case are neglect (36%), substance abuse by parent (32%), domestic violence in the child's home (12%), sexual abuse (8%), physical abuse (4%), and emotional maltreatment (4%) (U.S. Department of Health and Human Services, 2007). Based upon anecdotal evidence, Liberty County has typically seen cases of substance abuse by the parent and domestic violence. Reports are also frequently classified as "inadequate supervision." However, there has recently been an influx of child exploitation cases, to the point where CPS CMs are receiving additional training on how to deal with these atypical cases.

Child maltreatment can be split into two categories: child abuse and neglect. Child neglect is the failure to provide for a child's basic physical, educational, or emotional needs, including child abandonment. Examples of physical neglect include failing to provide necessary food and shelter, and lack of supervision, whereas medical neglect involves failing to provide medical and mental health treatment. Educational neglect includes truancy, or failure to educate a child or attend to special education needs (Child Welfare Information Gateway, 2013).

Child abuse is categorized into three main types: physical, sexual, and emotional. Physical abuse is defined as, "the non-accidental infliction of physical injury as a result of punching, pushing, striking, kicking, biting, burning, shaking, or otherwise harming a child". Sexual abuse encapsulates the "fondling of a child's genitals, intercourse, incest, rape, sodomy, exhibitionism, and commercial exploitation through prostitution or the production of pornographic materials." Emotional abuse includes acts that have caused behavioral, cognitive, emotional, or mental injury. While evidence of harm does not have to be proved before an investigation of emotional abuse can take place, often CPS is required to find proof of psychological injury which would allow DFCS to then intervene on behalf of the child. Other states also include substance abuse under child abuse and neglect, including prenatal exposure to illegal substances, the manufacture of methamphetamine in the presence of a child, selling, distributing, or giving illicit drugs or alcohol to a child, and a caregiver's use of a controlled substance that impairs the caregiver's ability to care for the child (Child Welfare Information Gateway, 2013).

Practice Roles and Responsibilities

The primary practice responsibilities of a Child Protective Services CM at Liberty County DFCS are as follows:

1. Assess the level of risk to children by conducting face-to-face interviews with alleged child victims and their caretakers

2. Assess the family's needs and strengths

3. Interview neighbors, friends, relatives, or professionals that have had contact with the family

4. Collaborate with law enforcement when children are physically removed from caretakers when the child is found by the courts to be at risk in the home

5. Review various pertinent documents such as police reports, criminal history, medical reports, school reports, or prior CPS case files

6. Testify in court as to the level of risk to children placed in the agency's legal custody

7. Be available for on-call scheduling

When a report of child maltreatment is made, that report is investigated by a CPS CM. If the suspected perpetrator is not a child's caregiver, the alleged abuse is classified as criminal and is investigated by legal authorities as opposed to CPS. Frequently, we work cases alongside of law enforcement when a child maltreatment case involves a possible criminal act, as the law requires (Cross, Finkelhor, & Ormrod, 2005). Once a case is opened, it is assigned either a 24-hour or 5-day response time-frame, depending upon the severity of the offense and the degree of dangerousness posed to any children in the home. If a call comes in at 8:30 P.M. and the case is given 24-hour priority, the CM who is assigned the case has until 8:30 P.M. the following day to make initial contact with the alleged victim or the entire family. We then begin investigating the alleged report of abuse or neglect to determine whether there is evidence to corroborate the accusation following our protocols for investigations.

First, we must assess the home to decide whether the child is safe enough to remain in the home, or if they should be removed temporarily to placement with a relative or foster home for the duration of the investigation. This can be a difficult call to make, as a child's, sometimes multiple children's, safety is at stake. Since calls are taken 24 hours a day, if a CM is on-call, they may have to respond to a call at 2 or 3 o'clock in the morning. It is not uncommon for law enforcement to make a call to CPS, requesting that the CM respond to a crime scene where child maltreatment is suspected or confirmed. In such cases, we must remain with the alleged victims until placement is found for all children. Meetings with the family often take place within the home, although we may also meet with children while they are at school. It is important to meet with the whole family to personally witness the actual family dynamics at work. We may take photographs and make notes to document the physical home environment. We then interview the child victim(s), alleged perpetrators, and remaining family members. Collateral witnesses must also be contacted to gather as much information as possible about the family. We typically have 30 to 45 days to close out a case, otherwise it becomes "overdue." At the end of our investigation process, CPS classifies the case according to the preponderance of evidence, meaning, "evidence which is of greater weight or more convincing than evidence which is offered in opposition to it; a 51% likelihood that abuse or neglect occurred" (Michigan Department of Health & Human Services, 2016). Family support cases, where financial assistance is provided or other services are brokered, are generally less intrusive and can take up to 60 days to complete.

We are trained to look for signs of abuse and neglect to corroborate our reported allegations. This involves looking for different symptoms in the child and the parent. We are looking for evidence of any sudden changes in the child's school performance, excessive absence from school, learning problems not attributed to physical or psychological causes, begging or stealing food, withdrawal, over-compliance, unwillingness to return home, reluctance to be around a particular person, or disclosure of maltreatment. Aside from changes in behavior, we document any unexplained burns, bites, bruises, or broken bones and pay special attention to any harsh disciplining for signs of physical abuse. A child who is consistently dirty, has severe odor, lacks weather-appropriate clothing, or who states that an adult is rarely at home may be exhibiting signs of neglect. Sexual abuse may have occurred if a child has difficulty walking or sitting, reports bedwetting, demonstrates developmentally inappropriate sexual knowledge or behaviors, or if the parent isolates the child from other children or is jealous or controlling of other family members (Child Welfare Information Gateway, 2013).

In caregivers, we look for the following signs of abuse or neglect: denial of the existence or blaming of the child for problems in school; asking teachers or other caregivers to use harsh physical discipline; seeing the child as entirely bad, worthless, or burdensome; demanding an unachievable level of physical or academic performance; relying on the child for care, attention, or fulfillment of emotional needs; inability to provide a reasonable explanation consistent with a child's injury; a history of abusing animals or pets; abuse of alcohol or other drugs; or constantly blaming, belittling the child. Additionally, we watch and listen to interactions between guardian and child to see how frequently they touch or look at one another, whether they say they do not like each other, and if they express their relationship is entirely negative (Child Welfare Information Gateway, 2013). CPS CMs must possess a keen eye for signs of abuse or neglect and pay close attention to all family members when conducting assessments.

Skills ingrained in the social work profession are essential to our client-centered work with children and their families. Of utmost importance is our ability to engage with clients. We often work against the clock to investigate cases of child maltreatment, limiting the amount of time we have to build rapport with the victims and their families. Critical to engagement with families is our ability to actively and reflectively listen, in which we give our full attention to the person speaking, and then mirror back what we heard to allow for clarification. To be effective at what we do, CMs have to quickly establish trust between ourselves and the families and victims we work with. This can be difficult because many families are often apprehensive about the investigative process. Being honest, forthright, and genuine goes a long way, and families can tell when a CM is not sincerely invested in their well-being. We balance expressing empathy for clients' situations, while maintaining a presence of authority that is crucial to drawing answers out in a timely manner. Using a mix of open- and close-ended questions is essential to gather the information we need. Often, some families will not open up and tell you their whole story, but they will give you bits and pieces that allow for the opportunity to ask follow-up questions that can give you more pieces to the puzzle to complete the 'big picture' of what is really going on. It takes a great deal of interviewing skill to navigate those first few interactions with the family, where the tone is set for the entirety of the investigation. At times, our families are very under-resourced and need help getting the basic services they need. Much of what we do is identifying families' needs and strengths: brokering services to provide them with the resources they need to succeed. This work is often unpredictable. We can go into work with a schedule in our heads of how the day will go and a call can come in and everything has to change to accommodate a new case. Flexibility and prioritization are skills most seasoned BSW and MSW social workers possess—skills that are taught through numerous experiences juggling multiple cases with competing client needs. The rapidly changing scene of CPS work requires that we work as a team—otherwise, you cannot get this job done in 40 hours a week.

In addition to the challenge of needing to be flexible while working within strict time frames, we often also have large caseloads. When I (the second author, Tiffany Johnson) first transferred to Liberty County, they were understaffed, which meant I had to wait 5 months to receive specialized training, while continuing to work with 40 active cases. There are currently only four CMs working in our investigative unit because two CMs are out on leave, meaning that everyone's caseloads are higher than usual right now. Prioritization and organization are the keys to being successful at this quick-paced job. As is the nature of this work, sometimes we have to work through the holidays. Last year, I was on-call and a case came in on Christmas Eve that I worked through Christmas day—allowing me no time to spend with my own family. We often carry a lot on our professional shoulders as CPS CMs; thus, it is extremely important that we take time out for ourselves. Self-care is a concept "lightly" taught in most social work programs, but it becomes even more important in the work that we actually do. We see things daily that can be difficult to leave at work and can easily get drawn into our client's lives, but we have to remember to set aside time to do the things we enjoy outside of work. It can be easy to make excuses for why we are not practicing self-care, but not making a commitment to self-care contributes to a high burnout rate in our profession. If we are not well, it is not possible for us to get our clients the resources that they need to keep their children safe.

Role Development Potential

Together, the social work BSW curriculum, on-the-job training, and work experience I received prepared me for my role as a CPS CM. My BSW generalist social work education laid the foundation for my work as a CM. Every day, I use what I learned in school, but my work responsibilities also moved beyond that. Courses on human development are incorporated into BSW and MSW curricula, and should remain a core course component to prepare students for work with children and adolescents. Knowledge of child development is also essential to child protective services work. CMs must understand the developmental abilities of children of all ages and tailor their questions when interviewing victims to fit their level of cognitive development. For instance, a 15-year-old child may be able to provide more precise information about specific dates of an incident, whereas a 5-year-old generally will not be able to. Family dynamics also play a critical role in our assessments, thus courses pertaining to appropriate engagement with families should be offered in CMG education. Furthermore, self-awareness exercises and self-reflection should remain central to BSW and MSW programs and continue to be practiced in the field. It is also vital that you be able to recognize your own self and your personal limitations. For example, from self-reflection I learned early on as a CM that I cannot take on too many sexual abuse cases, as those cases tended to weigh heavily on me. You really need to know what you can and cannot handle—we do not want to make things worse for families that we are here to help.

There are other valuable lessons learned working in CPS that can only be taught experientially. While self-care and the importance of setting boundaries is harped on in social work education, I never really understood how important it was, until I started doing CMG work. Nothing can really prepare you for everything you will see or every case you will encounter. I once responded to a 3 A.M. call for a domestic violence case, and walked into the home for an assessment to see blood splattered on the walls, broken glass everywhere, and pools of blood on the floor. Thus, we often arrive at the height of a crisis and how prepared you are to react in the moment is not something that can be taught through formal education, but is learned through experience. This job is very individualized and what strategies work well for one CM do not necessarily work as well for another.

Testifying in court is one CMG responsibility I also learned to do on-the-job, but it would have been helpful to learn more about in school. Additionally, time management is another critical skill to possess as a CM, and although it was taught at the BSW level, it was not stressed enough. The longer you do this type of work, the better you will be at prioritizing what is most important. Whereas those who work in foster care can take more time to get to know families, time is always at the back of your mind in CPS. I started out in criminal justice, so I feel comfortable being direct with clients and asking them a lot of questions, but you cannot be timid doing this kind of work. If you go into a home showing fear or being timid, people will pick up on that, and you will not get the answers that you need—you have to go in with confidence and set the tone for how this process is going to be, but in a respectful way. Confidence comes with experience. As a young CM, I face challenges working with clients because of my age. I carry myself differently when I go on a home visit, but if you show you are willing to go the extra mile to help them, and understand that they know their family best, they will respect you. Figure out what works best for you and your clients and stay committed to that. Furthermore, no two regional districts are the same—as I learned when transferring to a new location. One really has to take time to get to know the area and be knowledgeable about available resources—ask co-workers and supervisors for recommendations. Learn from your experiences, practice self-reflection, and be willing to accept criticism, and we believe you will be successful as a CM.

Concluding Remarks

Child maltreatment occurs across all family characteristics and demographics, but it is 100% preventable. As social workers, we uniquely understand the context and impact that environmental, social, and financial stressors have on families. Often, many of our families are under significant strain. While child abuse and neglect is never an acceptable result, with some support and guidance, children can remain with their families. For these reasons, CMs take on the important task of investigating alleged reports and carry the responsibility of ultimately deciding whether claims are substantiated on a case-by-case basis. Therefore, the rewarding, albeit challenging, work that CPS CMs do is necessary to protect children and preserve families. To be effective as a CPS CM, we contend that you must be flexible, engaging, respectful, and confident. Homing in on what works best for you requires a great deal of self-reflection, as well as external feedback and criticism. The work that we do is emotional in nature, thus self-care is perhaps the single most valuable lesson one can learn in this profession. In this line of work, know that you will make mistakes, and remind yourself that that is okay! Listen to your clients and your colleagues, seek out opportunities to continue learning, and show yourself as much compassion as you give to your clients.

Case Example

Some cases are memorable because they truly test your limits as a CM. The following case was a challenging one, as the initial call came in the middle of the night, as I was lying in bed after an already long day. As the 'on-call' CM, I responded to the call that came in at midnight on a cold, rainy night in October. I had very little information when I arrived at the house at 12:45 A.M., but law enforcement was already on the premises. The house had been raided for drugs, and the mother of 5 children who lived there was to be arrested, leaving the children with no place to go. The mother had allowed another relative to cook cocaine in the home, and there had already been a few drug transactions in and out of the home that night. As it turns out, the mother already had federal charges for drug trafficking. We needed to find a placement for all 5 children, three boys and two girls ages 3–15, immediately. In addition to the 5 children, the oldest daughter, who was 15 years old, also had a 6-month-old of her own. While the police were finishing up inside the house, I began my investigation by first questioning the mother and the children. I found myself asking the mother more close-ended questions, trying to get the issues tabled as quickly as possible. It was after midnight and we were standing outside in the rain, so I did not really have time for her to be evasive. I needed answers to very specific questions.

After getting all the information I could from the mother, I began talking to the children who were all in various states of alarm. The middle child was very emotional, so

I empathized with him and tried to hear and validate his feelings. I let him know it was okay to feel how he was feeling, but I made no promises that he would get to stay with his family. I let him know in that moment I was going to make sure that he was safe, and I did tell him that he would get to speak with his mother again. That much I knew. Next, I asked the 14-year-old some open-ended questions to get her side of the story. I got very different answers from her, as she conveyed the drug trafficking and crack production had been going on in the home for some time now. She seemed to be very honest and open, and to have grown tired of the situation. However, the 15-year-old daughter was more concerned with protecting her mother; she did not take my questioning seriously and would laugh or give me one-word answers. The youngest kids I questioned the least, asking only the standard questions like "Who cares for you most often?"; "Who disciplines you and how do they discipline you?"; "What would you describe as your daily routine?"; and filling in the gaps with information I had gathered from the oldest siblings. Knowing the younger children could not give me specific details such as dates, I did not want to distress them further by berating them with questions.

Next, I began making calls to everyone we could think of desperately trying to find placement for these children in the middle of the night. Thankfully, we were able to find a relative who would take all the children into her home, that night, temporarily. Ultimately, the three boys went with their fathers, one of whom was already going through the legitimization process before the drug raid to secure custody of his child. The 14-year-old and 15-year-old girls continued to live with the relative who had initially taken them in. At first, the 14-year-old really struggled to adjust to her new environment—she was not used to having any authority over her because her mother had not really been involved. The 15-year-old received parenting classes and counseling to deal with what had happened and to give her the chance to vent about things that had been going on that I did not have the chance to talk with her about. We often put in for counseling services because we have such little time to talk to the victims, and in some cases, it can serve as an extra set of eyes into the home as counselors and therapists are mandated reporters. Therefore, if abuse or neglect is still happening, we still have someone there to intervene.

Recently, I spoke with the 15-year-old, and she is doing really well. When we first met, she was failing every class in school, but now she is passing all but one. She is involved in doing more at school and not only seems happy, but tells me that she is happy living with her relative. I have noticed a positive change in her. However, after the children were all placed, their maternal grandmother began repeatedly calling in new reports on the relative who was keeping the children, reporting that food was not available in the home. It turns out that these reports were unsubstantiated, and that the grandmother just wanted the children to come stay with her to receive benefits for taking care of them. However, it was frustrating as a CM because I would have to go through the whole process each time of assessing the home and contacting collaterals to complete the investigation. This took time away from the many other cases I was working with at the time, which were also important. Although in this case, the children were not able to remain with their mother because she was serving time in jail, I do feel that we were able to help each of them get to a happier, healthier place in their lives.

REFERENCES

Child Welfare Information Gateway. (2013). *What is child abuse and neglect? Recognizing the signs and symptoms.* Washington, DC: U.S. Department of Health and Human Services, Children's Bureau. Retrieved from https://www.childwelfare.gov/pubpdfs/whatiscan.pdf

Cross, T. P., Finkelhor, D., & Ormrod, R. (2005). Police involvement in Child Protective Services investigations: Literature review and secondary data analysis. *Child Maltreatment, 10*(3), 224–244.

Division of Family and Children Services (DFCS). (2015). *Georgia state sheet.* Retrieved from http://dfcs.dhs.georgia.gov/sites/dfcs.dhs.georgia.gov/files/Georgia_StateSheet2015.pdf

Division of Family and Children Services (DFCS). (2016). Services. Retrieved from http://dfcs.dhs.georgia.gov/node/695

Michigan Department of Health & Human Services. (2016). Children's Protective Services investigation process. Retrieved from http://www.michigan.gov/mdhhs/0,5885,7-339-73971_7119_50648_7194-159484--,00.html

Primavera, J., & Jackson, S. A. (2014). Child abuse. Salem press encyclopedia of health, Research starters. Pasadena, CA: Salem Press.

Sedlak, A. J., Mettenburg, J., Basena, M., Petta, I., McPherson, K., Greene, A., & Li, S. (2010). *The Fourth National Incidence Study of Child Abuse and Neglect (NIS-4): Report to Congress.* Washington, DC: U.S. Department of Health and Human Services, Administration for Children and Families.

U.S. Department of Health and Human Services. (2007). Georgia Child and Family Services review final report. Retrieved from http://dfcs.dhs.georgia.gov/sites/dfcs.dhs.georgia.gov/files/imported/DHR-DFCS/DHR-DFCS_CommonFiles/CFSR%20GEORGIA%20FINAL%20REPORT%202007.pdf

ANCILLARIES

Internet Resources for Additional Reading

1. Child Neglect: A Guide for Prevention, Assessment, and Intervention. Retrieved from https://www.childwelfare.gov/pubPDFs/neglect.pdf

2. Child Protective Services: A Guide for Caseworkers. Retrieved from https://www.childwelfare.gov/pubPDFs/cps.pdf

3. Family-Centered Practice Guide: Engaging, Assessing and Building Strengths With Families. Retrieved from https://edocs.dhs.state.mn.us/lfserver/Legacy/DHS-4938-ENG

4. Making Meaningful Connections 2015 Prevention Resource Guide (Tip Sheets for Parents and Caregivers Available in English and Spanish). Retrieved from https://www.childwelfare.gov/pubPDFs/guide.pdf

5. Working with Resistant Families. Retrieved from http://dss.mo.gov/cd/info/cwmanual/section7/ch1_33/sec7ch20.htm

Hard Copy References for Additional Reading

Brittain, C., & Hunt, D. E. (2004). *Helping in child protective services: A competency-based casework handbook* [Electronic resource]. New York, NY: Oxford University Press.

Child Welfare Committee National Child Traumatic Stress Network. (2008). *Child welfare trauma training toolkit: Comprehensive guide* (2nd ed.). New York, NY: National Center for Child Traumatic Stress.

DuPre, D., & Sites, J. (2015). *Child abuse investigation field guide.* New York, NY: Academic Press, Elsevier.

Fontes, L. A. (2005). *Child abuse and culture: Working with diverse families.* New York, NY: Guilford Press.

Shovholt, T., & Trotter-Mathison, M. (2011). *The resilient practitioner: Burnout prevention and self-care strategies for counselors, therapists, teachers, and health professionals* (2nd ed.). New York, NY: Routledge, Taylor & Francis Group.

 **JOB DESCRIPTION**

STATE OF GEORGIA
Division of Family and Children Services

Nathan Deal
Governor

Bobby D. Cagle
Director

Social Services Case Manager/ CPS - F.A.S.T. Team
South District / Region 12 / Liberty County

Division of Family and Children Services

Position Number: 00022704	Job Code: 14204 (PL14); 14205 (PL13); 14203 (PL13); 14212 (PL12)	Posting Date: 01/30/16	Closing Date: 02/29/16 or until filled

Overview

The Georgia Department of Human Services (DHS), Division of Family and Children Services (DFCS) is seeking candidates for the position of **Social Services Case Manager**. This position will serve a designated county in a specific DFCS region. <u>The position requires the use of a car for travel and transportation of clients (children)</u>.

DHS delivers a wide range of human services designed to promote self-sufficiency and well-being for all Georgians. The department is one of the largest agencies in state government with an annual budget of $1.8 billion and approximately 9500 employees. DHS is comprised of three divisions and nine enterprise support functions.

DFCS is the division within DHS that investigates child abuse, identifies foster homes for abused and neglected children; helps low income and out-of-work families get back on their feet; assists with child-care costs for low income parents who are working or in job training programs; and provides a number of additional support services and innovative programs to provide aid to troubled families.

Summary of Responsibilities

This position reports to the Social Services Supervisor.

Under general supervision, the Social Services Case Manager/CPS - F.A.S.T.:

1. Assesses the level of risk to children by conducting face-to-face interviews with the alleged child victims and their caretakers; collaborates with law enforcement when children are physically removed from caretakers when the child is found by the courts to be at risk in the home; testifies in court as to the level of risk to children placed in the agency's legal custody.

2. May Serve as the case manager for children in foster care; ensures that the children are placed in permanent stable families within as short a time frame as possible; visits foster homes; supervises visits between children and parents; testifies regarding the status of the agency and/or parent's progress toward the court approved placement.

3. **Must be willing to be redeployed to any County &/or Region within the assigned District as needs arise. Districts consist of multiple Regions/Counties.**

4. Is available for on-call scheduling.

5. Engages in required state-wide travel.

6. Performs other professional responsibilities as assigned.

Core Competencies

1. Excellent oral, written, presentation, and interpersonal communication skills

2. Strong proficiency in the use of Microsoft Office Suite and/or standard software applications typically used in a corporate office environment

DHS provides services to ensure the health and welfare of all Georgians. In the event of an emergency, any employee may be required to assist in meeting the emergency responsibilities of the department.

Required Qualifications: Education, Experience and Credentials

1. **Job Code 14204:** Master's degree in social work from a School of Social Work accredited by the Council on Social Work (www.cswe.org) based in an approved, accredited college or university

2. **Job Code 14205:** Bachelor's degree in social work from a School of Social Work accredited by the Council on Social Work (www.cswe.org) based in an approved, accredited college or university

3. **Job Code 14203:** Behavioral Science degree (Bachelor's level or above) from an educational institution accredited by the Council for Higher Education Accreditation (www.chea.org) and/or the US Department of Education <u>and</u> one (1) year of social services work experience or a DFCS internship that involved a caseload **or** from an educational institution accredited by the Council for Higher Education (www.chea.org) and/or the US Department of Education <u>and</u> DFCS internship that included a caseload

4. **Job Code 14212:** Behavioral Science degree (Bachelor's level or above) from an educational institution accredited by the Council for Higher Education Accreditation (www.chea.org) and/or the US Department of Education **or** from an educational institution accredited by the Council for Higher Education (www.chea.org) and/or the US Department of Education <u>**or**</u> Bachelor's degree from an approved, accredited college or university

Foreign Credentials: Required Evaluation Reports

Persons who attended colleges or universities outside the 50 states in the United States or the District of Columbia will not be offered employment until they submit a foreign credential report which includes English translations and information showing detailed, course-by-course evaluations and appropriate US degree equivalency. The foreign credential report must be an independent review prepared by an agency approved by the GA DHS. These agencies are private enterprises that charge a fee for their services and the expense is that of the selected candidate. To find an approved vendor, visit http://dhsjobs.dhs.ga.gov/Main/Default.aspx. Go to Related Links and click on Foreign Credential Evaluation Report.

Preferred Qualifications: Education, Experience, and Credentials

The ideal candidate will meet the required qualifications as well as the following:

1. One (1) year DFCS Child Protective Services Case Management experience.

2. Child Protective Services Certification highly desirable.

3. Ability to provide transportation and evidence of a valid driver's license for required travel throughout the state

Competitive Total Rewards Package: Compensation and Benefits		
Pay Level 14	Starting Salary	$34,039.00 Master of Social Work degree
Pay Level 13	Starting Salary	$32,418.00 Bachelor of Social Work degree
Pay Level 13	Starting Salary	$30,869.00 Behavioral Science degree (Bachelor's level or above) + one (1) year case management experience to include one or any combination of the following work responsibilities: assessments, home evaluations, staffing, work with child safety or child welfare **-or-** Behavioral Science degree (Bachelor's level or above) + DFCS internship that included a caseload
Pay Level 12	Starting Salary	$28,005.00 Behavioral Science degree (Bachelor's level or above) **-or-** Bachelor's degree from an approved, accredited college or university Region 14: Bachelor's degree and at least one (1) year work experience in a social services delivery program

Salary is dependent upon DHS/DFCS salary practices, candidate's experience and/or available funds.

Current state government employees are subject to DHS and/or State Personal Board rules and practices regarding salary designations.

Benefits: Generous benefits package that includes an employee retirement plan, deferred compensation, 12 annual paid holidays as well as vacation days and sick leave. Flexible benefits include selection options for life, dental, and vision insurance and long-term health care.

Criminal Background Checks/Applicant Privacy Rights

All applicants may be subject to a drug screen and will be required to submit fingerprints to check for the existence of criminal history information through the Georgia Bureau of Investigation and the Federal Bureau of Investigation. Applicants have the right to challenge the contents of any criminal history record obtained for the purpose of employment with DHS. For an explanation of these rights, please read, "Applicant Privacy Rights" at: http://gbi.georgia.gov/sites/gbi.georgia.gov/files/related-files/document/ApplicantPrivacyRights.pdf

Georgia On My Mind: It Doesn't Get Any Better Than This

Georgians enjoy a quality of life that would be hard to find in any area across the nation. Lower taxes and a lower cost of living enable you to do more with the money you make and maintain a higher standard of living.

Within Georgia you will find an unlimited supply of recreational and cultural opportunities. Enjoy boating, camping, fishing, golf, hiking, picnicking, swimming, tennis, or just relaxing against Georgia's many scenic backdrops. Georgia is a 57,906 square-mile playground filled with natural beauty and immaculate resources.

From the mountains to the coast from ballet to baseball, Georgia offers you a livability and quality of life that can help you achieve your dreams.

Apply Now: Your Career is Waiting. The Only Thing Missing is You!!!

To begin your new career:

1. Scroll to the bottom of this page;
2. Cick on the CLICK HERE TO APPLY tab;
3. Upload a cover letter and résumé in Microsoft Word (.doc, .docx, .txt, or .pdf format) for the desired position. The cover letter and résumé will be used to initially assess written communication skills and the ability to effectively use standard software applications.

Interested applicants should adhere to these submission requirements and apply without delay. Primary consideration will be given to applicant packages that comply with submission guidelines. Vacancy advertisements are removed as soon as a viable applicant pool is established.

You will receive an e-mail to acknowledge receipt of your documents. Due to the volume of submissions received, we are unable to respond directly, either by telephone, letter, or e-mail, to requests to verify receipt of application documents. The e-mail acknowledgment will serve as confirmation of receipt of requested documents.

26

Manejadores de Casos de Salud Mental en el Sistema de Salud para Veteranos en la Región del Caribe*

*Yolanda Machado-Escudero and
Rafael Hernández-Ramirez*

The Clientele

The Veterans' Health Administration (VA) is the United States' largest integrated federal health care system, consisting of 152 medical centers, nearly 1,400 community-based outpatient clinics, community living centers, Vet Centers, and Domiciliaries (U.S. Department of Veterans Affairs, 2016a). About 235,000 individuals are employed at the VA, with approximately 9,000 of those being social workers, providing comprehensive care to more than 8.3 million active service members

---

*Mental Health Case Management at Veterans' Health System in the Caribbean Region.

and former combat and non-combat soldiers each year (Beder & Postiglione, 2013). The United States has 2.2 million active service members in all five Armed Forces' branches (Army, Navy, Marine Corps, Air Force, and Coast Guard—the latter does not belong to the Department of Defense, but to Homeland Security). Active members in the National Guard and the Army Reserve components are also considered part of the military in terms of their duties and eligibility for benefits. The number of veterans in the United States is estimated between 21.9 and 22.7 million, which represents about 7% of the U.S. total population (Hoffler, Deckle, & Sheets, 2014; Petrovich, 2012).

The VA Caribbean Healthcare System provides services to a population of 150,000 veterans in Puerto Rico and the U.S. Virgin Islands (U.S. Department Veterans Affairs, 2016b). In the 2008 fiscal year, 66,955 patients received inpatient treatment. For the same year, 927,072 outpatient visits were registered at all health clinics for this same region. The main VA hospital for the Caribbean Region is located in San Juan, Puerto Rico. The VA Medical Care Center in San Juan offers an amalgam of health services, including 348 hospital beds, 12 blind rehabilitation beds, and 150 nursing home beds. In addition, there are 8 outpatient clinics distributed across Puerto Rico, plus 2 located in St. Croix and St. Thomas in the U.S. Virgin Islands. Puerto Rico is home to over 93,000 veterans from all foreign wars (WWII, Korean War, Vietnam conflict, Persian Gulf War, and Iraq and Afghanistan conflicts).

The Mental Health Intensive Case Management Program (MHICM) is one of many options available to veteran patients living in the Caribbean Region with diverse mental health diagnoses. This program has been implemented nationwide at the VA health system since 1987, currently serving approximately 8,000 patients with severe mental illness (Mohamed, 2013). In Puerto Rico, this program started in 2006 as a pilot project, with the goal of reducing acute mental health hospitalizations for patients with histories of chronic mental illness. Currently, the MHICM program in Puerto Rico includes a staff of 11 case managers (CMs), three nurses, and eight social workers, with four CMs scattered across four outpatient programs, and seven CMs serving the metropolitan area of San Juan. Each CM has a caseload of 11–12 patients. This program serves approximately 125 patients, 90% males and 10% females.

The most frequent diagnoses among our patients are schizophrenia, schizoaffective disorder, bipolar disorder, and major depression with psychotic features. The great majority of patients admitted to MHICM have had a least two psychiatric hospitalizations before entering the program. Admission criteria for patients include 1) the primary diagnosis must be a severe and persistent mental illness such as schizophrenia, psychotic disorders, and severe post-traumatic stress disorder or PTSD; 2) dual diagnosis patients are accepted if their substance abuse has been in remission for at least 12 months, or they have completed a substance abuse program with success; 3) patients must present severe functional impairment; 4) patients must have been inadequately served by other available conventional treatments; and 5) an admission to a psychiatric acute inpatient care unit must have been reported for two or more occasions in the previous 12 months. Exclusion criteria for participation in the program include 1) diagnosis of substance abuse and or dementia; 2) patients who live further than 60 minutes away from the clinic where the CMG team is based; 3) patients